CW01003885

From
CORNER SHOP
to
GRAND MARCHÉ

From CORNER SHOP to GRAND MARCHÉ

A History of The Channel Islands Co-operative Society

by
KENNETH C RENAULT

with additions by
ALLAN SMITH

THE CHANNEL ISLANDS CO-OPERATIVE SOCIETY LIMITED

Published by The Channel Islands Co-operative Society Limited,
27 Charing Cross, St Helier, Jersey, JE1 1AS, Channel Islands

First published 2005

Project management, editing, proofreading and indexing
by Matthew Seal, MSServices

Typeset by Fakenham Photosetting Ltd, Fakenham, Norfolk

Printed in Great Britain by Cambridge University Press
University Printing House, Shaftesbury Road, Cambridge

British Library Cataloguing in Publication Data:
A catalogue record for this book is available from the British Library

ISBN 0-9550841-0-5

THE CHANNEL ISLANDS CO-OPERATIVE SOCIETY LIMITED

27 Charing Cross, St Helier, Jersey, JE1 1AS, Channel Islands
Tel: 01534 879822 Fax: 01534 768312

A Society incorporated under the Industrial & Provident Societies Acts 1965–2002

Contents

Foreword

This book began as an idea of Norman Le Brocq, who was involved with the Society for 35 years and President for 27 years. He wanted to recapture the early, undocumented history of the Society from those people who were there, before those voices were lost to us.

Sadly, Norman became one of those lost voices before the project was completed. The baton was then passed to Ken Renault who did an inestimable job, nearly completing the task that Norman had begun, before he himself was taken from us. Allan Smith, the current Chief Executive, took the final step and finished the first draft of the manuscript.

To all three of these people I want to say a sincere thank you for the time and effort they have put into this project.

It is only by looking back at our roots that we realise how far we have come, tracing the Society's history from small beginnings and early setbacks to become the successful business it is today. For this reason, if no other, I believe it is important that the history of the Society should be recorded.

The book reflects the position of the 'Co-op' as an integral part of the local community, adhering to its co-operative principles of serving shareholders, customers, members and the community. It seems only fitting that the history should be published now, in the 50th year of trading of the Society in both Islands.

To anyone who is interested in history, community or the 'Co-op', I commend this book to you.

June Le Feuvre
President
May 2005

Acknowledgements

Any book on the history of a co-operative is inevitably a collaborative endeavour of many people who in various ways support the writer who sets down the final draft. The present book is no exception, for without the willing help and shared memories of those who have been part of the story of the Co-operative Society in the Channel Islands, it could be no more than a recitation of dry facts.

This book was the inspiration of Norman Le Brocq. On retirement from the Board of the Society in April 1995, Norman began to record its history as he had witnessed and experienced it during his long service, first as a Board Member from 1960 and then, for 27 years, as President. He regarded this as his retirement project and set about it in his usual methodical way. By correspondence, telephone and personal contact he obtained a great deal of information from his contemporaries in management and from the staff. He compiled a notebook to which he could add his own personal experiences.

While continuing his researches in this way he wrote several draft chapters, which were to be the basis of his book. Regrettably, Norman Le Brocq died suddenly in December 1996 before he was able to prepare the book for printing and publication. His work lay unfinished for some months until, in early 1997, the present writer was invited to complete it. I freely and sincerely acknowledge my indebtedness to the notes and detailed information so carefully compiled by Norman, and those drafts he prepared for eventual publication. With the support of my wife Barbara and her precise and patient typing the work continued until, regrettably, Barbara died in 1997, just nine months after Norman. The work suffered another delay.

But with encouragement from Colin Davies, Society Secretary at the time, and the assurance of support from Ann Paul and Monica Le Maistre for the typing, and similar assistance, always cheerfully given, the work continued until at last completion is in sight. But it could not have reached this stage without many people who have contributed their experiences. Among them were Mrs Betty Murphy, who introduced me to No 2 Market Street, where as the young Betty Bishop, she joined Richen's staff before the Occupation and later the Co-op staff when the Guernsey Society was formed in 1947. Then there was Doreen Batiste, who, also as a young girl, was at No 2 and who I was privileged to visit in hospital during her last days; other key contributions on the early days came from John Dart, who joined Charing Cross in 1940, and Dick Shenton, who also came in at the beginning of the Occupation as office boy.

John Boucheré supplied the photograph (**3.6**), probably taken in the early 1920s, of the family hardware business in Georgetown, which was absorbed later into the purchase in 1947 of that group of properties from which sprang the first Co-op out-of-town venture. Michael Galway spent all his long Co-op service in butchery from that same period. A little later John Cuthbertson joined the staff in Guernsey and has offered photographs of his experience with the mobile shops in company with Doreen (**7.1**). Mrs Ruth Morris has spoken freely of her husband John's remarkable career with the Co-op through 45 years and contributed that photograph of him as the young clerk of 1940 (**2.5**) and the amusing sketch of him in later years (**9.1**). Mr Booth, whose name appears so frequently in the early post-Occupation Minutes, was happy to contribute his photograph too (**4.5**).

The *Guernsey Evening Press* and the *Jersey Evening Post* have offered advice and assistance on press reports and photographs, where available from their files. Stuart McAlister Photographers took the photographs of the 2005 stores and offices on both Islands reproduced in Appendix 3.

The Co-operative College contributed new photographs of the rooms at the College, which were refurbished from a donation by the Society and which commemorate the names of Norman Le Brocq and John Morris by a plaque at the door (**A4.11**, **A4.12**). Regrettably, the College has closed its doors at Stanford Hall, which was sold after 56 years of service to the interests of the Co-operative Movement in the training of management and staff of all levels.

Several members of staff gave me interesting details and photographs of early social activities, which illustrate their long-continuing loyalty to the Society and their own part in it.

Alfred Hamon spoke of his years of experience in the furnishing trade and particularly of the challenge he faced at the new Homemaker Store in Don Street when he became manager there in the early 1980s.

Robin Briault took a number of special photographs for me of work going on behind the scenes to illustrate to members and the reader those unseen disciplines and efforts by management and staff to ensure that the Co-op delivers the goods, not only to the supermarket shelves, but in many instances to the customer's front door.

KENNETH C RENAULT

Following Ken's death, we would wish to place on record the Society's gratitude to him for his dedication in producing this Society history. While others have assisted in the final editing and updating the book to 2005, this is Kenneth C Renault's book.

ALLAN SMITH MBE

Preface

At the beginning of 2005, The Channel Islands Co-operative Society had 60,783 shareholder/customers in Jersey and 32,919 shareholder/customers in Guernsey; annual turnover was in excess of £104 million and the surplus before distribution (the equivalent of profit before tax in a company) was over £7 million.

This successful commercial enterprise began trading in Jersey in 1919 and in Guernsey in 1947; a merger of both Societies in 1955 formed The Channel Islands Co-operative Society Limited. The growth of the Society is a testament to the dedication, business acumen and sheer hard work of generations of directors, managers and staff, loyally supported by Island shareholder/customers.

You will read how this book was set on its way by Norman Le Brocq, a Director for almost 35 years and President for 27 years of that term. Following Norman's tragic death Ken Renault agreed to complete the book, but before it could be published Ken too passed away.

With 2005 being the 50th anniversary of The Channel Islands Co-operative Society, we felt it fitting to re-edit the draft book so carefully and lovingly prepared by Ken and to publish it in this special year.

The Co-operative Society is unique in modern business in having shareholder/customers. Co-operative principles allow customers to become shareholders and take their share of the surplus (profit) in dividend related to their purchases in the financial year. This gives a total consumer ethos to the Society, and leads to a special relationship between the directors, management, staff and shareholder/customer that forms the basis of this history.

This book has been written, not by management but by a shareholder/customer, Ken Renault, and is the history of the Society through the eyes of a customer, who had access to the Minute books of the Society, interspersed with recollections collected from staff and customers.

In Chapter 13 I outline how the rapid growth of the Society since the 1970s has been 'directed' and 'managed': it did not grow like Topsy but was built on sound management practices and perceptive strategies.

We hope you will enjoy this book. It chronicles the growth of a business over some 86 years in Islands that have changed quite dramatically, both physically and economically, but which have retained within their people a character and soul based on honorary service and a generosity of spirit.

A Smith MBE
Chief Executive

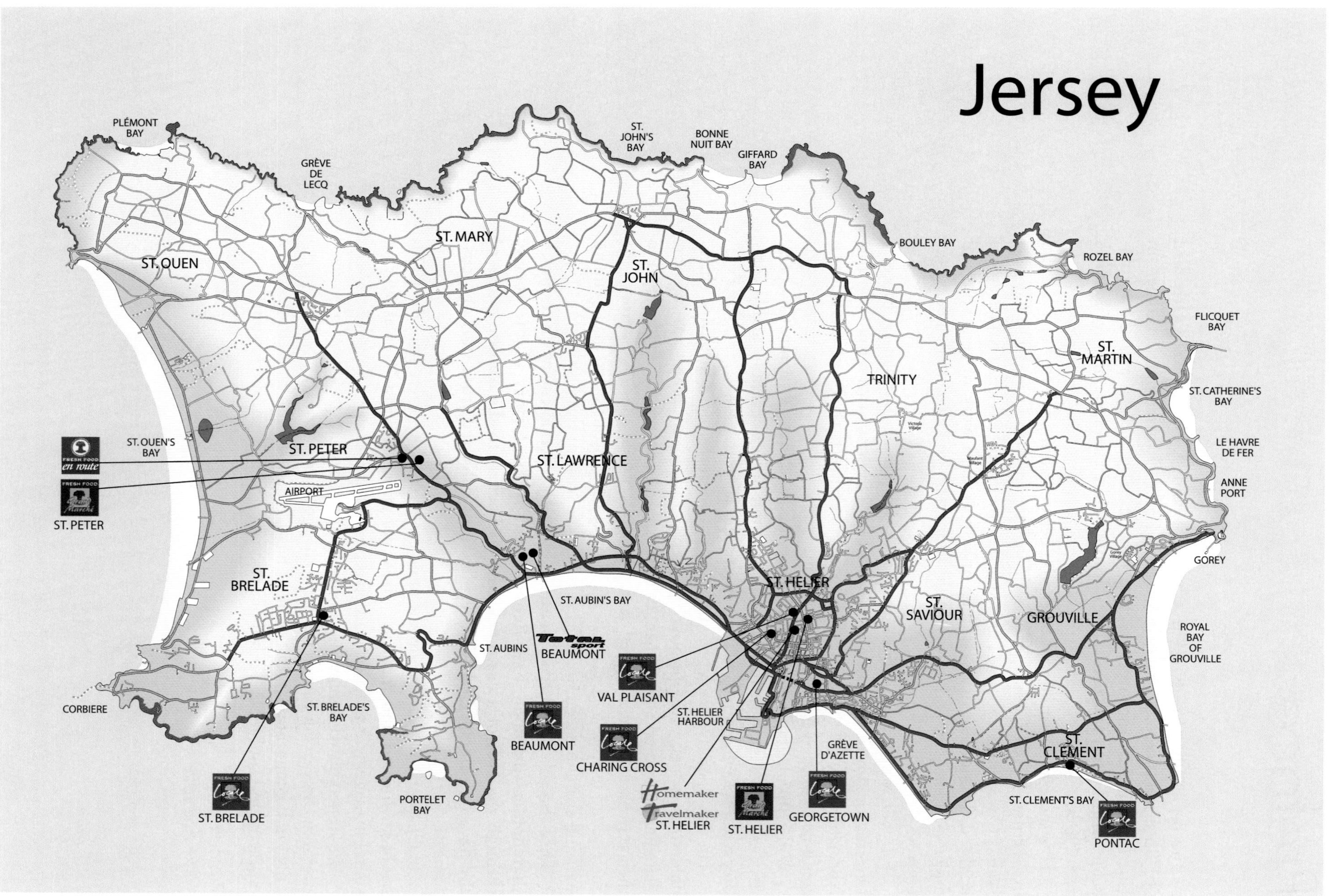

Jersey
PLÉMONT BAY
GRÈVE DE LECQ
ST. JOHN'S BAY
BONNE NUIT BAY
GIFFARD BAY
BOULEY BAY
ROZEL BAY
FLICQUET BAY
ST. CATHERINE'S BAY
LE HAVRE DE FER
ANNE PORT
GOREY
ROYAL BAY OF GROUVILLE
ST. OUEN
ST. MARY
ST. JOHN
TRINITY
ST. MARTIN
ST. PETER
AIRPORT
ST. LAWRENCE
ST. HELIER
ST. SAVIOUR
GROUVILLE
ST. BRELADE
ST. CLEMENT
ST. OUEN'S BAY
CORBIERE
ST. BRELADE'S BAY
PORTELET BAY
ST. AUBINS
ST. AUBIN'S BAY
ST. HELIER HARBOUR
GRÈVE D'AZETTE
ST. CLEMENT'S BAY
FRESH FOOD en route
ST. PETER
ST. BRELADE
BEAUMONT
BEAUMONT
VAL PLAISANT
CHARING CROSS
Homemaker Travelmaker
ST. HELIER
ST. HELIER
GEORGETOWN
PONTAC

Map 1 Jersey

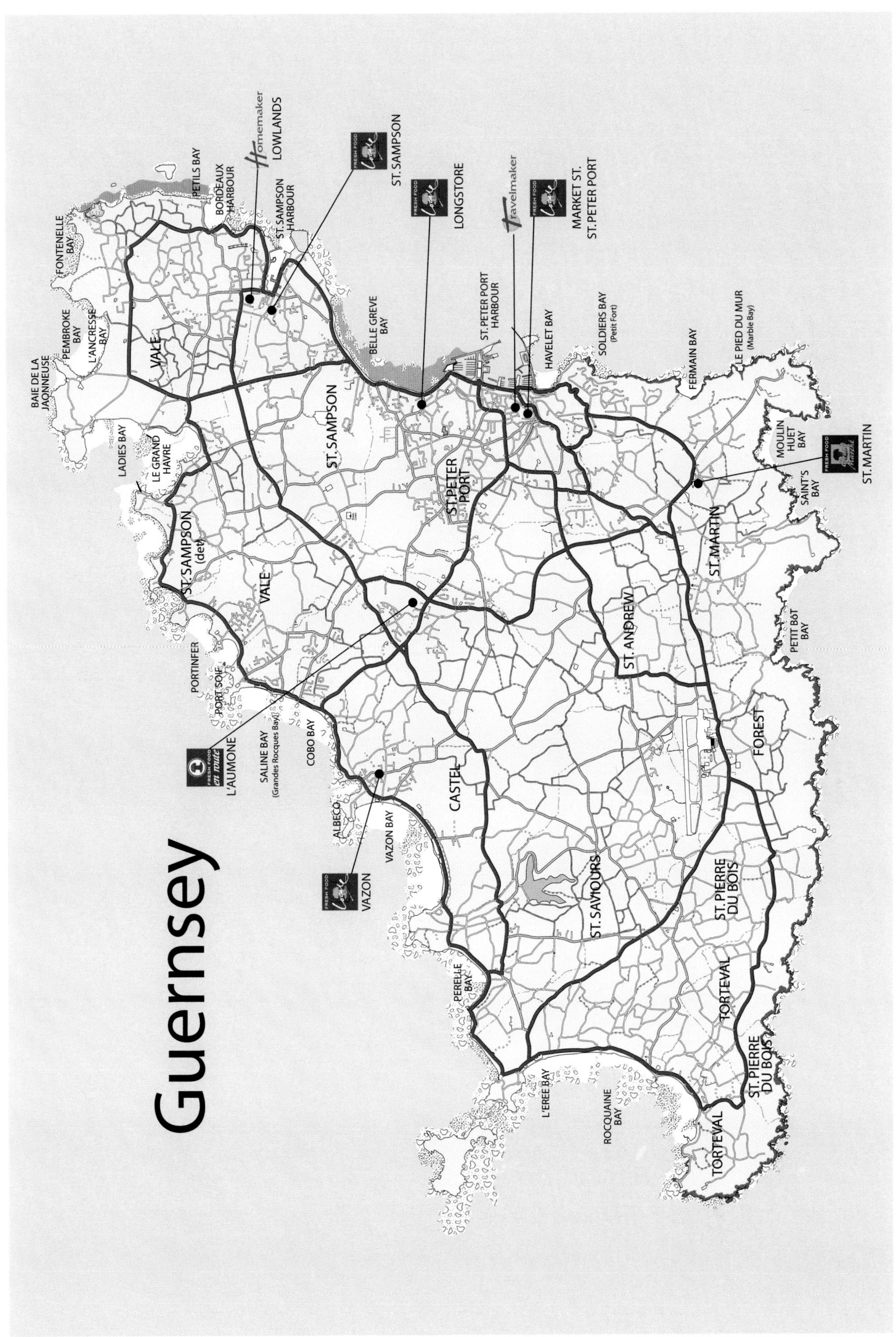

Map 2 Guernsey

Part one

Origins, Occupation and Post-war recovery

1.1 A group of managers and employees of the CWS taken at the entrance to one of the stores, posing with a sack of CWS potatoes bearing the branding 'British Produce, Grown in Jersey'. This photograph indicates the number of men (and a dog) employed by CWS in the late 1930s

Chapter 1

The Pioneer Spirit comes to Jersey

The month of May 1919, barely six months after the Great War had ended, was to prove a turning point in grocery trading practice in Jersey and later in Guernsey. This was borne out on 22 May when a significant meeting was held at the Oddfellows Hall in Don Street, the far-reaching effects of which could hardly have been imagined at the time.

That the meeting was of more than usual importance was indicated by the presence on the platform of Alderman W Devenay, JP and Mr B Williams, Secretary of the Co-operative Union of London, both of whom had come over from England to represent the CWS, the Co-operative Wholesale Society. Also present was Deputy Gray of St Helier, who was well known in the town for his energetic approach to progressive issues that were being debated in the States.

The objective of the meeting was to further the idea of a Co-operative Society in Jersey to cater for the needs of the working class. In this respect the timing was right, with demobilisation under way and thousands of men and women returning to civilian life, hopeful of better living conditions than their parents had experienced before the war. Despite the uncertainties of that early post-war period one outcome of that meeting was positive; with the backing of the CWS a way was opened for the working man and woman in the Islands to ease their anxieties over the weekly shopping for the family necessities, particularly in groceries.

The Co-operative Wholesale Society had been present in the Island for some years, occupying a merchant's stores at 27 Esplanade and trading in the usual import and export business of local produce. But there was a difference. In the CWS Annual Report of the First World War years Jersey is listed as a purchasing depot – it was a bulk buyer of Jersey potatoes and tomatoes for export to the Co-operative warehouses in Britain, with subsequent supply to the Co-operative Societies around the country (**1.1**). In this way the CWS was a forerunner of our present-day Potato Marketing Board and similar bodies supplying in bulk to the giant supermarket chains. The CWS also used its own shipping line for transport, *CWS Defiant* and *CWS Progress* (**1.7**) being two of its familiar ships in local waters.

Thus the CWS was well known among the farming and shipping communities. No doubt too the principles of co-operative retailing were often discussed while waiting around the Weighbridge. It would not be long before discussion turned to action, resulting in a modest group approach for support from the CWS on the mainland. That 1919 meeting in the Oddfellows Hall was the outcome.

During Williams's address he referred to the Rochdale Pioneers of 1844, and no doubt stressed the significance of the thrift they had demonstrated in furtherance of their ideal. The 40 original subscribers saved 3d a week (about 1p now) towards the total stake, until they had saved £28, a fair sum of money in 1844. From this sum they rented an old ground floor store at £10 per year for three years. With part of the balance essential repairs were carried out and fittings bought. Then, with only £16 left for stock, they bought 28 lb of butter, 56 lb of sugar, 6 cwt of flour, a sack of oatmeal and some tallow candles. At the end of the Rochdale co-operators' first year their total takings were £710, membership was 74, capital had grown to £181 and they held a surplus of £22.

Let us reflect for a moment on the symbolism between that determined effort of the Pioneers, with their first shop in 1844, and the closing minutes of that meeting of 1919, an interval of 75 years. The tossing of those shillings onto the table was indeed history repeating itself. Little did our own pioneers of 1919 appreciate the significance of their modest contribution to Jersey's first truly co-operative store, the story of which we are about to read.

On 23 May 1919 the morning quiet of Duhamel Place, St Helier, was broken, not only by the opening and latching of window shutters but by the chat across the street and talk of what had gone on in the Oddfellows Hall the night before.

The word 'co-operative' was not unknown in the town at the time – there was a shop in Waterloo Street, known as Co-operative Stores, which advertised boldly in the local press (**1.2**) – but this was a privately run shop selling soft goods and clothing. As far as we know, it did not trade in wholesale or co-operative terms but as a normal retail outlet.

Very New Stock of Goods
AT THE
CO-OPERATIVE
STORES,
WATERLOO STREET.

Very large stock of very new Millinery, remarkably cheap.
A very large stock of Sports Coats in all shades.
Blouses in large variety.
Blouse Materials.
Very large stock of Navy and Black Costume Serge & Dress Materials
Ladies' and Maids' Costumes and Rain Coats.
Girls' Stockings all sizes and prices.
Ladies' Stockings all sizes and prices
Men's Stockings and Socks, all sizes and qualities.
Blankets, Sheets, Sheetings.
Calicoes, Long Cloth, Flannel, Prints
Long Lace Curtains, 1/6, 1/1½, 2/3, 2/6 to 7/6

1.2 Typical advertisement of the Co-operative Stores of Waterloo Street as displayed in the *Morning News* of 1 June 1916

Then there was the CWS, the Co-operative Wholesale Society, a trading branch of the Co-operative Movement on the mainland. From its farming and business contacts among our local communities would have sprung the local interest in the Co-operative Movement and the desire to know more of its retailing possibilities if it were one day to become established in the Islands.

The *Jersey Evening Post* report of that May evening at the Oddfellows Hall (**1.3**) indicates the interest shown by the listening audience. But as those rumours spread around the town and the press report was read that evening – it occupied a long column, alongside an advertisement headed 'Demobilisation' in which Au Gagne Petit offered men's trench coats and raincoats, 'perfect in cut and finish for every occasion' for 'Service men returning to Civil Life' – reaction and response may well have been lukewarm and confused. 'After all, who wants another Co-op? We've got two already' might have been heard. But equally quickly, as the full facts became known, it would have been appreciated that individuals, friends and acquaintances were paying a shilling each to become members and a Management Committee was being formed from well-known personalities and local businessmen. This information would have signified, more fully than rumour, that something fairly serious was going on.

Membership of that first Management Committee included the names of H Allix, J de Gruchy, W du Feu, PN Gallichan, J Hardman, E Le Quesne and E Moignard. Hardman and Moignard were prominent trade unionists in Jersey at this time, indicating an early guiding influence in the shaping of the embryo Society. Le Quesne was also a strong man for the times, being the Secretary of the Master Plumbers Association. Shortly afterwards, in 1922, he was elected to the Poor Law Commission, which he served for many years. He also became involved later in early labour disputes with local companies and gained a reputation for skilful negotiation, a reputation that served the Island well when, twenty years later as a Deputy and Committee President, he took over the invidious and challenging task of organising the Department of Labour during the Occupation.

The *Morning News* also published a very brief report of this meeting, ending with the comment that a similar Society had already been formed in Guernsey and that it hoped to commence operations within a few days. No supporting evidence

Co-operation in the Channel Islands.

Big Meeting at the Oddfellows' Hall.

The Oddfellows' Hall was crowded last evening when Mr. B. Williams, of London, spoke on the formation of a Co-operative Society in Jersey.

Mr. E. Le V. du Durell presided. With him on the platform were Deputy Gray, Mr. Williams and Alderman W. Devenay, J.P.

The audience was composed chiefly of working-men, but it included a number of ladies and a sprinkling of well-to-do tradesmen.

Mr. Williams, having been introduced by the Chairman, began his address by urging the working-men of Jersey to submit no longer to oppression and injustice. He instanced the case of Robert Smillie who at 18 was supporting six brothers and sisters by long and laborious toil, and so improved his mind in the little spare time he had that to-day "dukes and earls toed the line in front of him." "That is the sort of thing," said Mr. Williams, "that you want in Jersey. You want to make these people toe the line, and make them realise that they are not worth more than you are. There is too much subservience and servility in these islands; for Heaven's sake throw all this over and show these tyrants that they can't trample on your liberties. When they attempt to do so resent it at once with all your force and you'll be victorious."

Mr. Williams having got that much off his chest now started on the subject of co-operation, and said it was a matter for the working-classes. They needed no bosses or bullies to help along the scheme he was about to outline; it could be started and maintained by the coppers of the rank and file. He had not come to establish a business, but to tell them how to do it.

If any millionaire came along to establish it for them the thing to tell him was "Hands off! We don't want you in this." He had already done that in England in at least two cases. What they wanted was a Co-operative Society based on the firm will of the people; if they were trustworthy and loyal to it no millionaire with all the power of his millions would be able to shake it.

It was a simple matter to get hold of the basic principles of the scheme. The complications came afterwards when one had to deal with the complicated peculiarities of human nature. He had been told that the people of Jersey were a peculiar lot of people to deal with, but as a matter of fact he had been told that sort of thing at pretty well every place he had visited. The truth was that people were the same everywhere. Jersey had got plenty of the right sort, he was sure of it.

The Society he was there to advocate was a Society formed for the purpose of purchasing goods at wholesale rates instead of at the retail rates paid in the shops. Whatever margin there was between the two rates they saved. They would want a shop and a man to manage it, and they would, of course, have to pay rent, rates, etc. It would also be advisable to set aside, quarter by quarter, a certain sum to form a reserve fund for a rainy day, and for depreciation at 10 per cent. People would buy their goods at the local market price. There would be no opposition to tradesmen and no cutting of prices, but they would have a shop of their own. The business would be run for say three months, and at the end of that time the chances were that they would be able to declare a dividend of 1s. in the £.

Mr. Williams then gave a very interesting account of the history of the movement since the formation of the Rochdale Co-operative Society in 1844. As an instance of the growth of the movement he pointed out that the organisation now has a total capital of twenty million pounds, disposes of forty million pounds of tea annually, owns 18,000 acres in Ceylon for the growing of tea, and has the biggest flour mills and the largest boot factory in the world. The whole organisation was run by and for the working-man, and the Chairman of Directors of that huge concern only received £600 a year. In the whole of the Society he did not think there were more than five men getting more than £1,000 a year.

When the farmers of England wished to start a co-operative society they received an annual grant of £13,000 from the Government, but the working-man had done without grants and had run his business without patronage from anybody. There was just the same kind of human nature and ability in Jersey as there was in London, and they could run a society successfully if only they stood together. Unless they did that their money and their Society would go.

"Stick together," said Mr. Williams, "Go to your own shop, and to no other, and you'll succeed. You don't want to get a lot of money from any man. The thing to do is to get a thousand people to subscribe £1 each and then you can make a start. What you must do is to bring in the man with £1 and a big family, for he'll do better out of it than the man with £20 and no family, seeing that he'll buy more. People with big families can go along and eat themselves into a fortune, for the more they eat the better off they'll be. (Loud laughter.) So far as I can see there are very excellent prospects indeed for co-operation of this kind in Jersey. If co-operation of the right kind gets rooted in Jersey, other things will grow out of it which will benefit you and help you to fight those enemies of yours who are always trying to keep you in a state of subjection. (Cheers.) You want Jersey for the people of Jersey. I don't see why the whole of the Island can't belong to the whole of the people. You can do it if you make up your minds." (Cheers.)

Alderman Devenay having given the history of a Co-operative Society successfully run by Trade Unionists, Deputy Gray, who was given a particularly cordial reception, said they must adopt co-operation if they wished to be true to themselves, for co-operation would be the death-knell of profiteering. It would stop cabbages at 1/2 and swedes at 8d. each. (Applause.) Such a state of things could not exist with co-operation, and once their society was established he could foresee a flag day being organised on behalf of the poor profiteers. (Applause.) A few years back Jersey butter was 1/- per lb., while now it was 3/6—all on account of grass not growing because of the war. (Cheers and laughter.) He did not wish to see private enterprise done away with altogether, but he wanted to see their co-operative society the means of bringing profiteers to book. They must not go away and forget about it; that was a way they had in Jersey, unfortunately.

"We passed your Franchise Bill to-day," continued Deputy Gray. "It has taken a nine-months' offensive, but we went over the top to-day and captured the enemy trenches. (Cheers and laughter.) Do it Now! There is too much 'wait and see' in this Island; make up your minds before you go away that this co-operative society is going to be an accomplished fact. It will be an enormous success, there is not a doubt of it. As a Docker in full benefit I suppose I am entitled to put down my shilling." (Here Deputy Gray threw a shilling on the table amid laughter and applause.)

A vote of thanks having been passed to Mr. Williams, the meeting closed, but numbers stayed behind to put the shilling, which makes them members of the Society.

1.3 A contemporary report of the historic 'big meeting' at the Oddfellows Hall, at which the Jersey Co-operative Society was born (retyped from the Jersey Evening Post, 23 May 1919)

LA HAULE,

To Let for Xmas, 1919.

THE FARM known as **"VERMONT,"** situate at the top of La Haule Hill, St. Brelade, consisting of a good dwelling house, outbuildings and V.28½ of VERY EARLY LAND, being one of the best farms in the parish.

For all particulars apply to G. F. D. Le Gallais, Solicitor, 6, Hill Street.

To Let for September 29th.

3 LARGE STORES, STABLES & YARD, all adjoining, situate at Springfield Place, Town Mills, now tenanted by Messrs. Dennis and Sons, Limited.

Apply to Mr. T. G. Gaudin, 3, Salvandy Terrace.

Sale by Public Auction.

ON WEDNESDAY, the 2nd July, 1919, Miss Clara Elsie Emily will offer for sale by public auction the property known as "AURORA COTTAGE," comprising dwelling-house, outbuildings and about V.3 of land. The said property situate near Trinity Parish Church.

The sale will take place on the said day at 3.30 p.m. at the offices of Le Masurier and Giffard, 23, Hill Street, where all particulars may be obtained.

Sale by Public Auction

ON WEDNESDAY, the 2nd July, 1919, Miss Irene Marguerite Emily will offer for sale by public auction the Farm known as "LA CHASSE," comprising dweling-house, outbuildings and about V.28 of land. The said property situate Vingtaine de la Croiserie, in the Parish of Trinity.

The sale will take place on the said day at 3 p.m. at the offices of Le Masurier and Giffard, 23, Hill Street, where all particulars may be obtained.

FOR SALE

THE beautiful freehold property known as **Longueville Manor,** with gardens, lawns, small lake, woods, and arable land adjoining measuring altogether about 38 Vergées, or 17 Acres, situate at St Saviour.

For particulars and permission to view apply to Messrs. Bois & Bois, Solicitors, 16, Royal Square, St. Helier.

PROPERTY FOR SALE AT ST. LAWRENCE.

THE property known as "LA FONTAINE," consisting of good dwelling-house with about one vergée of garden planted with fruit trees in full bearing; the whole situate in the Parish of St. Lawrence.

For particulars apply to Crill and Benest, Solicitors, 16, Hill Street.

Sale in Perpetuity, or TO LET ON LEASE.

ON WEDNESDAY, the 25th June, 1919, W. J. Orier, Esq., will put up for sale in perpetuity his Farm, comprising a good dwelling-house and farm outbuildings with the land belonging thereto, the whole adjoining and measuring 50 vergées, the whole being known as MAUFANT FARM, Parish of St. Saviour.

Possession at Christmas next.

The sale will take place the said

QUEEN STREET.

By Permission of the Bailiff.

Grand Australian Carnival Night and Fancy Dress Ball,

WEST PARK PAVILION, MONDAY, JUNE 30

SPECIAL PRIZES. EXCELLENT MUSIC by a specially-selected Orchestra directed by Mons. H. De Lavaux.

Look out for a Great Australian Scena descriptive of one of the famous Ned Kelley's "Hold-Ups." Nothing like it has ever been produced in Jersey.

ADMISSION, 1s. Tickets (including admission to ball and dance area), 2s. A limited number of Reserved Seats, 6d. extra.

M.C.: Mr. JACK SOPER.

Tickets may be obtained from the office of "Jersey Topics," or from Messrs. W. Gallichan, Baymont House, St. Aubin's; H. Piper ("Lofty"), and others.

Be sure to obtain your tickets EARLY. Catering by Maison Tolcher (Aurora Hotel)

Jersey Co-Operative Society.

The Society's Office will be **OPENED** on **MONDAY,** June 23rd, at **41, NEW STREET,** when the Secretary will be in attendance from 11 to 1 and 6 and 8 each day to receive instalments and applications from intending members.

A. LE QUESNE, Secretary pro. tem.

WILLS, 39, Halkett Place,

THE HOUSE FOR

SPORTING & PHOTOGRAPHIC REQUISITES

Cricket, Lawn Tennis Golf & Sporting Goods in Great Variety.

The attention of **Amateur Photographers** is specially called to the supply of Photographic Requirements, including **Kodaks, Films & Accessories.**

Amateurs' Plates Developed, Printed and Enlarged at short notice.

C. T. MAINE, 35, King Street.

Sun Glasses

Cinema Glasses

When you have been out in the glare of the sun—or when you have been to the pictures—is your pleasure spoilt by Eye-strain or Headache?

THE BEST DAYS ARE HERE—ENJOY THEM.

Our Optician, GEO. ALLEN, F.S.M.C., F.I.O., will advise you **FREE OF CHARGE.**

Crookes Glasses, Smoke Glasses, Blue Glasses in Stock.

OPTICAL REPAIRS.

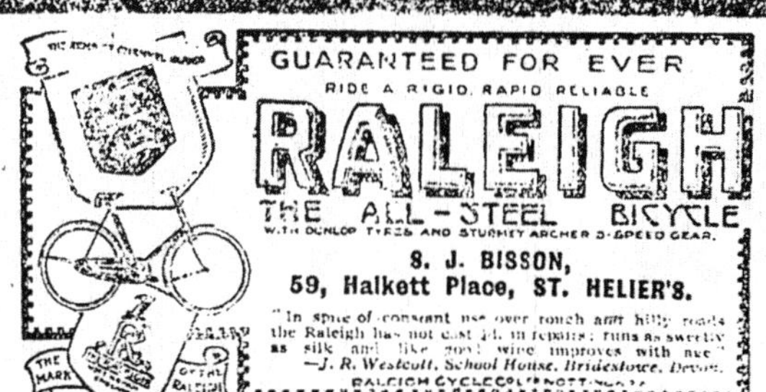

Make Your Ford Car Into a One-Ton Lorry

SPECIAL OFFER TO FORD OWNERS

WE will fit the "BAICO" ONE TON ATTACHMENT to your Ford Chassis and give you the use of it for one week entirely free of any charge. At the end of that time you can either purchase the attachment at the advertised price— or return it to us without it costing you a penny.

First Come. First Served.

CORSETS 'LA CYBELE'

DISTINCTIVE MODELS FOR EVERY TYPE OF FIGURE.

SEE DISPLAY.

6d, 9d, and 1s. (including seat).

Concert to be followed by a

Grand Bal de Nuit

ALL THE LATEST DANCES & MUSIC.

Dancing to commence at 10 p.m. Tickets, 1s. Onlookers, 6d.

Refreshments, including ices, will be obtainable at the Buffet.

TICKETS may be obtained from Mr. J. Lindsey, or any member of the Committee.

THE

KING'S FUND

and the LOCAL FUND for our Disabled Service Men, and the Widows and Dependents of those Heroes who fell in the Country's Service.

FLAG DAY

Saturday, June 28, 1919.

—:o:—

REMEMBER, and, Remembering, Give as freely as these Heroes gave for you.

—:o:—

REMEMBER THE ISLAND FETE AT "THE GROVE," ST LAWRENCE.

In aid of the above Funds.

Parochial Stalls, Entertainments, Band, Merry-Go-Rounds, Novel Competitions for children, etc., etc.

RESERVE THIS DATE FOR THE KING'S FUND.

ROYAL ACADEMY OF MUSIC,

YORK GATE, MARYLEBONE ROAD, LONDON, N.W.1.

Instituted 1822. Incorporated by Royal Charter 1830

THE METROPOLITAN EXAMINATION OF MUSICAL COMPOSERS, PERFORMERS AND TEACHERS.

Successful candidates are created LICENTIATES of the ROYAL ACADEMY OF MUSIC, and have the sole right of appending the letters L.R.A.M. to their names. The Examinations are held during the Summer and Christmas vacations. Last day of entry for the Summer Examination, June 30th. Entries can be received until July 15th on payment of a late fee of 5/-.

Syllabuses, entry form and all further information may be obtained on application to Alfred Lichtenberg, Esq., 26, West Park Avenue, St. Helier, Hon. Local Representative, or to The Secretary of the R.A.M.

Miss Mary Haynes,

L.R.A.M. SINGING, L.R.A.M. PIANO,

REMOVED TO

4, Canterbury Place, Stopford Rd.

Comrades of the Great War

WANTED: SECRETARY

ANY Comrade desirous of taking up Secretarial duties is invited to send in a form of application addressed to the Commandant, C.O.G.W., 7, Mulcaster St.

Full particulars required, also stating capabilities.

Applications to be sent in by Monday, 23rd inst.

Victoria Garage, Bagot.

TAXIS to and from Steamers, or for Touring, at MODERATE TERMS.

TELEPHONE - - 289

NOTICE.

I THE UNDERSIGNED, Curator to the property and person of Mr. Philip Le Feuvre, son of Francis, of "Grantez," in the Parish of St. Ouen, give notice to all persons not to give credit to the said Mr. Le Feuvre, nor to contract any business with him on pain of same being null and void.

And all persons having claims against the said Mr. Le Feuvre are requested to send me a detailed statement of same within a fortnight from this date, and all who may be indebted to him are requested to settle with me without delay.

GEO. F. D. LE GALLAIS.
6, Hill Street, Jersey,
21st June, 1919.

1.4 Two notices in the `Jersey Evening Post` classifieds in June 1919 announced the opening of the Society's Office at 41 New Street on the 23rd, and the first Jersey Co-operative Society shop at the same address on the

WEST'S PICTURES.

MONDAY NEXT & Two Following Nights,

OLGA PETROVA

IN

TEMPERED STEEL

—:●:—

BOOK AT DE GUERIN'S HALKETT LIBRARY and Avoid Disappointment.

Good Things to Eat at Guiton's

Here are two tasty things denied you during the War:

New Season's Freshly Made Seville Orange Marmalade,

The genuine pre-war kind in 1 lb. Jars 1/- 2 lb. Jars 1/8

Luscious Chinese Figs

in Wooden Drums 2/- each —a fruity confection that never cloys the appetite.

Guiton's is headquarters for good things to eat.

We have large supplies— but do not expect them to linger long on our shelves. Order in time.

P. Guiton

GOOD THINGS TO EAT

31, Bath Street and 12, Queen Street.

SMALL QUANTITY

Stone Lime for Tomatoes

Ready for IMMEDIATE DELIVERY.

Apply, Building Yard, Le Geyt St.

Seasonable Provisions

JAPANESE CRAB, per tin 1/11½
CRAYFISH, per tin 1/10
COLLARED HEAD, per tin ... 1/3
HAM & TONGUE PATE, per tin 1/3
BEEF & TONGUE, glasses ... 2/6
OX TONGUES, large ... ...6/11 & 8/6
LUNCH TONGUES, per tin ... 3/6
SALAD CREAM, bottles ... 1/6 & 2/6

Complete Stock of Pickles, Sauces, Salad Oils, Vinegars, Sardines, Salmon and Cooked Meats.

Large Assortment of POTTED MEATS, each ... 6½d. & 10½d.

—:0:—

ESTABLISHED OVER 80 YEARS.

BICHARDS

CHARING CROSS SUPPLY STORES.

FRESH ARRIVAL OF FINE

OLD POTATOES

(LARGE SAMPLE.)

SUITABLE FOR CHIPS

CHEAP. Apply:—

Frederick Baker & Sons, Ltd.

QUEEN STREET.

C. KENT & Co.

WE BUY
ALL CLASSES
FAT CATTLE
FOR CASH.

BUY WAR CERTIFICATES. £1 FOR 15/6

Tel. 70

9, 10, 11,
MARKET

Meat Merchants

Deliveries Everywhere Every Day.

Jersey Co-Operative Society.

THE Society's Bakery and Confectionery Departments will be OPENED on the 30th inst., at **41, NEW STREET.**

BREAD will be retailed **11d. per 4lb.** loaf over counter, 1s. delivered.

Branch Establishment : 24½, CHARING CROSS.

CUT THIS OUT AND KEEP IT.

MOTOR BUS SERVICE

SUMMER SERVICE, JUNE 29th, 1919.

SUNDAY	10 am		6 0 pm		For St. John's, St. Mary's and St. Ouen's
MONDAY	8 am	12 noon	5 10 pm		,, St. John's and St. Mary's
	8 am	12 noon	5 10 pm		,, St. Ouen's
TUESDAY	8 am		5 10 pm		,, St. Martin's to Faldouet
	8 am		5 10 pm		,, Trinity, Les Becquets
WEDNESDAY	8 am	12 noon	5 10 pm		,, St. Ouen's
	8 am	12 noon	5 10 pm		,, St. John's and St. Mary's
THURSDAY	8 am	2 pm	5 10 pm		,, St. John's and St. Mary's
	8 am	2 pm	5 10 pm		,, St. Ouen's
FRIDAY	8 am		5 10 pm		,, St. Martin's to Faldouet
	8 am		5 10 pm		,, Trinity, Les Becquets
SATURDAY	8 am	12 noon	4 25 pm	7 10 pm	,, St. John's and St. Mary's
	8 am	12 noon	4 25 pm	7 10 pm	,, St. Ouen's

The 'Bus will start from 37, BATH STREET, at the above-stated hours, and the return journey from each Terminus one hour later.

FARE

St. Ouen's direct ... 1s.	each way	St. Martin's direct... 9d.	each way
St. Peter's direct ... 9d.	,,	Faldouet direct ...... 10d.	,,
St. Mary's direct ... 10d.	,,	Trinity direct .... 9d.	,,
St. John's direct ... 9d.	,,	Les Becquets direct... 10d.	,,

SUNDAY: Only Return Tickets Issued. Fare, 2s.

The Termini are so arranged that **VISITORS** can reach the principal PLACES OF INTEREST, all of which are within easy walking distance.

St. Ouen's—For Plemont Caves, l'Etacq, Grève-de-Lecq, Crabbé, etc.
St. Mary's & St. John's—For Bonne Nuit Bay, Wolf Caves, Devil's Hole, Grève-de-Lecq
Trinity & St. Martin's—For Bouley Bay, Rozel, St. Catherine's and Anne Port.

SOLE AGENT for the Famous

Willeys' Overland.

Before deciding to purchase a new car, wait and see the new **Model 90 Willeys' Overland**, fitted with Electric Light and self-starter.

I have secured a permit to import a Demonstration Model direct from the works in America, and expect it to arrive in the island in about 4 weeks.

G. BENETT.

SOLE AGENT FOR **FORD CARS.**

NOTICE.

On and after SATURDAY NEXT, June 28th, 1919:

Through Bookings

Between the Two Companies

Will Cease.

BY ORDER.

Royal Jersey Agricultural and Horticultural Society

AGRICULTURAL DEPARTMENT.

JERSEY HERD BOOK.

AN EXAMINATION OF CATTLE eligible for qualification will be held on TUESDAY, July 1st, as follows:—

At the Show Grounds, at 9 a.m.
At St. Peter's Parish Hall, at 10 15 a.m.
Near St. Ouen's Parish Hall, at 11 a.m.
At Haut des Buttes, St. Mary, at 11. 45 a.m
Near Les Capelles, St. John, at 12.15 p.m
At the Haute Croix, at 12 45 p.m.
At Bouley Bay Hotel, at 2.30 p.m.
At St. Martin's Arsenal, at 3 p m.
At Prince's Tower, at 3 45 p.m.

ENTRY FEES (Bulls and Heifers):—
Members of the Department, 3/- each entry.
Non-Members, 4/- "
Entries on Day of Examination, 4/- and 5/- respectively.

ENTRIES will be received at the Society's Office. No. 3, Mulcaster Street, DAILY UNTIL SATURDAY NEXT, the 28th inst.

H. G. SHEPARD Secretary.

LONDON.

57, Torrington Square, British Museum, W.C.1.

Magnificent central position. Room and breakfast from 5s. daily. Recommended. A. A. James (Mrs.).

COSWAY STUDIOS,

Bath Street.

Mr. Horace J. Ramon

HAS pleasure in announcing that having engaged the services of an Operator of exceptional ability, he is able to undertake sittings without a previous appointment if desired.

Proofs will be submitted in 3 days and complete orders within a fortnight.

CLOVERS and RYE GRASSES,

Swedes, Turnips,
Sprayers, Raffia,

SULPHATE OF COPPER.

C. A. SORMANY

19, BATH STREET.

VALUE

Cheer Up!

If you've been reading reports on "World Shortage of Woollens," "Tailors' Exorbitant Charges," etc., HIPSLEY advice is, CHEER UP! See our wide range of Suitings. Sterling quality. Then notice Hipps' prices.

There's no shortage of Tailoring Value at Hipps.

Our Style No. 1529

To measure - - from 70/-

2/- in the £ Discount to all demobilised men.

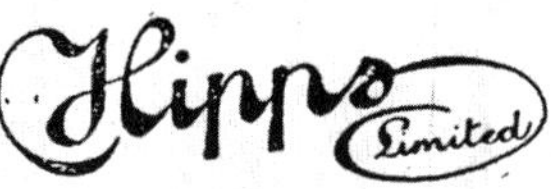

44½, King Street,

Jersey.

30th. The shop offered bakery and confectionery departments, with bread sold at 11d per 4lb loaf in the shop or delivered for a penny extra at 1 shilling (about 5p now) was quoted and, as we shall read later, the Guernsey Society, as it was before amalgamation, did not come into being until after the Occupation – though there were, as in Jersey, shops using the name Co-operative Society some years earlier.

The newly formed Management Committee wasted no time in putting theory into practice. Just a month after the founding meeting, a notice appeared in the classified section in the *Evening Post* of Saturday 21 June notifying the public that the Society's office over the shop at 41 New Street would open on the following Monday to receive applications for membership. This was followed by a further notice on 27 June that trading would commence on Monday 30 June in bakery and confectionery at the same address, and at a 'Branch Establishment at 24½ Charing Cross' (**1.4**).

In fact, considerable activity had been going on behind the scenes during the preceding month, for the energetic members of the Committee had quickly succeeded in renting these two shops, probably with the friendly help of their business contacts in town and the backing of the CWS. No 41 New Street had been confectioner's prior to 1919, run by a Mr James Wright, so a similar business could move in with a minimum of interior shop and office fittings needed (**1.5**, **1.6**).

It may be wondered how the newly fledged Society could rent premises and buy a considerable amount of stock for the new shop, and then, only two years later, in June 1921, purchase premises in the centre of town at a cost of £4,000. That early local Committee must have been wide awake to future possibilities and have shown great faith in its ability to shape the new Society by the purchase of No 3 Pitt Street and Nos 27 & 28 Charing Cross, a prime site in the centre of town. How did they do it?

The press report of that first meeting in May 1919 gives a clue in its references to the oration of Mr Williams on the formation of the Co-operative Movement in Britain and his presence that night on behalf of the Co-operative Wholesale Society. The CWS were clearly to be the local backers of the scheme in Jersey in furtherance of a guiding principle of the movement, namely to give financial backing and support to their individual stores which, though operating independently, are an integral part of the whole.

The CWS had been well established in Jersey for some time as a trading partner in the agricultural life of the Island, operating, like other local merchants, from stores near the harbours. It first occupied No 27 Esplanade, which it shared with L'Union Agricole de Jersey, and later No 60 Kensington Place. An indication of CWS influence on the farming and trading world before the Occupation is given by the photo-

1.5 No 41 New Street, an impressive corner shop for the Society's first venture into the local commercial world. In recent years it was the home of Jersey Cancer Relief and is now The Daily Grind coffee bar (1998 photo, Ken Renault)

1.6 An elegant No 41 suspended over the main door (1998 photo, Ken Renault)

graph, taken probably in the 1920s, which shows the CWS coastal steamer *Progress* of Manchester at the Albert Pier loading potatoes from a lorry and trailer of the Jersey Trading Co. Ltd (**1.7**). In addition to the export business they imported fertilisers, barrels and trays for general agricultural needs.

It was no doubt in the confidence born of CWS support that the Jersey Society, still at its Registered Office, No 41 New Street, was able to purchase from the Le Monnier family 3 Pitt Street and 27 & 28 Charing Cross, the first major move towards the final establishment of the Co-op in that important block development (**1.8**). No 27 would eventually become the Society's Registered Office.

An interesting personal factor comes into focus here: Mrs Rosalie Le Brocq, widow of the late President, Norman Le Brocq, was born above No 28 Charing Cross where her father, John Le Riche, occupied the premises as an ironmongers and general hardware shop. Later, the Le Riche family lived in Val Plaisant, where John Le Riche ran a garage business. In a contract dated 23 September 1950 the Jersey Society purchased the freehold house and garage, No 55 Val Plaisant (see **3.3** below), from Mr John Le Riche for the sum of £7,000. This continued as a garage and workshop for the Society's use until 1967, when it was rebuilt and opened in January 1968 as the Val Plaisant supermarket.

Evidence of that financial and practical CWS support in the early days can be seen in extracts from the archives of the Midland Bank in London as early as May 1919. Here we read that Mr AJ Aubin of the Hill Street branch had opened up the question with his head office and had remarked 'we should like to get this account if possible', a positive indication of early action to establish the Society financially.

By January 1920 formal application has been made for '£500 at 5% as a limit agreeably with client for business purposes', presumably as a loan, though with some guarded warning recorded – 'Returns £3,505, Present balance £111 Dr.' – possibly a reference to the trading account of the first shops.

1.7 The CWS coastal steamer *Progress* of Manchester moored at the Albert Pier loading Jersey potatoes from a lorry and trailer of the Jersey Trading Co., probably during the early 1920s

An interesting paragraph on Proposed Security and Guarantee then gives the names of the Management Committee of that time. These were:

- Ernest Le Vavasseur dit Durell, who 'keeps a satisfactory account with us'
- Walter du Feu, 'assessed @ 51 quarters, average balance of £500 current account at Jersey Bank'
- Arthur Le Quesne
- H du Heaume Allix, 18 quarters 'account with us and keeps average £550 at Jersey branch'
- Edward Le Quesne, 45 quarters
- John Vernon de Gruchy, 42 quarters
- P N Gallichan, 60 quarters
- Messrs E & A Le Quesne wish to invest their share of their late father's estate, which was assessed at 502 quarters St Helier and 92 quarters St Martin.

Within a few days some minor changes had been made in the formation of the Committee. This meant a fresh application was required. Interesting observations are made, among them that Philip Nicole Gallichan was a Builder, 'respectable and considered good for four figures', and that Allix was a partner in Allix's Tobacconists of Queen Street – this well-known shop was closed only recently – while Philip Hamon Junior 'is Chief Clerk at Messrs Le Masurier and Giffard our Bank Solicitors'.

So, in those few simple but interesting entries in the Midland Bank files we glimpse the modest beginnings of the Jersey Co-operative Society. It would establish itself and expand during the 1920s, slowly as opportunity occurred, but with a determined optimism and enthusiasm.

The Jersey Co-operative Society Limited.

Telegrams: "JERCOP, JERSEY"

Kindly address all communications to THE SOCIETY, not to individuals.

Reference:

—LD 15775—

Registered Office—41, NEW STREET, ST. HELIER, JERSEY,

COUR ROYALE 6 AOU 1921 JERSEY

August 3rd 1921.

At a Meeting of the Committee of Management of the Jersey Co-operative Society Limited, held at their registered office, No 41 New Street, Jersey, on the 22n d.day of June 1921.

It was resolved that Philip Orde Sandilands President, William Frank Gale, Secretary, and Frederick Hubert Fisher, Manager, be and are hereby named Mandatories and representatives of the Society in order to pass before the Royal Court for and on behalf of the Society, the Contract or Deed of purchase of the premises Nos 27 & 28 Charing Cross, bordering on Charing Cross and Pitt Street, from Mr Louis Charles Le Monnier and Mrs Jane Le Monnier, née Penny, his mother, for the sum of £4000 payable in cash, the property being free from rentes.

Signed for and on behalf of

JERSEY CO-OPERATIVE SOCIETY, LTD.

P. Sandilands ...President.

W. F. Gale ...Secretary.

F. H. Fisher ...Manager.

1.8 The Resolution of the Management Committee dated 3 August 1921 by which the main buildings of Nos 27 & 28 Charing Cross were purchased and which is still the Society's central store and also the Registered Office of the Society

The first Annual Meeting, held in 1921, reported to members that trade turnover had amounted to £10,400 for the previous year (at least £250,000 at present-day values) and membership was about 300. This was an impressive result, achieved in only two years' trading.

Also in 1921 we find that first major property purchase when, as we have seen, the Society bought 27 & 28 Charing Cross and 3 Pitt Street, an adjoining property. It could then concentrate the grocery trade in one larger store in a more prominent shopping area in the town centre. The rented property at No 41 New Street was retained for the time being as the bakery and confectioners, with the Society's offices continuing upstairs.

In this context we read that the Society wrote to the Royal Court in August 1921 from its Registered Office at No 41, in order to pass contract for this purchase of Charing Cross, naming as mandatories and representatives Philip Orde Sandilands, President; William France Gale, Secretary; and Frederick Hubert Fisher, Manager. This welcome expansion allowed eventually for the construction of a bakery in Pitt Street, when the confectioners was transferred to No 28 and tenancy of No 41 New Street was relinquished.

At that time the north side of Charing Cross consisted of a row of small shops extending to the corner of Dumaresq Street. Readers may remember them as they were gradually purchased by the Society, particularly during the 1960s and 1970s, to form part of the present Co-op frontage from Pitt Street to Dumaresq Street.

1.9 Nos 27 and 28 Charing Cross, taken in about 1930. Bread and confectionery are prominent in the two windows, but also precautionary timberwork on the front face, a presage of difficulties ahead

Nos 24 & 25 Charing Cross were a modest grocery and greengrocery owned by a Mr Bichard. It was to be a very suitable place from which to set up a more permanent base, and no doubt Mr Bichard had permitted a short-term rental of No 24 – 'the branch establishment' – to enable the Society to open for business while Nos 27 & 28 were being fitted out as their permanent premises.

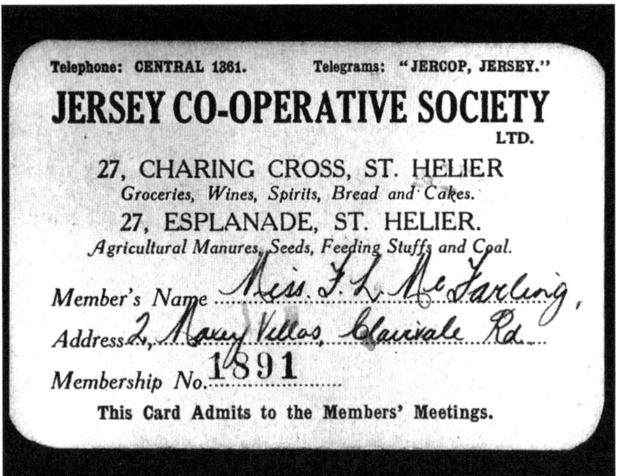

Telephone: CENTRAL 1361. Telegrams: "JERCOP, JERSEY."

JERSEY CO-OPERATIVE SOCIETY LTD.

27, CHARING CROSS, ST. HELIER
Groceries, Wines, Spirits, Bread and Cakes.

27, ESPLANADE, ST. HELIER.
Agricultural Manures, Seeds, Feeding Stuffs and Coal.

Member's Name Miss F. L. McFarling,
Address 2, Mary Villas, Clairvale Rd.
Membership No. 1891

This Card Admits to the Members' Meetings.

1.10 A member's card of the pre-war period, indicating not only the member's address and membership number, but also the continuing close relationship between the Society and the CWS

The 1920s saw the still young Society continuing to establish itself in the public eye, and the accompanying illustration shows the solid-looking frontage of 27 & 28 Charing Cross in about 1930, with its full business name prominently displayed above the fascia and on the wall above (**1.9**). The confectionery department is clearly visible in the corner window, with groceries in the adjacent window. The upper windows display in gilt lettering typical of the period 'Show Rooms' and 'Boot & Shoe Departments', while on the glass panel of the front door the initials JCS are already intertwined like a modern logo.

However, behind that substantial façade there were ominous indications of difficulties ahead, unknown perhaps to the shopping public, perhaps even to the members (**1.10**). The Depression of the early 1930s was to affect Jersey, not perhaps as seriously as in Britain but sufficiently to cause financial problems in our Islands.

We no longer have the Society records of that period but we can read of these difficulties in the CWS Minutes of 10 March 1931:

1.11 The original building, 27 and 28 Charing Cross, demolished in preparation for the rebuilding, which when completed would reveal an architectural style in great contrast to the previous structure. The Cumings butcher's shop can just be seen to the left of the timberwork

> Jersey Society (Under Supervision) –
>
> Resolved:
> that we request the Committee of the Jersey Society to hand over the control and management of their affairs to a representative to be appointed by the CWS on our usual conditions. That, subject to Society agreeing to give us control of their business, we agree to pass to them a trade credit of £500, so as to enable them to write down the debts owing, amounting to £2,260.2s.6d. It is estimated that £294 are bad and £464 doubtful.

And again on 7 July:

> Jersey Society (under supervision) –
> The Final Meeting of Society's Members was held on 24th June, when the necessary resolution giving the CWS complete control was passed by the necessary majority –
>
> Resolved:
> that this be noted, and that we agree to a trade credit of £500 being passed to the Society, so as to enable them to write down the debts owing amounting to £2,260.2s.6d.
>
> That Mr Newman be appointed Supervisor of this Society.

Regrettably, all Society minutes and records of those formative two decades from 1919 to 1939 were lost or destroyed during the Occupation. In the absence of documentary evidence we can only presume that possibly owing to weakness or lack of experience of the local management and the accounting procedures, accentuated perhaps by the effects of the Depression on trading, the Society had allowed debts of £2,260 to build up, necessitating an appeal to the CWS for help.

Such a move as this, a complete takeover by CWS, must have been a serious blow to the new Society, only 11 years after its auspicious start. However, a serious situation had arisen and CWS assumed control for some time, in fact, up to the eve of the Occupation. Presumably the local Management Committee continued in office to deal with its usual duties of supervising the daily shop routines but was unable to exercise any financial responsibilities.

Linked with this situation was the problem, forced upon them, of dealing with the precarious state of the corner building at Nos 27 & 28. The Surveyor's reports on this structure when contract was passed, only 15 years before, must have been extremely lax for serious defects are visible and more were to be exposed in the course of demolition. Heavy temporary struts were clamped to the wall between windows on the first floor, intended to give support against possible collapse.

However, towards the end of the 1930s, the financial situation must have eased sufficiently for the CWS to have agreed to a full rebuilding of the corner. This decision to rebuild was most probably inevitable, for in its current management and financial role CWS would have been duty bound to safeguard their main premises.

A Mr Gladden of St Martin was the builder who undertook the contract to rebuild. Demolition of the old building was carried out in 1937 (**1.11**), revealing even more serious trouble, for areas below ground were filled with water. Gladden must have been dismayed, to say the least, at the state of the foundations and cellars. It had been known for many years that this area of Charing Cross and York Street was liable to flooding at the peak of spring tides, and only in recent years has the town drainage been improved sufficiently to avoid this occasional flooding of the streets and basement areas.

In 1937 the problem was serious enough to incur considerable additional work and cost. The builders succeeded in rendering the whole basement area watertight so that it could be used for storage, but in a comparatively short time dampness began to seep through the new work. Cliff Pinel recalls that the cellars were not a long-term solution to the storage of perishable goods. As we shall read later, this matter of storage was to become an acute problem, added to by the Society's welcomed and continuing growth and the greater number of shops to be kept supplied from a central source. Very shortly after the new building was completed, when the German bombers raided the town in June 1940, the basement became the staff air raid shelter, fortunately for only a very short time, until the Germans arrived.

To enable normal business to continue while building was going on, temporary shops were opened in the storerooms in Pitt Street (**1.12**, **1.13**). In very cramped conditions stock was shelved or just stacked on the floor (**1.14**, **1.15**). It was business as usual as far as was possible, and the local committee and staff deserved praise for their patience, though how customers managed to

1.12 Aerial view of the temporary shop in Pitt Street opened during the rebuilding

complete their purchases in such conditions is a testament to their loyalty.

After demolition the architectural design of the new shop followed the modern/art-deco style of the period. Flat concrete-faced walls, with Crittall pattern steel windows and a black polished fascia displaying a classic Co-operative Society name were up-to-date and top of the range, and possibly one of the first such designs in Jersey at that time (**1.16**, **1.17**). Fortunately, the rebuilding was completed just before the Occupation, thus allowing

1.13 Close-up of window of the Pitt Street shop (on bottom left of **1.12**), showing a neat display of confectionery despite the lack of space

the restocking of the shop from CWS sources in Britain before restrictions were introduced. The temporary premises in Pitt Street were closed.

Harry Kinnish, who joined the staff in 1938, was involved in the pre-Occupation period and would have experienced the companionship of the small friendly shop staff of just four or five at Charing Cross. He also would have known the work involved in stocking the shelves and arranging the counter displays. As we see from the illustrations much of the stock came from CWS sources in bottles, cans or boxes, with a hint of Australian produce and New Zealand cheese and butter, the latter a great favourite of the period at 1/- a pound (about 5p today).

Those main domestic items of butter, lard, margarine, sugar, dried fruit, etc, were delivered in bulk to be weighed and packed individually for the customer. Some shops of that period had large blocks of butter on marble slabs at the back of the counter from which the assistants would estimate and cut a portion with wooden butter pats and dextrously bring it to the scales to be checked before packing it neatly in greaseproof paper. Sides of bacon, which were delivered wrapped in linen, were often hung behind the counter before being cut into

1.14 Inside Pitt Street: temporary grocery department, indicating a determination to display the stock as invitingly as possible, despite lack of space

1.15 Temporary confectionery department

1.16 The new building at 27 Charing Cross, with keen but well-organised queuing. It looks like the first day of trading

1.17 A grainy shot of the façade of 27 Charing Cross, reproduced with a story in `Co-operative News` on 12 September 1942, which gave an update on life in the Islands during the Occupation

manageable pieces for the bacon slicers. This would have been the typical grocery and provision scene of the time, though regrettably we no longer have a record of Co-op practice during that period.

Despite the difficulties the young Society was compelled to face and to endure during the 1930s, progress continued, no doubt with the active support of CWS, which had both to consider the temporary failure of a new Society, which it had so strongly backed only ten or twelve years previously, and for which it now had financial responsibility. Accordingly, we see that by contract of 12 May 1932 a property in Don Road, opposite Royal Crescent, was purchased for £2,500 (**1.18**). This was used as a coal store from which deliveries were made to members, coal being a necessity in those days for the cooking ranges and open fires that were commonplace in most family homes. The mandataire nominated to pass contract in the Royal Court was George Ernest Williams, who signed the contract as Manager and Secretary.

This further requisition of property was to prove of considerable value to the Society in various guises for the next 38 years, as we shall read in later chapters.

At about this time bakery rounds were also introduced. The original Pitt Street bakery could not cope with the increased demand, so the coal department was transferred from Don Road to a

13 1933 237

A la Cour Royale de l'Ile de Jersey.

L'An mil neuf cent TRENTE-DEUX, LE QUATORZIÈME JOUR DE MAI.

PAR DEVANT Charles Edward MALET DE CARTERET, Ecuier, BAILLI de l'Ile de Jersey, assisté de Philip de Carteret Le Cornu et Guy Fortescue Burrell de Gruchy, Ecuiers, Jurés.

SOCIÉTÉS À RESPté LIMITÉE

Sur la demande de la Société avec responsabilité limitée incorporée sous le nom de "The Jersey Co-operative Society Limited" en vertu des prescriptions de l'Acte de Parlement dit "Industrial and Provident Societies Act 1893" (lequel a été enregistré dans cette Ile) comme paraît par certain certificat en date du 3 Juillet 1919 portant le sceau du Registre dit "Registry of Friendly Societies Central Office" et faisant commerce en cette Ile, la Cour a ordonné l'enregistrement dans le livre du Registre des Sociétés à responsabilité limitée, de certaine résolution des Directeurs de ladite Société portant la date du 29e jour d'Avril 1932 par laquelle résolution Monsr. George Ernest Williams est nommé Mandataire de ladite Société aux fins de passer certain contrat héréditaire spécifié dans ladite résolution et ce afin que ladite résolution tire son plein et entier effet selon sa teneur.

DE LAQUELLE RESOLUTION LA TENEUR SUIT:-

12th May, 1932.

The Committee of Management of THE JERSEY CO-OPERATIVE SOCIETY LIMITED. at a Meeting held on the 29th April, 1932.

RESOLVED -

That George Ernest Williams, Manager and Secretary of the Jersey Co-operative Society, Ltd., be

238

be and is hereby named Mandatary and Representative of the Society in order to pass before the Royal Court of Jersey on behalf of the Society the Contract or Deed of Purchase of the premises No. 26, Don Road, for the sum of £2,500 payable in cash, and also to be a party to the necessary Deed for the commutation of the seignorial rights in respect of the aforesaid property. -

Signed for and on behalf of the
JERSEY CO-OPERATIVE SOCIETY LTD.
(Signed) A. E. Newman
Minute Secretary.

- 2 -

1.18 The Resolution of the Society presented to the Royal Court on 14 May 1932 by which No 26 Don Road was purchased, a building that was to serve the Society in a variety of guises for the next 38 years

merchant's store in Anley Street and a new bakery was installed at Don Road. It is not easy now to contemplate the work involved and the nuisance of dust when delivering coal around the town and to and from the harbour and the store, but the writer can remember as a boy watching the colliers moored at the top of the New North Quay just opposite the old JRT terminus. Coal was unloaded from the holds, hauled up by little steam cranes swinging around from ship to shore, to be loaded into horse-drawn carts, a cloud of dust rising to shore from every basketful.

Anley Street was not the easiest place for storage, a narrow thoroughfare with traffic in both directions. It was not an easy place for coal lorries to gain access; this was proved when, as we read later, the coal was transferred again to the CWS store at No 27 Esplanade, which remained in operation until 1948. At that time the Georgetown purchase was made and the coal business was brought up to Elizabeth Street, creating the same nuisance of dust and noise in close proximity to the new Co-op shop.

This brief résumé of the early years of the Society, before, during and after the Occupation, will give us some idea of the difficulties faced by the management and staff as they persevered in that initial endeavour to establish and embed Co-operative ideals in Jersey.

2.1 A shadow falls across the Islands (Jersey Heritage Trust, © Société Jersiaise)

Chapter 2

The Occupation Years

The 1930s were a testing time for the Jersey Society, for, apart from the unexpected, and no doubt unwelcome, total control by CWS in 1931, the necessary rebuilding of the old Charing Cross corner block Nos 27 & 28, and the uncertainty over future financial arrangements, the closing years of the decade witnessed the spectre of war spreading across Europe (**2.1–2.4**).

The Society was suddenly being made aware of changes to come. A young man by the name of John Morris was to find himself at the centre of those changes. John was born in Wellingborough, Northants, in May 1915 during the First World War. He left school at 15 and entered Co-operative Society employment in 1938. Still a young man but already showing his abilities, he became Chief Clerk at the Market Harborough Society and was obviously a candidate for further progress.

After this lapse of time we can only guess at the train of events that brought John to Jersey. It is likely that the CWS Supervisory Committee members, though still in financial control, were planning some strategy to enable the Jersey Society to become more self-supporting again. To this end they may have enquired in the UK for candidates who might exercise some greater responsibility within the Society.

2.2 German regiment marching in St Helier, while a policeman watches (Jersey Heritage Trust, © Société Jersiaise)

Whatever the circumstances, John Morris was offered the position of Chief Clerk/Accountant with the Jersey Society. He arrived in 1939, aged only 24, at the outset of the war already being waged in Europe. Quickly settling into Island life as a keen and popular young sportsman, he little realised the responsibilities that were to face him just months ahead.

During those early months in St Helier John and George Townend shared a flat together, then John moved into digs at the Caesarea Hotel in Cattle Street. As he settled into business routine at Head Office in Charing Cross, he would have become aware that much needed to be done if the Society was to recover its previous local control.

With the worsening news of the war in Europe during the early months of 1940 another question loomed: what would the Society do in any future emergency? It was the CWS Supervisory Committee that made all senior management appointments. As June drew nearer the decision was taken for them, as all CWS staff and senior management left the Island with the general evacuation. John Morris was now in charge, a heavy responsibility for a young man only recently arrived from England.

However, he was helped by the presence of another young man, George Townend, who had been sent over by CWS just a few months before Morris. These two young members, new to Jersey, got on well together, and, faced with the inevitable, they shared responsibilities amicably. Townend took over as Food Manager while Morris remained

2.3 View of Noirmont Point, showing German control tower (Occupation Memorial Image Library, © Société Jersiaise)

2.4 Part of the front façade of The Forum cinema, St Helier, with swastika flags and banners (Occupation Memorial Image Library, © Société Jersiaise)

in the office as Chief Clerk, the appointment that had brought him to Jersey.

How serious this fortuitous situation might have become for both the Society and Morris can only be guessed at, when we recall that John had previously volunteered successfully for the Royal Navy as a writer during the winter of 1938–39 but had been told officially to await instructions! An accompanying photograph (**2.5**) shows the youthful John Morris dressed for the occasion when he was best man at the wedding of Ralph Le Herissier, a colleague in the office.

The early days and weeks of the Occupation saw little disturbance to the normal shop routine once the panic of evacuation had died down. Of the Island's population of 50,000 about 6,600 had chosen to leave (**2.6**), so for the first few months stocks of the usual foodstuffs were ample. Locals could buy their normal supplies, but the Germans, settling in after their first British conquest, could also take advantage and buy quite freely. It must have been a strange period of quiet, almost normality, through that first summer before rationing was introduced in October 1940.

But by that time stocks were becoming seriously depleted and the Co-op, along with the other big food retailers, Le Riche and Orviss, began to experience difficulties in ordering normal supplies. In fact, the Co-op probably had greater difficulties because of its normal reliance on assured deliveries from the CWS Retailing Division, deliveries that were now denied.

Mrs Joyce Moignard, née Coleman, of Yorkshire recalls those difficulties and retains a clear picture of her part at Charing Cross where she began, in 1939, her many years' service with the Society, mostly in the general office. Among Joyce's colleagues of that early period she remembers Ralph Le Herissier, Patricia Aldous and Dick Shenton, also Eileen Jenner, Dot McDermot, Olga Huelin, Harry Kinnish, Audrey Le Clair, Aileen Duquemin and Winifred Sinclair, who she believes continued working at the Co-op for many years.

Dick Shenton retains vivid memories of his early life during those demanding years. An 'Old Boy' of de la Salle, he left school at 15 and joined the Co-op staff as office boy at 15s per week (now 75p). He cycled into town every day to and from St

2.5 Photograph of the young John Morris, as best man at Ralph Le Herissier's marriage during the Occupation (photo Mrs Rose Lewis)

2.6 Queuing to register for evacuation, June 1940, outside the Town Hall (Occupation Memorial Image Library, © Channel Islands Occupation Society)

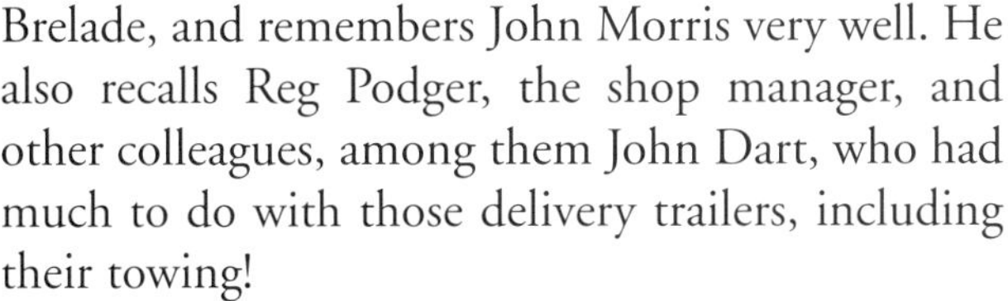

Brelade, and remembers John Morris very well. He also recalls Reg Podger, the shop manager, and other colleagues, among them John Dart, who had much to do with those delivery trailers, including their towing!

Dick remained with the Co-op for four years and remembers the family share number: 215. Looking back on his brief spell at the shop, he particularly recalls the friendly relationships among the staff and ever-helpful contacts they maintained with members and customers. In his own words, 'the Co-op really was a shop for the people in those difficult times, a true reflection of the Co-operative spirit that gave it birth'.

Mary Beuzeval, recalling the early 1950s, echoes those sentiments when she says 'the old Co-op was a friend and a great help to many, I'm sure. Shopping now is so impersonal.' She still remembers 'Dennis, who called every Monday morning for the grocery list, which would be delivered on the Wednesday, and the blue "divi" stamps that were such a help at Christmas.'

Throughout the Occupation the dividend continued to be paid to members. Joyce Moignard remembers that one of the many routine jobs in the office was counting up the coupons that were clipped off the ration books by the counter staff, to be entered in the ledgers and from which the dividend was calculated at the end of the year.

Used ration books had then to be taken, with the necessary forms, to the Food Control Office to obtain new books. If, as sometimes happened, a ration book was lost, the essential forms had to be completed again and taken to a Jurat, who would witness Joyce's signature and countersign before she could collect a replacement book from the Food Control Office.

The late Mrs Parkman, née Patricia Aldous, who also joined the Society in 1939, spent most of her time in the Cashiers Office at Charing Cross coping with the arrival of the cash containers sent up to her by the counter staff on the overhead wire carrier system. The containers held the ration coupons, which were passed on to the general office, with the customer's payment.

During the early days of the Occupation, when the Germans introduced their own currency, Patricia found marks and pfennigs rather confusing when counting up the change due to the customer, and there were occasions when she ran out of change temporarily. She would then return to the counter whatever currency she could with an IOU for the balance! She also recalled with a touch of nostalgic amusement the presence of Dick Shenton in the shop. It is said that a number of the girls were agreeably impressed by the 'smart, good-looking young man on the bread counter'.

Both Joyce and Patricia remembered that for the most of the Occupation period the Co-op was

2.7 A German soldier looks forward to an ice cream, outside the Charing Cross shop (Jersey War Tunnels Mayne Collection Bunderarchiv. Courtesy of the Jersey War Tunnels)

restricted to selling mainly the weekly grocery rations and bread – until the flour ran out – while a vegetable and produce shop was opened in Broad Street and managed by Muriel de la Mare. This occupied the old ABC café premises at the Charing Cross end, conveniently opposite the 'big' shop' as it was known among the junior staff.

Winifred Watson, née Sinclair, joined the Co-op in 1943 aged 16, and her first position was with Muriel, both doing their best with whatever vegetables and fruit could be found during that increasingly difficult period. Because of inevitable shortages the shop opened only from 10 am to 12.30 pm and 2 pm to 4 pm, with a half-hour extension on Friday and Saturday.

Potatoes became rationed and, for want of anything else, would often be cooked in seawater and eaten on their own as a treat. Another more satisfying treat was the occasional apple pie or even a little surplus fat from the Sand Street Bakery brought to the shop by George Townend, carefully wrapped up from view. Another delight was a sugar beet syrup when it could be produced.

When not on duty the German soldiers would wander through the town (**2.7**). They seemed to be fond of apples and would come into the shop and point to their choice – so the girls naturally found it necessary to keep the best apples and tomatoes out of sight, reserved for members and regulars, the Germans' selection being restricted to those left on display.

Despite the hardships of those years there were the usual social gatherings to look forward to. Perhaps on three or four summer Sundays during the year a horse and van would be borrowed or hired from Pitchers' stables in Kensington Place to take a party to the nearest beach that was open for swimming, or to Gorey, Rozel or St Brelade, where there were open areas for the horses to rest and graze.

During the winter months there were occasional evenings out to the First Tower Institute for dancing or perhaps to Boudins cycle shop in Bath Street, which had a big room on the top floor used for dance classes. It was an ideal place to relax, though as the evenings were short everyone hurried home at the last moment to avoid being caught out after curfew.

It was a difficult time to be a young girl out in the world, but Winifred Watson looks back on that period with pleasurable memories, though tempered by the occasional reminder of the tragedy of war, as when a group of prisoner of war (POW) workers would be marched past the shop by their German guards. Often the prisoners were in shabby, ragged clothes, perhaps with only sacking around their feet (**2.8**).

2.8 Forced workers under German guard, Jersey (Occupation Memorial Image Library, © Société Jersiaise)

Winifred left the Co-op after Liberation, but little did she know that Cliff Pinel would call on her one day years later to persuade her to return. This she did in 1963 and continued until 1988, one of her first shops being the old Georgetown premises.

The first major blow to the Society's business occurred quite early in the Occupation, with the requisition of the Don Road Bakery by the Germans to provide bread for their troops. The Germans later built their own bakery at Beaumont, which would figure again in the Society's history, as we shall see (**2.9**). As one of the main suppliers of bread to their customers by delivery, this requisition was serious for the Co-op. Eventually, through the medium of the Essential Supplies Department, an arrangement was reached with Lipscombe in Sand Street to share their bakery. This necessitated considerable shift work at Sand Street to ensure that all customers received their bread.

It should be remembered that until supermarkets took over in recent years the staples of bread

2.9 The German Bakery on Goose Green Marsh, Beaumont, St Peter. Built by the Todt Organisation (the letters O.T. Backerel can be seen) as a bakery for the German garrison, it continued in the same role for the Co-op for many years after the Occupation. It is now the location for the IT Centre and Total Sport (Occupation Memorial Image Library, © Société Jersiaise)

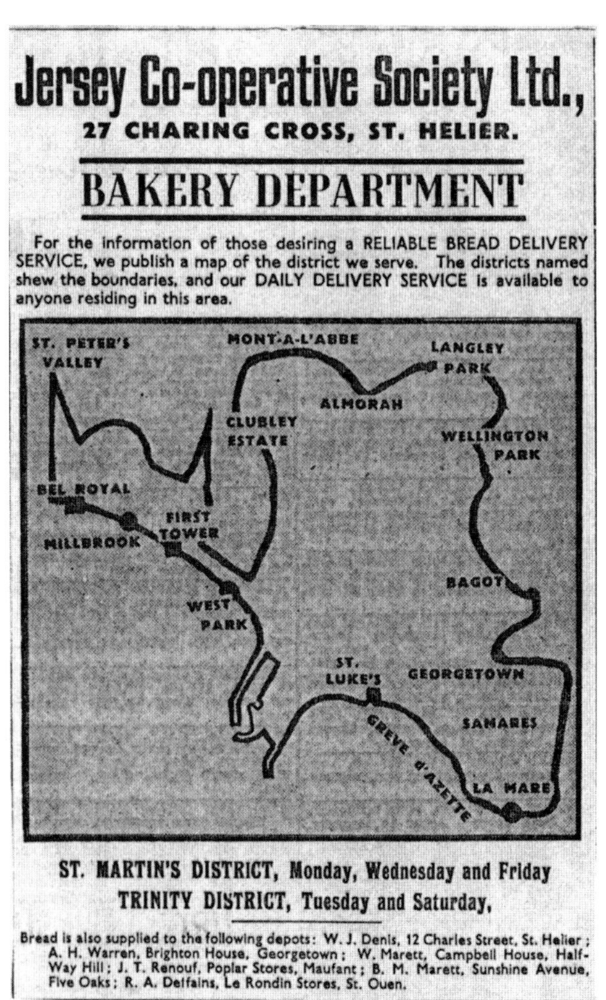

Jersey Co-operative Society Ltd.,

27 CHARING CROSS, ST. HELIER.

BAKERY DEPARTMENT

For the information of those desiring a RELIABLE BREAD DELIVERY SERVICE, we publish a map of the district we serve. The districts named shew the boundaries, and our DAILY DELIVERY SERVICE is available to anyone residing in this area.

ST. MARTIN'S DISTRICT, Monday, Wednesday and Friday

TRINITY DISTRICT, Tuesday and Saturday,

Bread is also supplied to the following depots: W. J. Denis, 12 Charles Street, St. Helier; A. H. Warren, Brighton House, Georgetown; W. Marett, Campbell House, Half-Way Hill; J. T. Renouf, Poplar Stores, Maufant; B. M. Marett, Sunshine Avenue, Five Oaks; R. A. Delfains, Le Rondin Stores, St. Ouen.

2.10 A Society notice in the Evening Post of 19 December 1941, showing the route of the Co-op Bakery delivery round covered by the bicycle trailers

and milk were delivered. Few people had cars, and petrol was rationed. The Society had contracts with the hospitals, prison and the Little Sisters' Home for their bread supply so were allowed petrol for one van for most of the Occupation.

Relations between Islanders and Germans were not easy, as the experience of Don Road baker Mr Geoff Delauney (**2.11**, **2.12**) highlights.

Deliveries of bread to the Society's members were to become more difficult, particularly to the country parishes. The sketch map (**2.10**) shows the extent of the main town delivery circuit and the route to Bel Royal and up St Peter's Valley. This restricted delivery round of the early Occupation period was curtailed still further when petrol rationing was tightened.

Then someone had the novel idea of continuing deliveries by means of lightweight trailer towed by bicycle. Apparently seven such trailers were built by Underhills, the coach-builders in Victoria Street. These were little more than boxes of plywood, or whatever material was available, mounted on light motorcycle wheels. They were towed around the town and as far out as Bel Royal and St Clement. The hilly roads must have called for a great deal of muscle power! Several 'depots' were set up in the country areas so that the van could deliver a bulk supply to each while the bicycle trailers could take over from each 'depot' and so economise on the meagre supply of petrol.

The face of defiance

2.11 Geoff Delauney's Occupation ID card picture

2.12 Mr Delauney in 2005

Islander Geoff Delauney was 15 years old and working with his father at the Co-operative Bakery in Don Road when the Germans arrived in June 1940. Now aged 80, Mr Delauney recalls how his scorn for German authority landed him in trouble and eventually led to his deportation to France.

'When the Germans arrived, nothing happened really,' he said. 'They were here and you were there. As long as you kept your nose clean, nothing happened. We had a curfew, of course, but apart from that life went on.'

The first time he came to the notice of the Germans was on the day English-born Islanders left by ship. Mr Delauney was among the crowd at Mount Bingham watching the departure.

'There was a lot of shouting and singing,' he recalled. 'Then the Germans came on the scene with fixed bayonets and revolvers and tried to get the crowd to disperse. The troops rushed in and it got nasty. Some of us were collared and they took us down to the Pomme d'Or, took our particulars and then sent us home.'

With a smile of his old defiance, Mr Delauney commented: 'I am not sure whether I was in the wrong place at the wrong time, or just shouting too much.'

He continued in the bakery, now moved to Sand Street, until he had another brush with the Occupation authorities. One day he was cycling with some friends past the Royal Hotel. A group of German soldiers came out the worse for drink, and one pushed him off his bike. Mr Delauney says: 'I got up and called him a Deutsche swine. They all rushed towards me, and I hopped off my bike and did a bunk.'

Unfortunately for Mr Delauney, he came face to face with the same officer again in a café in Colomberie a few days later, and after a commotion Mr Delauney was marched at rifle point to the secret police HQ at Silverside.

There he was beaten up and found himself in Newgate Street prison. Soon afterwards he was sent to Saint Lò prison in Normandy. Other adventures followed, including digging up unexploded bombs for the Germans in Paris, joining the Free French army as they marched into the city in August 1944 and finding his way back to Southampton and the Islands as a hero.

Mr Delauney got his wish to join the Royal Navy in September 1944 and worked in the North Atlantic convoys. After the war, he returned to Jersey and resumed work as a baker in partnership with his father. He met his wife Marge (née Pigeon) at a dance at the Milano, L'Etacq, and they have been married for 52 years.

Despite being beaten up, locked up and used as expendable labour by the Germans, Mr Delauney says he has never felt animosity towards them. 'It was war, and life was cheap. We have now got some great German friends.'

(With thanks to Mr Delauney and *Jersey Evening Post*, 28 April 2005)

Cliff Pinel, who joined the staff at Charing Cross in 1943 as a 'bacon boy' at 30s (£1.50) per week, also remembers these trailers with particular distaste. His normal round was up Vallée des Vaux as far as the Harvest Barn, through Grand Vaux and up Langley Park to Five Oaks – a hilly route indeed. Apart from the effort needed to tow them on the limited food rations available, Cliff still remembers the discomfort of the bumping experienced on the bicycles when tyres were worn out, and makeshift rope or old hosepipe were the only available replacements.

But the trials of the bread round and other discomforts of the times did not deter him, and we shall read more of Cliff in later chapters. These trailers were an example of the initiative and the ingenuity shown by our Jersey Society, and other shops too, to cope with the severe restrictions encountered in the course of normal and essential business – serving the customer.

Similar ideas surfaced when the Society took over the CWS packing station. Quantities of the flimsy paper used for lining the tomato trays in normal times could be cut into squares and packed to make serviceable toilet paper to sell in the shops. Old flour sacks were cut down and stitched to serve as shopping bags. The later years of the Occupation were indeed a period of trial for everyone, with initiative and ingenuity stretched to the limit.

Some of our present members may remember hearing of Lord Justice du Parcq, whose home on St Saviour's Hill was later to become Hautlieu School. He headed the Channel Islands Refugees Committee in London, whose main purpose was to assist the many thousands of Islanders who had evacuated to England while there was still time before the Germans arrived, and later, to establish and maintain whatever means of communication was possible with those who had remained in the Islands. This seems to have occurred early in 1941, when messages began to arrive in response to those sent by the British Red Cross.

The *Co-operative News* of Saturday 12 September 1942 (printed for the CWS in Manchester) gave prominent coverage of the situation so far as it was known from the details gathered from one of the early escapees. This account was headed 'Jersey Co-operators carry on under Nazi Supervision' and accompanied by a photograph of the rebuilt Charing Cross shop, Nos 27 and 28. The photo used was actually from pre-war (see **1.17**). A picture taken during the Occupation shows the anti-bomb protection added for the windows (**2.13**).

This *News* report mentions that 'up-to-date authentic news of the Jersey Co-operative Society is very scanty indeed'. But it was believed that 'its headquarters at St Helier are still undamaged; that trade is still being carried on under the supervision of the Nazis, although the shelves are almost empty, and the stocks in its warehouse are now very small indeed'. There was 'very severe' rationing in force under the Germans, although 'Early on, some essential supplies were obtained from France, by buyers sent there from the Islands.' Those early missions to France by Island buyers were initially permitted by the Germans on an ad hoc basis but eventually a permanent Purchasing Commission was set up to cover both Islands. This was then based in Granville and consisted of a representative from each Island – first Raymond Falla from Guernsey, later replaced by George Vaudin, and JL Jonault from Jersey – both under the supervision of a German officer.

These two men were required to travel long distances and worked seven days a week to meet and discuss with the French authorities the supply and exchange of critical items to and from the Islands, items which were not available elsewhere. The French were naturally reluctant to sell, believing of course that every pound sent away was a pound less for their own people who were also beginning to suffer, but they were required to do so under the arrangement with the German command. Generally speaking the two representatives found the suppliers themselves to be co-operative.

In the course of their many journeys Vaudin and Jonault were able to acquire a wide-ranging selection of urgently needed items in addition to the scarce foodstuffs, among these being insulin and also X-ray films for the hospital. In return the Islands were required to send what could be spared from their produce, and many thousands of tons of potatoes and tomatoes went off to France. It could fairly be said that in the absence of the normal export market to Britain, now closed off, much of the quantity still being grown could be spared without depriving the Islanders and that in exchange the Islands were receiving other essential foodstuffs and urgently needed items no longer available elsewhere.

We cannot say what immediate effect these arrangements would have had on Co-op stocks as everything received in this way would have been absorbed into the overall rationing, but obviously

2.13 Façade of the Charing Cross shop during the Occupation, showing anti-bomb blast window protection. The small cart on the left was used by ex-servicemen, who would push it around the streets and play gramophone records (Occupation Memorial Image Library, © Société Jersiaise)

the Society was gaining some relief from the efforts of these two tireless men in Granville. The arrangement worked tolerably well for some time but eventually was a victim of the difficulties experienced during the Allied advance through Normandy. A particularly happy recollection of the period was that of the eventual arrival of the ship *Vega* (**2.14**) and the delivery to the shop of the Red Cross parcels from which the Co-op could distribute a little additional food and other necessities.

Another item in the September 1942 *News* report mentions the use of wooden soles for boots in place of leather, which was becoming difficult to obtain. Old car tyres were also used for resoling.

The *Co-operative News* also reported that leaders of the Channel Islands Refugees Committee in Britain were to visit Manchester to discuss problems of present urgency with Directors of the Co-operative Wholesale Society. So it was with a certain feeling of relief that the Islands' problems were being conveyed to the CWS, though circumstances prevented any immediate and useful action.

So, improvisation became a part of life during that difficult period until Liberation (**2.15, 2.16, 2.17**). This indeed helped the still young Society, barely twenty years old, to maintain its presence in the Island community, not yet quite accustomed to a Co-op shop in its midst. But there is no doubt that the enthusiasm and resourcefulness of the youthful John Morris, assisted by George Townend, enabled the Management Committee and the members to maintain a service to the Island that would have pleased the Jersey pioneers of May 1919. In Dick Shenton's words, 'it really was a shop for the people', and the nostalgic recollections of those who lived and laughed through their years at 27 Charing Cross are testament to that sentiment.

2.14 The Red Cross vessel *Vega* in St Peter Port, Guernsey, December 1944 (Occupation Memorial Image Library, © Société Jersiaise)

2.15 Celebrating Liberation, 9 May 1945 (Jersey Heritage Trust, © Société Jersiaise)

2.16 Queuing to change marks back to sterling (Jersey Heritage Trust, © Société Jersiaise)

BUCKINGHAM PALACE

To my most loyal people in the Channel Islands, I send my heartfelt greetings.

Ever since my armed forces had to be withdrawn, you have, I know, looked forward with the same confidence as I have to the time of deliverance. We have never been divided in spirit. Our hopes and fears, anxieties and determination have been the same, and we have been bound together by an unshakable conviction that the day would come when the Islands, the oldest possession of the Crown, would be liberated from enemy occupation. That day has now come and, with all my Peoples, I cordially welcome you on your restoration to freedom and to your rightful place with the free nations of the world.

Channel Islanders in their thousands are fighting in my service for the cause of civilisation with their traditional loyalty, courage and devotion. Their task is not yet ended; but for you a new task begins at once—to re-build the fortunes of your beautiful Islands in anticipation of reunion with relatives, friends and neighbours who have been parted from you by the circumstances of war. In this task you can count on the fullest support of my Government.

It is my desire that your ancient privileges and institutions should be maintained and that you should resume as soon as possible your accustomed system of government. Meantime, the immediate situation requires that responsibility for the safety of the Islands and the well-being of the inhabitants should rest upon the Commander of the Armed Forces stationed in the Islands. I feel confident that the Civil Authorities, who have carried so heavy a burden during the past years, will gladly co-operate with him in maintaining good government and securing the distribution of the supplies which he is bringing with him.

It is my earnest hope that the Islands, reinstated in their ancestral relationship to the Crown, will soon regain their former happiness and prosperity.

(Signed) GEORGE R. I.

2.17 The proclamation from King George VI to 'my most loyal people in the Channel Islands' following Liberation (Jersey Heritage Trust, © Société Jersiaise)

Chapter 3

A New Beginning

The last General Meeting of the Jersey Co-operative Society before the Occupation had been held in the Wellington Hall, Union Street on 14 December 1939. This meeting had reported a successful trading year and a healthy financial position following eight years of supervision by the CWS.

Now, in 1945, the Society was free from the restraints of the Occupation period and was eager to resume normal business once more. The first post-Occupation General Meeting was held in the Town Hall on Wednesday 5 December 1945, when 110 members attended. This encouraging turnout was an indication of the interest still being shown in a resurgence of the Society and the shop – many members of the 1930s had evacuated, and some were deported, so the pre-war membership had naturally been depleted. Many families had not yet returned to the Island so the attendance suggested a strong continuing support for the Co-operative ideal.

At this first meeting following the Occupation, A Davies was in the chair, supported by RS Edwards and SL Kassell of the CWS Supervisory Committee. Also on the platform were George Townend and John Morris, as Manager and Chief Clerk respectively, and JH Dunford as Secretary. The Chairman opened the meeting with a reference to those members who had lost their lives during the war and called for a minute's silence to their memory.

The Report and Accounts for the previous six years ending September 1945 were introduced. It appeared that despite the difficulties of the Occupation the Society was already enjoying an improved financial position. The members were no doubt delighted to hear that the dividend was to be 1s (5p) in the pound and the bonus 3d (about 1p) in the pound.

It was agreed that the appreciation of the meeting on behalf of all members would be extended to the Board of the CWS and to the members of the Supervisory Committee. For a Society still in effect in its early stages, and recovering from six years of hardship, this continuing support was welcomed – though, as we shall see, there were to be embarrassments ahead. Tribute was also paid to the services and the loyalty of management and staff. An enquiry was raised from the floor on whether there could be some compensation for the loss of wages and bonus arising from the financial difficulties of those six years. No details or response to this request are recorded.

No doubt an expression of the desire of the staff to exercise a greater formal influence on the affairs of the Society, proposals were put forward for a local committee of five members of which one member could be an employee of the Society. In the ensuing election the Local Committee of Messrs Kinnish, Downer, Foley, Gladden and Mrs Le Rougetel was established, with Mr Kinnish being the elected employee. Several of these members were to continue serving the Society for many years ahead.

Successive half-yearly meetings through the late 1940s gave welcome news in the Reports of a continuing increase in membership and a continuing dividend of 1s in the pound, with a bonus of 3d in the pound.

However, changes were in the air. As the Occupation years receded and social and family hardships diminished – though food rationing was to continue till 1954 – a more positive outlook

Opposite page **3.1** Doreen Batiste, who pioneered the use of mobile shops in Guernsey in 1950, followed up later in Jersey, seen here with her first mobile or travelling shop (© Guernsey Evening Post)

emerged in both Islands. This was made apparent in Jersey by the fact that increasing business made an expansion of premises essential. The CWS Supervisory Committee then entered into contract with a Mr Cuming, butcher, of 26 Charing Cross, for his property and for the lease of a garage and store in Old Street.

This transaction aroused considerable anger in the new Local Committee so soon after its election, and its response certainly justified its existence on behalf of the membership. This incident was recorded in the Minutes of the Meeting of 23 January 1946, which are worth quoting here in full –

> RESOLVED that the local Committee protest at the manner in which the purchase of the adjoining premises, the property of C J Cuming Esq., had been brought about. Having been elected by ballot at a General Meeting of the Society, to look after the interests of all members, we very strongly resent the fact that the first notification we receive of the purchase should be through the medium of the press. As matters have proceeded so far on this occasion, we agreed, under protest, to the Contract being passed, but maintain that in all future dealings which the Society might contemplate, the Committee should be made aware of the facts and fully consulted before any final decision is made.

Strong words from that new Local Committee, considering that it was the CWS that was paying the purchase price, but having made its point it was naturally happy to seize this first opportunity to expand next door.

The gross purchase price of 26 Charing Cross was £4,125. It was interesting from an historical viewpoint that George Townend was named Mandatory and Representative of the Society in order to pass contract in the Royal Court for the purchase and for the deeds for the commutation of Seigneurial Rights. Few members, or the public in general, realise as they push their trolleys around that the floor they walk over, was once, some sixty years ago, subject to such feudal custom.

The more relaxed air of the late 1940s now encouraged increasing business in those very areas had prompted the establishment of the Society in 1919 – the family needs of groceries and provisions. We read in the minutes of March 1946 of the limitations of existing accommodation for motor vehicles and the possible need for a branch butchery. During the same period the military contract held by the Society for the supply of bread to the Garrison was terminated, necessitating some adjustment to the bakery output. Eventually the old bakery, which had been moved from Sand Street to Georgetown, opposite the New Era, now Barclays Bank, was demolished in 1946 to make room for the new Grasett Park Estate.

The baking and confectionery business was then transferred to Don Road, which, until mid-1946, accommodated the Grocery stores and Despatch; this of necessity was moved back to Charing Cross. But a more effective solution was on the way.

It was fortuitous that at this time of expansion, and the reallocation of departments to make the most effective use of limited space, that it became known that the German bakery building on Goose Green marsh at Beaumont was to be offered for sale by public auction. This was an opportunity not to be missed. Arthur Jacobs, the then manager, was named Mandatory to represent the Society at the auction, which took place on 11 May 1950. His bid for the Society was the highest, at £7,500, for the purchase in perpetuity of the land, a part of the marsh and the building thereon – the bakehouse (**3.2**).

This was quite a heavy financial commitment so soon after recovery from the Occupation, together with the purchase of Val Plaisant coming up in the same period (**3.3**). But it no doubt had the

1933

481

A la Cour Royale de l'Ile de Jersey

L'An mil neuf cent CINQUANTE, LE DIXIEME JOUR DE JUIN.

SOCIETES A RESPONSté LIMITEE.

Sur la demande de la Société avec responsabilité limitée incorporée sous le nom de "The Jersey Co-operative Society Limited" en vertu des prescriptions des Actes de Parlement dits "Industrial and Provident Societies Acts, 1893 to 1928" (lesquels ont été enregistrés en cette Ile) comme paraît par certain certificat en date du 3 Juillet, 1919, portant le sceau du Registre dit "Registry of Friendly Societies Central Office" et faisant commerce en cette Ile, la Cour a ordonné l'enregistrement dans le livre du Registre des Sociétés avec responsabilité limitée, de certaine résolution des directeurs de ladite Société passée à une réunion desdits directeurs tenue le 15 Mai, 1950, par laquelle résolution Monsr. Arthur Harold Jacobs est nommé mandataire de ladite Société aux fins de passer certain contrat héréditaire spécifié dans ladite résolution et ce afin que ladite résolution tire son plein et entier effet selon sa teneur.

DE LAQUELLE RESOLUTION LA TENEUR SUIT:

"That Mr. Arthur Harold Jacobs be and is hereby named Mandatory and Representative of the Society in order to pass before the Royal Court of Jersey on behalf of the Society the contract or deed of purchase of the premises known as "The German Bakery" St. Peter's Marsh, St. Peter from the tenants of St. Peter's Marsh for the gross price and sum of £7500 Stg."

3.2 Contract of 10 June 1950 by which the Society bought the Bakery, a building of Occupation memory that still serves the Society in modern fashion, as the IT Control Centre upstairs and the Total Sport shop below

3.3 The Val Plaisant Motor Garage, which the Jersey Society bought in September 1950 for £7,000. Mr John Le Riche, the previous owner, and father-in-law of the late Norman Le Brocq, is standing in front of the petrol pump. The building would become the Co-op Locale Val Plaisant (photo Mrs Le Brocq)

approval and support of CWS for it was discussed at the committee meeting on 2 June 1950 when formal approval was shown, and it was agreed that when possession was obtained on 11 November, the bakery would be transferred to its new home, enabling Grocery stores, Despatch and the General Offices to return to Don Road, where they remained until the late 1960s.

Referred to in colloquial terms as the old German Bakery, it was in fact built for the Todt Organisation. Little could it be imagined at the time that this building would not only continue to serve its original purpose for some years ahead but that it would eventually enter the IT world as the offices for the Society's Central Computer Operations.

In retrospect we can imagine the time and effort required of the hard-pressed staff as these decisions were made to accommodate several departments in their transfers from place to place.

The bakery, once settled in the old German building, continued to flourish. The Society, true to tradition, had always taken great pride in its products. The encouraging circulars sent out by Mr Peach (eg **5.2** below), extolling the quality of a wide range of bread and cakes and the regular door-to-door delivery service, gave considerable satisfaction to the Society and to the members.

However, some twenty years on, doubts began to emerge as to the justification for continuing such production and service in the face of the increasing competition, particularly from the supermarkets that were just beginning to emerge in the 1960s as the shops of the future. The building was in need of an overall modernisation, there are mentions in the minutes of the necessity to replace the ovens and the likely costs – not surprisingly, perhaps, as the original German ovens had been in use for some 25 years when the matter was first raised. And in such a semi-industrial building there were many health and safety hazards for which there were at that time no statutory regulations in place. Staffing difficulties arose also, for, perhaps unknown to members, who welcomed their early morning deliveries of fresh warm bread, the bakery was virtually a 24-hour operation in sometimes unpleasant conditions. It was becoming obvious that skilled bakery staff were not easily recruited for such unsociable hours and conditions.

Eventually the Board was compelled by circumstances to accept the inevitable and with some regret pass the business over to Le Brun's, as is explained in greater detail in Chapter 6.

One early member of the bakery staff was Mike Carter, a contemporary of Michael Galway, who joined the Co-op in 1954, barely 15 years old, at the end of his school summer holidays. With no training in trade or business Mike was asked for his preference and choice of workplace. Having, surprisingly for a young boy, an inclination towards bakery and confectionery, he opted for the bakery and spent eight years there until, his interests having moved towards engineering, he transferred in 1962 to the garage and workshops in Val Plaisant. Later he went with the workshops to 60 Kensington Place.

Mike has vivid recollections of his experiences in the bakery and speaks of them now with mixed feelings – satisfaction with his work but an awareness of the unpleasant conditions at times, particularly during the summer months when the heat, the dust and the wasps could be very unpleasant (the wasps were attracted to the smell of the bread).

The ovens were of German origin, the manufacturer's name embossed around the heavy cast-iron doors. They were coke-fired, the coke being delivered in sacks by truck to the rear of the building from whence the sacks were hoisted by chain and pulley to the floor above. One can imagine the coke dust in the air as the truck was unloaded by the windows, which were probably always open because of the heat. The upper floor of the main block, now occupied by the IT Centre, was the flour loft. Here a similar hoist was used to bring the flour, imported in sacks, up to the storage area from which it was fed through a hatch and chute to the dough and bread-making staff below.

Mike recalls the routine for bringing the loaves out of the ovens. The floor plate, fitted with rails, was drawn out from the base of the oven as a support for the baking plate. This was fitted with wheels to ease its movement over the lower plate. All this was not only heavy work, but hot too, and in the absence of proper asbestos gloves (perhaps a blessing!), the men made up thick gloves of sacking to protect their hands from the hot metalwork when pulling on the bar.

The bakery day was a matter of shifts. The dough mixers came on in the afternoon to mix the dough for the baking staff, who worked the night shift till 5 am, when the day staff arrived to prepare and pack the loaves and rolls for delivery.

In 1960 the Annual Report announced the intention to modernise the bakery by converting the old coke ovens to oil-fired units and installing an automatic bread-making plant. Bread and confectionery had long been a staple of the Co-op, and the Society was not in the mood to consider giving it up despite the costs involved.

Obviously, baking was an onerous and expensive business by traditional methods, but changing circumstances and social needs inevitably introduced an easier and more convenient means of providing the customer with an all-day supply of bread and rolls of equal quality and now of an even wider range. The refurbishment of stores and the perfection of the compact in-store ovens enabled bread to be baked with greater ease, and quickly to order. We shall read more of these developments in later chapters.

The minutes of the 1946–47 period show how rapidly the Society was moving towards accommodating the demands of increasing business. In May 1946 considerable discussion centred on a possible purchase of Hamon's Ltd drapery business, which was then for sale at £50,000, a very considerable sum at the time. The Committee decided that the premises were not ideal, being suitable only for drapery and clothing – a rather surprising view as the Society was actively considering the development of the business of 'dry goods' as they were called then. However, the possible acquisition of Falle's, 3 Beresford Street was considered more suitable for those needs, the premises being larger and thus more accommodating for a 'Men's Department and for boots and shoes'. This was a clear indication of the Local Committee's active introduction and development of the dry goods trade. This had been raised as early as December 1945, at the first post-Occupation meeting. In the end, this possibility of acquiring Falle's was not pursued.

Such attempts to create a full clothing and furnishing and hardware department were inevitably thwarted by the many difficulties already seen in

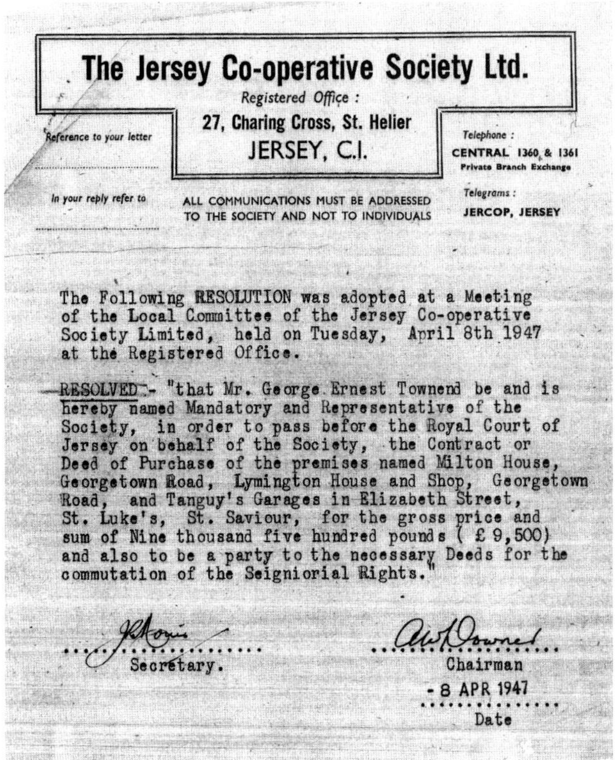

The Jersey Co-operative Society Ltd.
Registered Office :
27, Charing Cross, St. Helier
JERSEY, C.I.

Reference to your letter ....

In your reply refer to ....

ALL COMMUNICATIONS MUST BE ADDRESSED TO THE SOCIETY AND NOT TO INDIVIDUALS

Telephone : CENTRAL 1360 & 1361 Private Branch Exchange

Telegrams : JERCOP, JERSEY

The Following RESOLUTION was adopted at a Meeting of the Local Committee of the Jersey Co-operative Society Limited, held on Tuesday, April 8th 1947 at the Registered Office.

RESOLVED:- "that Mr. George Ernest Townend be and is hereby named Mandatory and Representative of the Society, in order to pass before the Royal Court of Jersey on behalf of the Society, the Contract or Deed of Purchase of the premises named Milton House, Georgetown Road, Lymington House and Shop, Georgetown Road, and Tanguy's Garages in Elizabeth Street, St. Luke's, St. Saviour, for the gross price and sum of Nine thousand five hundred pounds (£ 9,500) and also to be a party to the necessary Deeds for the commutation of the Seigniorial Rights."

.... Secretary.

.... Chairman

- 8 APR 1947
.... Date

3.4 Before the Royal Court of Jersey, the Resolution of the Management Committee, dated 8 April 1947, covering the purchase of properties in the Georgetown area. These were to form the basis of the first Georgetown shop and eventually the Locale Supermarket and car park in 2002

3.5 One of the properties of the Georgetown purchase, which became the Coal Store, Elizabeth Street and the cause of a considerable nuisance owing to dust and noise so close to the shop (photo taken in January 1967). The Georgetown Food Centre stands on this site, having begun trading in April 1969

the normal run of Co-op business at this time, the lack of suitable premises, and thus the lack of the additional space required to display the stock. CWS made some attempt to alleviate the problem and offered the service of its Mail Order Department so that customers could order by mail from the catalogue, an early example of a practice very popular today, but the main objection remained lack of space for stock and display, particularly in the area of clothing and materials.

Mid-1946 was a time of intense activity by the Local Committee on behalf of the Society as it attempted to cope with increasing business, the demand for expansion of existing premises and the acquisition of new ones, difficulties over the occasional shortage of supplies from the mainland, and the allocation of goods on points, often from a competitor in the Island, at the same time as membership continued to increase.

A résumé of the activities of this very busy period in the early post-war days can be read in the minutes of 1946. It included the purchase of Cuming's butchery business, the move of the Bakery from the wartime premises in Sand Street to Georgetown and its eventual closing down and demolition, the constant need to expand and acquire additional premises and maintain existing premises to acceptable standards (**3.4, 3.5, 3.6**).

That Cuming's butchery business, just purchased, was but one of several small individual shops with houses over that formed the curved frontage of Charing Cross from the Co-op to Dumaresq Street. Little did the Society appreciate in the 1940s that only ten years later, as the business grew, so did the need for additional premises, a natural expansion to house the widening range of goods becoming available and about to be demanded by members and public alike.

The days of bicycles and wireless sets were over, and once rationing and quotas ended in 1954, more sophisticated tastes developed. The Society would be hard pressed for space to cope with this continuing demand. This row of little shops was to

3.6 The Boucheré family's hardware shop, which originally occupied the site at Georgetown and the frontage on the road, now identified by the decorative wall arches, finished in green and cream (photo John Boucheré)

prove invaluable in the future for a modest extension, shop by shop, from the original corner Nos 27 and 28, but for the moment with CWS financial control still in place our still modest Jersey Society had to exercise patience.

On the staff and social side also there was much to report. A request was received from the Jersey Labour Party asking if the Society would hold Labour Party application forms and receive completed forms and subscriptions on its behalf. The proposal was made that the committee recommend to the Supervisory Sub-Committee that this request be granted, but this was not seconded. However, the proposal that the Society might show sympathy with the objects of the newly formed United Nations Association of Great Britain and Ireland was accepted, and an annual subscription of £1 was paid on that occasion; no further record of continuing membership is known.

As an example of closer links with the Co-operative Movement in Britain, George Townend was appointed the Society's representative to the Annual Congress of the Co-operative Union Limited at Blackpool. He was later thanked for his interesting report on the business of the Congress, though whether this link continued over a period is not recorded.

By this stage, following the successful partnership with John Morris through those difficult years, George Townend was considering his future. In 1947 he resigned and emigrated to Tasmania. His place as Manager was taken up by AH Jacobs, who came over by arrangement with CWS to further the Society's progress. John Morris continued as Chief Clerk.

At this point, we see the emergence of Co-operative feeling in Guernsey, doubtless brought about by social and business contacts between the Islands. With the example of Jersey already in mind there seemed to be no necessity for a public meeting. The only publicity that did appear was a very brief note on the front page of the *Guernsey Evening Press* of 15 February 1947. The CWS were in Guernsey already, probably as successors to the short-lived Guernsey Growers Co-operation Society, which had been registered in 1910 under the same Industrial and Provident Societies rules as applied to the Jersey Society.

At that time there was a fundamental difference between the Islands in their respective agricultural practices. Jersey concentrated on the outdoor crops of potatoes and tomatoes, backed up by a well-established dairy industry; Guernsey, facing north, depended on glass for its main crops of potatoes and tomatoes plus grapes and flowers. More than his Jersey counterpart, the Guernseyman thought of himself as a grower, which no doubt accounted for the different emphasis in the name of the Society. There appeared to be a minor retail business in Guernsey under the Co-operation Society umbrella; one of these did not hesitate to use the title Co-operative in its publicity. However, registration of that Co-operation Society was cancelled in 1916, the Society having ceased trading. It was not until after the Occupation that the desire for a Co-operative shop began to take positive shape.

Also in Guernsey at this time was the Co-operative Insurance Society's Guernsey Agent, Derek Falla, of whom we shall hear more in the years to come (**3.7**). The CIS Regional Manager, Harry

3.7 Derek Falla, who discovered No 2 Market Street and made the first approaches towards purchase (photo 1998, Ken Renault)

3.8 No 2 Market Street, The Guernsey Groceteria, shown shortly before the Society took it over in February 1947. Jimmy Batiste is on the left and Betty Bishop on the right

3.9 Duncan MacMillan and his wife, happily settled in Canada

Beatham, was consulted, and he asked Derek Falla to find suitable premises from which to establish the first Guernsey Co-operative shop, which was to be the basis of the first Guernsey Co-operative Society. It was agreed that it would operate in the same manner as the Jersey Society, with a CWS-appointed Supervisory Board and a local Advisory Committee.

As a local insurance man with business contacts around the town, Derek Falla's search was quickly rewarded. He very soon found a small but flourishing grocery shop in Market Street known as the Guernsey Groceteria (**3.8**). It was owned by a Mr MacMillan, who, very conveniently, was contemplating emigration to Canada and was willing to sell (**3.9**). So, with little delay, Guernsey's first Co-operative shop was opened in March 1947, and with the shop came Betty Bishop, one of MacMillan's staff. She was then in charge of the Provision Section, and was to remain with the Society in various capacities for several years, becoming a popular and valued member of the Co-op staff (**3.10**).

A more convenient and potentially profitable site could not have been found than 2 Market Street. Derek Falla's intuition in such circumstances was to serve the Guernsey Society very well indeed for many years. Right opposite the Market and near the Arcade, it was at the hub of the town's domestic shopping area, for groceries and similar needs, And so, before the Royal Court on 28 February 1947 Contract was passed conveying 2 Rue du Marché from Duncan Cameron MacMillan and his wife to the Co-operative

3.10 Betty Bishop on the Co-op produce stall in the market, 22 June 1949: yes, we have bananas! (photo Betty Bishop)

Wholesale Society Limited for the sum of £6,000. MacMillan had made a shrewd investment, for he had bought No 2 for £4,300 only nine months earlier (**3.11, 3.12**).

The Guernsey Co-operative Society was born, though its registration did not take place until later. With this contract came Jimmy Batiste, the Manager, to be joined soon after by his sister Doreen Batiste.

The first Advisory Committee included Derek Falla; his father, Walter Falla, who was a prominent Methodist preacher; Ernie Saunders, a leading trade unionist; and JRD Jones, a manager at the Guernsey shipping terminal of the GWR, later to become British Rail.

It was of considerable help to the budding Guernsey Society to have Duncan MacMillan's continuing management of the shop until he left for Canada later in 1947 and also Betty Bishop's supervision on the grocery side. Added to these advantages were their customers, who were a reservoir for future membership of the Society.

The Guernsey Society quickly established itself and adopted the same pattern as in Jersey, with half-yearly members meetings, held in the Guille-Allez Hall. So successful were the first two years of trading that consideration was being given to the purchase of the Golden Grain Bakery, but eventually the price was considered too high. By 1949 the Society had already outgrown the capacity of Market Street and was searching for another outlet. In that same year a small shop was found in Nocq Road, St Sampsons, a semi-urban area that promised good returns. This was purchased in March 1949.

The 1949 minutes show a strong seven-member Advisory Committee consisting of JRD Jones, in the Chair, supported by Walter and Derek Falla, E Saunders, John Mills, HK Foley and W Marquis. The financial results showed good form, with a dividend paid of 1s in the pound. So strongly placed was the Society that already by 1950 the Nocq Road shop was proving inadequate for the business it was generating and a further search was made. This resulted in the purchase of a shop on the Bridge in 1949 of roughly double the size.

In 1949, encouraged no doubt by such financial success, Guernsey members were pressing, and the Local Committee recommending, the opening of additional departments other than the traditional grocery business. Obviously there was an opportunity here to expand, but it could not be followed up at the time, for the final opinion expressed by the committee stressed the need to find suitable premises and the necessary capital before such hopes

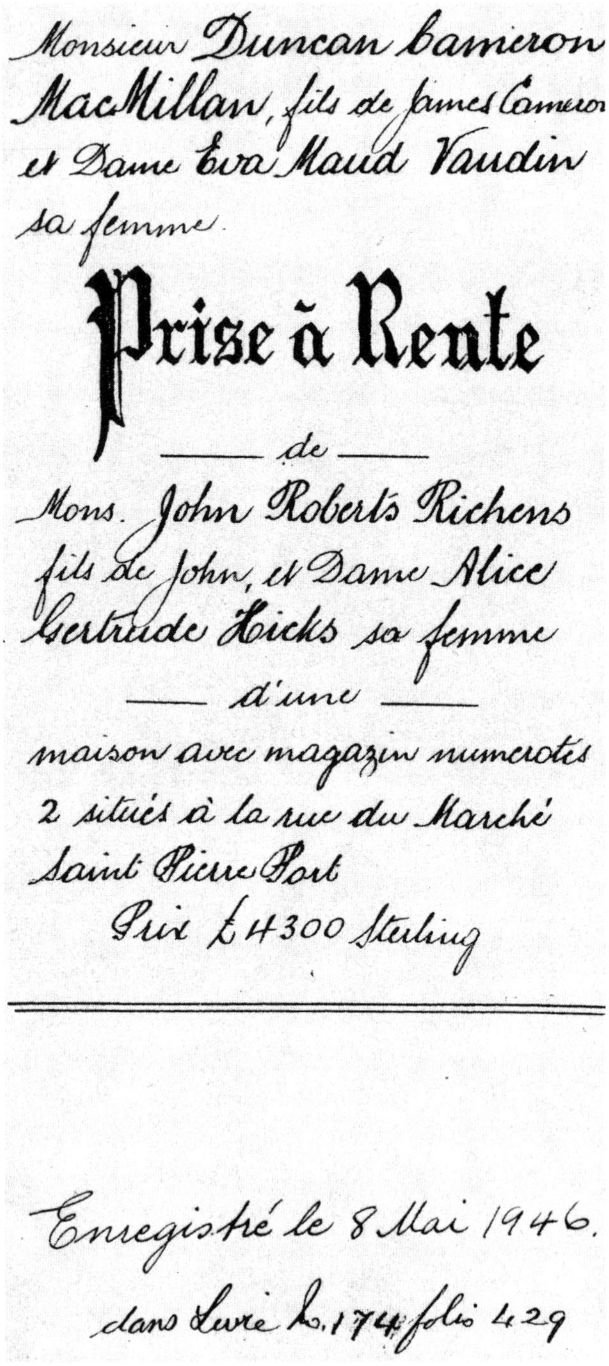

Monsieur Duncan Cameron MacMillan, fils de James Cameron et Dame Eva Maud Vaudin sa femme

Prise à Rente

— de —

Mons. John Roberts Richens fils de John, et Dame Alice Gertrude Hicks sa femme

— d'une —

maison avec magazin numerotés 2 situés à la rue du Marché Saint Pierre Port

Prix £4300 Sterling

Enregistré le 8 Mai 1946.

dans Livre No. 174 folio 429

3.11 Contract of 8 May 1946 by which Duncan MacMillan and his wife bought No 2 Market Street, Guernsey from John Richens for £4,300

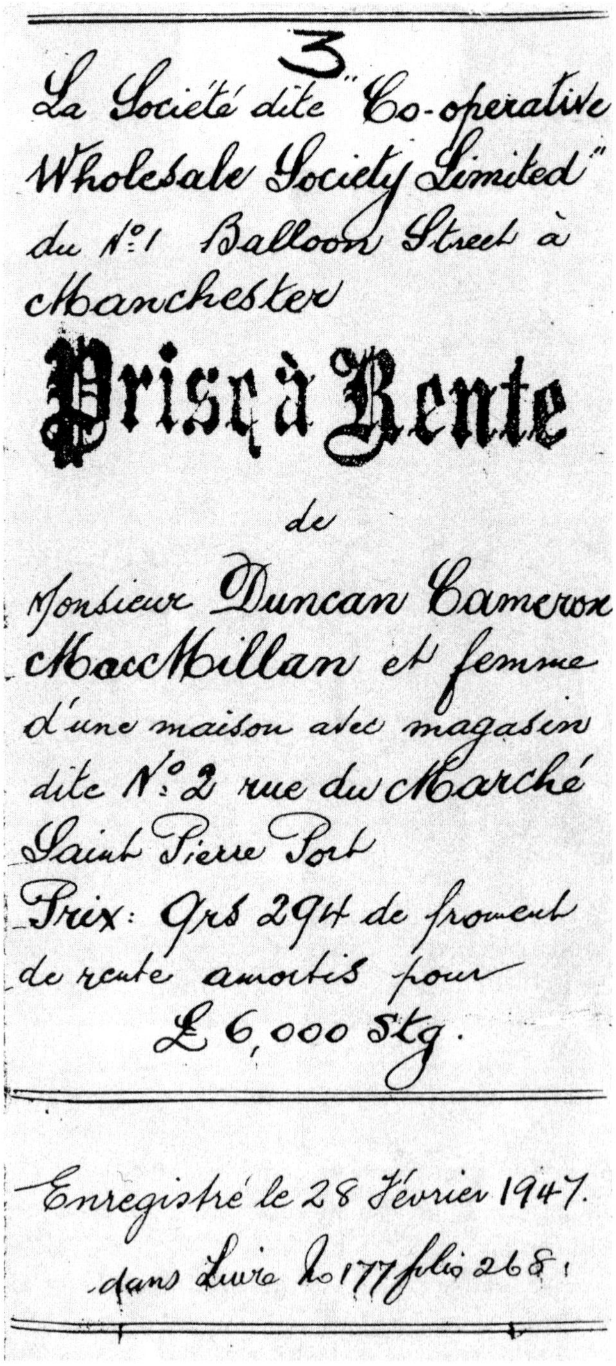

3

La Société dite "Co-operative Wholesale Society Limited" du No 1 Balloon Street à Manchester

Prise à Rente

de

Monsieur Duncan Cameron MacMillan et femme

d'une maison avec magasin dite No 2 rue du Marché Saint Pierre Port

Prix: Qrs 294 de froment de rente amortis pour £6,000 Stg.

Enregistré le 28 Février 1947.

dans Livre No 177 folio 268.

3.12 Only nine months later, by contract dated 28 February 1947, the CWS purchased No 2 Market Street from Duncan MacMillan on behalf of the newly formed Guernsey Co-operative Society for £6,000

could be implemented. On this issue of raising additional capital it was decided to insert advertisements in the local newspapers, drawing attention to the rates of interest offered by the Society on share and loan capital in the hope of encouraging more members and thus more deposits.

In May 1952 the disposal of the original Nocq Road shop and premises was still an issue to be decided, and at the half-yearly meeting this was raised again. Mr RA Jennings, who was then managing Nocq Road, reported that application had been made for an off-licence in the name of the Society, and if this was granted the Nocq Road premises could be used as a warehouse for the liquor stock.

It was probably this application that caused the resignation of Walter Falla in 1952, for his Methodist principles and upbringing prevented him accepting the idea of the Society taking up a liquor licence. His son, Derek, had by then moved

3.13 The Jersey Society's mobile shop, complete with onboard scales, produce and fire extinguisher, and a tempting display of muscatel grapes, dates and cakes, at an exhibition in the early 1950s (photo Speed Photographics)

to Jersey in connection with his work with CIS, and in pages to come we shall read of his considerable work with The Channel Islands Co-operative Society Limited after the merger of 1955.

In the meantime the Nocq Road problem remained unresolved, and after some considerable delay there were still no buyers at a reasonable price, the highest offer being £1,000 for a property shown on the balance sheet at £2,074. It was then decided to rent it on short-term lease.

Concurrent with the extension of trading into the Bridge area and the obvious wish to extend still further into the country parishes – few of the country folk had cars in those days and there was business to be had out there – the idea of travelling shops was discussed and quickly implemented.

The first 'shop on wheels' was introduced towards the end of 1950. These travelling shops, as they were called, were already in use with several Co-operative Societies in Britain around 1950, so it was not surprising that the idea quickly filtered down to Guernsey, where the need was greater than in Jersey. Doreen Batiste, who spoke patois and French, was promoted to Mobile Shop Manager and she took the shop around the Island every day from Tuesday to Saturday (**3.1**). The first recorded accounts showed sales from the mobile as £55 for the first week and £140 for the second. Mr Jennings, as Foods Manager, was requested to maintain details of running expenses. These were sufficiently satisfactory for a second mobile shop to be ordered and to be on the road by early 1951. Jersey followed suit with its own mobile shop, shown (**3.13**) fully equipped on an exhibition stand in the early 1950s.

At this same period, around the end of 1950, the Local Committee again drew attention to the deteriorating situation at Market Street, where already, only three years after purchase, the lack of space to expand and accommodate the increasing turnover was creating difficulties. The committee had apparently mentioned this some time previously and had recommended that the garage adjoining the manager's house, then itself in great need of repair, should be reconstructed as a warehouse and garage. This property in Longue Rue, in St Martin's Parish was bought in 1951 to serve as rented accommodation for Jennings.

It was emphasised to the CWS Directors that whether or not the garage was reconstructed it would certainly have to be repaired, having been reported as unsafe to use. The Directors promised that these points would be considered. Here we can see two aspects of the 'growing pains' of the Guernsey Society – in this instance the need to deal with the residual neglect, suffered by so many Island properties as a result of the Occupation, and also to modernise and expand with limited capital. Alongside were the more personal difficulties that inevitably must have occasionally arisen between the Local Committee and the Directors to whom all major matters had to be referred. To a rapidly growing concern this must have seemed irksome at times, although it was appreciated that it was a result of the initiative and support of the CWS only four years previously that such progress had been made. This frustration was to surface in other ways in the near future.

Another such issue, though seemingly of minor importance nowadays, was the protest that the date chosen for the half-yearly meeting was 'very inconvenient if it fell on a Thursday'. Thursday was the traditional half-day for all shops and trades. The writer recalls the time when on a Thursday afternoon everything in town was closed, there were very few restaurants, the holidaymakers were out and about around the Islands and the town was virtually silent!

Obviously the Local Committee members, some of whom were staff, were not in favour of giving up their half-day to discuss business that could just as conveniently be dealt with on another day. An amusing close to this discussion was the note that the date of the next meeting should be left with the Supervisory Committee to decide – the Directors were maintaining their position!

As late as May 1951 this need to satisfy members' requests and stock a wider range of dry goods, as they were still called, had still not been met, but mention was made of moves in that direction by the Jersey Society, which it was hoped would add momentum to these similar hopes in Guernsey.

These occasional references to apparent delays in implementing members' wishes indicate the extent to which the Societies in both Islands were under firm control of the CWS Supervisory Committees, despite the local business experience of some of the members of the Local Committees.

This overall responsibility of the CWS, though at times irksome to the Local Committee members, was an essential element and principle of the Co-operative Movement. It did enable the smaller Co-operative Societies, particularly in their early years, to draw on the wide experience, and, at times, the financial support of the CWS. This was to be shown in practical terms in 1953 when two items of particular importance were raised at the May meeting of the Guernsey Society: the Chairman of the Supervisory Committee, Mr HH Flynn, referred to the item in the current balance sheet indicating the financial help given to the Society for that period. Under the heading of 'Financial Assistance' the Minute states:

> the financial assistance which the CWS has afforded the Guernsey Society amounts to £3,376 and this would be repayable to the CWS, should it be decided at any time in the future that the CWS should relinquish responsibility for the management of the Society. The assistance was, therefore, a contingent liability and while the CWS had no desire whatever to alter the existing relationship, the Supervisory Committee had been informed by Counsel that the liability must be shown on all published Balance Sheets of the Society.

The second item raised was that of liability to Income Tax. The Minute stated:

> Liability for United Kingdom Taxation:
> The Chairman informed the Local Committee of the negotiations, which had taken place with the Board of Inland Revenue on the Mainland regarding Jersey Society's liability for United Kingdom taxation. The advice of Counsel had been sought and it would now seem that there was little doubt that because control of the Society was exercised on the Mainland the Jersey Society was liable for the payment of United Kingdom tax.
>
> Exactly the same position obtained in the case of the Guernsey Society but, in this instance, the taxable surplus has so far been insufficient to give rise to a liability.

We shall read more later of this issue of liability to UK tax and of the interesting result that led to a revolution in the Co-op situation in the Channel Islands.

The ongoing dilemma over dry goods was at last resolved during 1951 when sufficient capital was available to undertake the refurbishment and maintenance of Market Street and the rebuilding of the garage at 'Roselyn' as a grocery warehouse. This enabled space, now made available, to be used for a future Drapery and Hardware Department on the first floor of Market Street. This period, only four years after the formation of the Society in 1947, was one of considerable expansion with limited resources, and the Local Committee warned members that additional capital would still be required for future developments.

One suggestion proposed that rates of interest on share and loan capital might be increased from 3⅓% to 3½% on shares and from 2½% to 3% on loans as an inducement to members to increase their savings. This was to be considered by the Supervisory Committee.

Needless to say, these periods of expansion and upheaval must have placed a heavier burden on the staff at all levels. In the absence of a firm management policy in these matters – personnel management was still an ideal for the future – it was inevitable that serious cases of misconduct would surface from time to time.

The first such case concerned a Mr Thomas who was appointed as Branch Manager at St Sampsons, despite evidence of a recent charge before the Magistrate's Court prior to his appointment to the Society on three months' probation. Regrettably, within a year serious deficiencies were discovered in the sales receipts at St Sampsons and the matter was referred to the Chairman and the General Supervisor with power to act. No further action is recorded in the minutes, presumably it being suggested to Mr Thomas that he should resign.

In Jersey an interesting appointment came up early in 1953 when the still young John Morris found himself, at this critical period in the Society's history, promoted to the post of Acting General Manager in April. He had obviously proved himself to the Board and was to take up the General Manager's position on the departure of Jacobs.

We read from the minutes of the Half-Yearly meeting of the Local Committee of 14 May 1953 that some disquiet was again being expressed among members over the Society's liability to UK taxation and that legal advice had been sought, but with similar results to the previous attempt.

The minutes of the post-Occupation period record several instances by both Societies of some minor frustration and impatience on the part of members at the apparent unwillingness of the CWS Supervisory Committee to deal with practical issues that they, the members, thought were necessary or at least desirable in the local interest. This no doubt led to the occasional firm exchange of views between the two committees.

Here we can sense how relationships were being stretched, after five years of repression and inaction during the Occupation, added to the Islanders' innate feeling of independence. The earlier years of the Jersey Society were no doubt quieter in terms of interaction with the CWS; now, twenty years on, in the 1950s, members and their committees were expressing firmer opinions on the future of their Society, and that working relationship was being questioned. At the same time there was always an acknowledgement of the debt, both practical and financial, owed to the CWS, from that enthusiastic first meeting of 1919 onwards.

For example, in 1951 the Jersey Society agreed to subscribe to 'a Bond in the Capital sum of £30,000 (thirty thousand pounds) in favour of the Co-operative Wholesale Society as security for advances and interest thereon which have been made or which may be made ... against the real estate of the Society ...'. This is just one instance of that continuing support by the CWS without which the Society could not have reached its full potential.

The Special Rule IX referred to later by Mr Quincey is worth quoting in part, as it stood in 1938, to show the terms of that relationship and the inability of the Local Committee to depart from its principles:

> The Committee of Management shall consist of such persons as may from time to time be appointed by the Board of Directors of the Co-operative Wholesale Society to manage the Society ... this Special Rule is hereby declared fundamental and no resolution for the alteration of this Special Rule which would have the effect of removing the Management of the Society from the persons appointed from time to time by the said Co-operative Wholesale Society Limited shall become operative until the

> Society shall have repaid to the Co-operative Wholesale Society Limited, a sum equivalent to the total amount of pecuniary assistance … afforded to the Society.

Reference to the Rules of the period (1938) will show that this Special Rule IX was fundamental and confirmed the role of the CWS in its supervisory control of the local Society, a fact that was perhaps not fully understood or accepted by the Local Management Committee.

It is interesting to read between the lines, as it were, that the CWS was unwilling to vary the existing relationship with both Societies by which liability to UK tax must be shown in all published balance sheets. It is worth repeating the relevant clauses from the Minutes of the Guernsey Society's half-yearly meeting of 14 May 1953:

> (5) Liability for United Kingdom Taxation:
> The Chairman informed the Local Committee of the negotiations, which had taken place with the Board of Inland Revenue on the Mainland regarding the Jersey Society's liability for United Kingdom taxation. The advice of Counsel had been sought and it would now seem that there was little doubt that because control of the Society was exercised on the Mainland the Jersey Society was liable for the payment of United Kingdom taxation. Exactly the same position obtained in the case of Guernsey Society but, in this instance, the taxable surplus has so far been insufficient to give rise to a liability.

However, though committee members reluctantly accepted the position as set out to them, the matter did not rest there, at least only temporarily. For by 1955 the objections to this liability were brought up again, more strongly perhaps by members and their increasing pressure on the Local Committees. It is very likely indeed that this pressure for change by the more vocal members did prompt a fresh look at the situation and how it might be varied to avoid UK tax, which to the average Islander was an imposition unsupported by our constitutional position.

In this reaction they were ignoring, or were unaware of, the legal link of CWS control and supervisory management of the Local Committees by which the Jersey and Guernsey Societies were regarded as 'branches' of the Co-operative system in England and thereby liable to tax. No doubt in deference to this increasing pressure, the Chairman mentioned the reference contained in the balance sheet for the half-year ended 28 March 1953 to the financial assistance that the CWS has afforded the Guernsey Society. This amounted to £3,376, and this would be repayable to the CWS should it be decided, at any time in the future, that the CWS should relinquish responsibility for the management of the Society.

The assistance was, therefore, a contingent liability, and while the CWS had no desire whatever to alter the existing relationship, the Supervisory Committee had been informed by Counsel that the liability must be shown in all published balance sheets of the Society.

At this point if we look back at the progress of the Guernsey Society before the amalgamation we can gather some idea of its initial successful establishment within just six years since registration by reference to the twelfth half-yearly meeting in May 1953.

From the Report of this meeting we see that the Registered Office was at No 2 Market Street, presumably over that first shop, and that the Committee of Management consisted of the Supervisory Committee, Messrs Quincey, Flynn and Schofield, who were Directors of CWS Limited, and the Local Committee of seven, headed by Mr Jones as Chairman and including two ladies, Mrs Brown and Mrs Kimber. The Secretary was H Atkins and the Manager RA Jennings. Membership had reached 2,042 and the dividend was 9d in the £1 (about 4p). Mention was made of the opening of the new Drapery Department on the first floor of the Market Street shop, with an appeal to members to support it.

However, despite this initial success it was becoming obvious that it could be increasingly difficult for such progress to be maintained. Surprisingly perhaps, the membership total began to decrease quite rapidly from that 2,042 in May 1953 to a fluctuating figure of around 1,600 during the next three years. Trading sales remained fairly static at around £41,000 to £50,000 per annum during the same period. This was such a modest increase that the dividend was reduced to 6d in the pound (about 2½p). In fairness, it must be said that the Society was having difficulties over the maintenance of Market Street, which was in need of major refurbishment, without which it could not present an attractive front to the public or an easy working environment for the staff.

But in addition to the practical aspect there were also some limiting factors on the personnel side, for the Local Committee exposed certain shortcomings in management and accounting. It took a firm line in its criticisms of this weakness, which may well have had a detrimental effect on the public support of the shop, even among members, which could explain the decreasing membership figures. Paradoxically, this decreasing membership was actually increasing its investment in shares, loans and small savings from £13,000 to nearly £19,000 during that same period, possibly a result of the appeal to members to increase their savings.

Despite this disappointing situation the Guernsey Society did try to overcome this apparent inertia in 1954 with the opening of a new Butchery in the Meat Market. It was conveniently close to the main shop, which, it was no doubt thought, could, with the new Drapery, offer a wider range of goods and thus boost the annual sales figures.

By contrast, and with the backing of 35 years' experience, the Jersey Society was in a stronger position, in spite of the rigours and shortages of the Occupation period. The half-yearly Report and Balance Sheet of March 1954, just a year before the decisive amalgamation came under active discussion, continues to show a similar Supervisory Committee to that in Guernsey, with the three CWS Directors, and the Local Committee members, with Mr Atkins as Secretary and John Morris as General Manager.

But change was in the air for Jersey as well as for Guernsey. The Jersey Society membership for 1954 was over 4,000 and sales for the half-year totalled £115,374, an increase of over £5,000 for the half-year period. Dividend remained at 1s (5p) in the pound.

At last the Jersey Society was gaining a sound base for independence, and it is noteworthy that those sometimes restrictive controls exercised by the CWS Directors were now nearly at an end. Their names would no longer appear on the half-yearly reports, and the first Channel Islands Co-operative Society Half-Yearly Report of March 1956 shows a strong Committee of Management team: JRD Jones as Chairman, supported by HK Foley, J Mills, Mrs J Kimber, Mrs MA Rothwell, Mrs L de Ste George, W Foley, JG Dunstan, DP Cheeseman and E Brouard-Mumford. John Morris was shown as Secretary and Manager.

Though we no longer have the evidence, it is a reasonable conjecture that during that uneasy period of uncertainty for the Guernsey Society there would have been telephone calls and possibly visits between the Islands, with discussion of the possible advantages of a merger. Both Societies had much to gain: Jersey would be free of that irksome Inland Revenue taxation, and Guernsey would gain the support of the much greater membership and the stronger financial position that Jersey could offer.

And CWS, in full knowledge of the position in both Islands, was prepared to offer formal support for the idea of a Channel Islands Society. So, from this interim position arose the positive decision of all three parties – CWS and the two Island Societies – to merge and so to present a stronger image in both Islands.

That this second approach of 1955 was more positive and meaningful on both sides is borne out by the Minutes of the Jersey Society's Half-Yearly meeting of 18 May 1955, just two years later when the CWS did appear to be more conciliatory in its response. The Minutes, given in full in **3.14**, show a change of heart.

This resolution of agreement by the CWS to the amalgamation was confirmed by the unanimous vote of both Societies. The way was now clear for the formal amalgamation of the two Societies.

Matters were moving quickly now. At special meetings held in both Islands in August and September 1955 the resolution proposing the amalgamation of the two Societies was passed without a dissenting vote.

Minutes of the proposed amalgamation were repeated at these special meetings and are given in **3.15**. The wording of each resolution is identical, except of course, for the transposition of the words Jersey and Guernsey as the text required. Again, the formal details of the amalgamation were agreed unanimously at both meetings.

With the contentious issue of liability to UK tax once settled, this led to a clearer understanding of the extent of CWS supervisory control, and lightened that control without unduly affecting the willingness of CWS to continue offering advice and assistance as needed.

Appreciation of this past and continuing advice and assistance was readily acknowledged by the new Society. At the General Meeting of Members

Future of the Society

The Chairman outlined the position in regard to Jersey Society's liability to United Kingdom tax and the steps that had been taken to investigate the possibility of avoiding tax. He said that from investigations that had been made and advice that had been received from Counsel, it would now seem certain that so long as control of the management of the Society was exercised by CWS Directors meeting on the Mainland, the Society would, for purposes of United Kingdom tax, be deemed to be controlled from England and profits of the Society would be subject to United Kingdom tax in the same way as other Co-operative Societies in Britain.

As regards the present method of management, Mr Quincey pointed out that a Special General Meeting to alter or delete Special Rule IX (which places the management in the hand of CWS nominees) could only be called by direction of the Committee of Management or by means of a requisition signed by not less than three-fourths of the Members of the Jersey Society. He further pointed out that no resolution which would have the effect of removing the CWS nominees from the Management Committee would be enforceable unless and until the Society repaid to the CWS the total amount of assistance it had received since the Rule was registered in February, 1938.

As regards the assistance, the total sum received from the CWS amounted to £8,035. However, £4,281 had been granted prior to February, 1938 and, therefore, the sum repayable by Jersey Society was £3,214.

Mr Quincey went on to say that a similar situation with regard to United Kingdom tax existed in Guernsey and that it would seem necessary, if a solution were to be found, to consider some modification in the form of control of both Societies.

In considering this matter the Supervisory Committee had to keep primarily in mind the more important question of the future conduct of the Society and the development of co-operative trade generally. After careful thought they were of the opinion that the best solution would be the creation of a Channel Islands Society, comprising the Jersey and Guernsey Societies, and they had decided to submit this proposal to the Local Committees in Jersey and Guernsey for consideration.

Further, the Supervisory Committee had consulted the CWS Board and Mr Quincey had been authorised to say that if the Jersey and Guernsey Societies were agreeable to the proposal, then the CWS Board was prepared to co-operate by –

giving consent to the deletion of Special Rule IX and the appointment of a new Management Committee comprising elected members of both Societies;

waiving their right to the repayment of assistance by both Jersey and Guernsey Societies;

continuing to give assistance by way of advice and guidance to the new Society, if it were so desired. The matter was considered by this Committee and after a full discussion it was unanimously agreed –

That this Committee is agreeable, in principle, to the creation of a Channel Islands Society by the amalgamation of the Jersey and Guernsey Societies, and recommends that a Joint Meeting of the Local Committees of the two Societies be held at an early date to consider the matter in detail.

3.14 Minute of the Jersey Society's Half-Yearly Meeting of 18 May 1955 (retyped) at which the position regarding UK income tax was resolved and the decision to amalgamate with the Guernsey Society was taken

Proposed Amalgamation with Guernsey Society

At a Special General Meeting of the Society held on 25th August, 1955, the following Resolution was passed by 19 votes for the Resolution and nil against – 'that this Society and the Guernsey Co-operative Society Limited shall be amalgamated on the conditions following:

The name of the amalgamated Society shall be The Channel Islands Co-operative Society Limited;

The Registered Office of the Society shall be at 26 Don Road, St Helier, Jersey;

The Rules of the Society shall be the rules as now submitted to this meeting;

All members of each of the amalgamating Societies at the time when this Resolution is registered shall be the members of the amalgamated Society, each of whom respectively shall be credited in the books of the Society with the like amounts of shares, share capital, loans, deposits, dividend and interest, as are standing to his or her credit in the books of the Society of which he or she is a member at the date of such registration;

The amalgamated Society shall be credited with all the assets of each of the amalgamating Societies at the date of the registration of this Resolution, and shall undertake all the obligations affecting either of the said Societies at such date'.

3.15 Minute of the Special Meeting of 25 August 1955 (retyped) at which the recommendation to amalgamate the Jersey and Guernsey Societies was unanimously agreed on 22 November 1955 this was expressed in the Minutes as follows:

> Assistance rendered by the Co-operative Wholesale Society Limited
> The Chairman referred to the assistance given by the Co-operative Wholesale Society Limited, and members of the Supervisory Committee, over the past 24 years, and added that the CWS has agreed to advise the amalgamated Societies of Jersey and Guernsey, under the name of The Channel Islands Co-operative Society Limited.

And, as a welcome bonus, the new Channel Islands Co-operative Society emerged a stronger force in the retailing market, particularly in food and drink, and was now able to consider active competition with similar businesses already established in both Islands, though, as we shall see, this would not be achieved for some years to come. In Part Two we shall read of that progress towards a full recognition of the new Channel Islands Co-operative Society in the business and social life of the Islands.

Part two

The Channel Islands Co-operative Society

1955–2005

4.1 The late 1950s saw a new type of advertising used by the Society, with an attractive American-style model and tempting free offers here launching the Jersey Food Hall in 1959 (photo Robin Briault)

Chapter 4

FIRST FOOD HA
OPENS JULY 9th, 19
22 - 23 CHARING CRC

A New Society

The amalgamation of our two Societies, achieved at last in 1955 (in legal terms at least), would bring the Society's shops and properties into closer partnership but, naturally, integration of the administration and staff of both Islands needed a breathing space for adjustment to the new overall control. This would be achieved in very good time, which given recent problems in Guernsey in particular was to the credit of all involved.

Guernsey's challenges soon featured prominently at the joint half-yearly meetings and in the published Reports to the Members. In December 1955, for example, items discussed included the desirability of buying or building additional premises for a garage. The Market Street shop needed modernising, but this would depend on the possibility of moving the new Drapery department, which was occupying space on the ground floor. The Nocq Road premises were to be reorganised to allow the stocking of the mobile shops to be carried out more efficiently and at less cost.

Certainly there was a new impetus, a fresh enthusiasm to get things done, though, as always, the costs involved and the imponderables to be overcome did not always offer or allow an easy solution. However, optimism for the future was shown in the first Half-Yearly Report of the new Channel Islands Society in March 1956. This reported an impressive membership of 6,154 and a total trading figure of £178,114, while the Members' investment in Shares and Loans had reached £101,392. For the first time the new Society was able to publish detailed Accounts with its Reports.

During this first year the Management Committee's Report detailed the improvements being made in several departments. Refrigerated counters were to be fitted at Georgetown, Charing Cross and in the Jersey Market – that is, in all those shops selling meat; another new mobile shop was to be purchased for Guernsey; furniture and television were to be displayed in Charing Cross; and hire purchase facilities introduced.

In this Report we read the first hints of self-service as an integral feature of the modernisation of the Market Street shop, though there was discussion of the respective advantages of counter service and self-service. An interesting issue was revealed as a result of this item – that CWS were the owners of the property and 'would probably agree to install a new shop front'.

During this period of the mid-to-late 1950s the Society showed its first emergence into the competitive commercial world of publicity by taking a stand at the Springfield Trades Exhibition in St Helier, an opportunity that was used to display furniture and furnishings. This apparently proved highly successful in bringing the idea of Co-op shopping to a wider public who may not yet have seriously considered using the Co-op for home furnishings as well as traditional groceries.

The value of the mobile shop was still apparent; a new one was purchased for Guernsey in 1956 to replace an older model and another was purchased for Jersey to serve the needs of the country parishes – this was still a period of cycling in and out of town or using the JMT for major shopping trips. Even though petrol was now freely available car ownership was still the exception for most country residents, so the mobile shop still played its full part in parish life. The accompanying illustration (**4.2**) shows one of the more unusual hazards faced by the Co-op mobile: being stuck in the snow!

The ongoing problem of the Market Street shop was about to be eased, if not yet solved. News had obviously been received that nearby premises, Rectory House, were likely to become available but

4.2 Getting mobile shopping to the customer was not always easy: stuck in snow, Jersey, 1962 (© Jersey Evening Post)

4.3 Rectory House in St Peter Port, as it was before conversion by the Society to a new shop front with showrooms and offices above

the situation became complicated by the conflicting views of the Management Committee, the Members and CWS.

It emerged that while the CWS had adopted a more conciliatory attitude following the previous arguments over the Inland Revenue tax, and the subsequent formation of the joint Society, as owner of the properties the CWS was in a strong position to disagree with Committee wishes or intentions. This shows up clearly in the following extracts from minutes of July 1957, when Mr Booth, a Director of CWS and a former member of the old Supervisory Committee, spoke to the members on this exciting prospect of expansion into an existing and nearby property.

Obviously eyes and ears had been alive to nearby possibilities and committee members must have enquired about Rectory House, and the fact that the CWS Architect had actually inspected the property and given an estimate for alterations indicates a preview by the CWS. It is not difficult to appreciate the air of excitement and hopeful anticipation before the meeting at which Mr Booth spoke with cautious optimism. One can almost see the twinkle in his eye as he reported on the latest development regarding the shop premises and the five floors of Rectory House, Guernsey.

> The Architect's estimate for the proposed alterations at Rectory House was approximately £13,500, and Mr Booth stated 'that under normal circumstances the capital charges would be too high for the proposed business to be an economical proposition.
>
> 'It must be remembered however that conditions and values are not the same as on the mainland, and if these standards are applied there never will be any development in the Channel Islands.' The Manager was very enthusiastic about the purchase and 'as possession could not be obtained for four years, this would enable us to depreciate the property considerably. It must also be remembered that this property is one of the very few in the main shopping centre that are ever likely to be offered for sale, and the price asked is not unreasonable' – the Committee were firmly of the opinion that the offer should be very seriously considered, and strongly recommended the purchase. 'Should any more suitable property be offered before 1961, it is most unlikely that any loss would be incurred in re-selling.'

The members' interest and management's enthusiasm at the prospect can be appreciated when it is seen how convenient a property Rectory House would be, so near to No 2 and, at the top of Market Steps, even closer to the Arcade and the town centre. Rectory House, previously known as the Old Rectory, was in fact the old parish Rectory of St Peter Port, and as it already had a shop frontage, and was in such close proximity, this would make the transfer of stock from No 2 a simple matter (**4.3**).

It will be noted that the redevelopment of 1999 is known as No 2 Rectory House, there being a fine distinction in name between Market Street and Market Place: the latter is the very short frontage beside the Steps and connecting to the Arcade.

At the September meeting members could sigh with relief as they heard a letter from CWS Directors being read, 'approving the purchase of Rectory House, the purchase price not to exceed £15,000'. The Manager informed the meeting that on behalf of the Society he had agreed to purchase for the sum of £13,500 and had paid a deposit of 10% to the Agent. John Morris then appeared before the Royal Court in October 1957 to pass contract for the purchase of all that property known as Rectory House, Market Place, St Peter Port, Guernsey, together with the dwelling houses immediately to the rear, situated in Arcade steps, from Mrs Stone (Dame Winifred Carrie Fuzzey) for the gross price and sum of £13,500 (**4.4**). It was found later that the two cottages at the rear were in too poor a condition to consider restoring and they were sold after some delay to a Mr Hooker for £1,000.

But the Market Street saga was destined to continue for some time yet. At the July 1958 meeting a member enquired about the Artisans Institute property and when was it likely to be sold as States approval to sell had been granted. From the minutes we read:

> The Manager, John Morris, stated that he had heard nothing, but assumed that it would be sold by public auction. He also stated that in a conversation with Mr Booth on the question of purchase, Mr Booth was of the opinion that it was doubtful if the Society could now afford further capital outlay on development, and he considered that once the Drapery Department had been moved to Rectory House, the present premises would be adequate. Opinions

Date: le 8 Octobre 1957.

Channel Islands Co-operative Society Limited

Prise à Rente

de Dame Winifred Carrie Fuzzey, veuve de Monsieur Vernon Ewart Stone,

(1) d'une maison avec boutique, appelée "Rectory House" édifices et jardin, situés Place du Marché, St Pierre Port.

(2) d'une maison appelée "Prospect House" et numérotée 1 et d'une maison y joignant numérotée 2, avec belle, situés dans les escaliers conduisant à l'Arcade Commerciale, à Clifton, St Pierre Port.

Prix: Qrs 661.2.0 de froment de rente amortis pour £13,500 stg.

REGISTERED 8th October 1957

BOOK 207 NO. 585.

4.4 Contract of 8 October 1957 by which the then recently formed Channel Islands Co-operative Society brought Rectory House from Dame Winifred Carrie Fuzzey for £13,500

expressed by members were not in agreement with the views expressed by Mr Booth. Present premises were too small, to modernise would be costly, and it would be most difficult to continue business whilst alterations were carried out. It was unlikely that we would be granted an off-licence for wines and spirits in the present premises, as there was no room for frozen food, or a cold room. Members expressed the view that we would probably never again have such an opportunity, and it should not be missed, even if it meant some other development had to be postponed. Mr Brouard-Munford asked if there was any possibility of the Co-operative Wholesale Society Limited buying the property and renting it to the Society. It was suggested that the question be discussed with Mr Booth, but should the property come on the market before such meeting could take place it was the opinion of the Committee that the property should be purchased, if available at a reasonable price.

As with the Rectory House purchase in 1957, this fresh initiative of 1958, just a year later, aroused great interest, bordering on impatience on the part of members, who saw the advantages of acquiring another very convenient property adjacent to the original Market Street store, and no doubt opening up the possibility of obtaining an off-licence for wines and spirits, which could not be entertained at No 2. In retrospect their impatience at the caution being expressed by Mr Booth of CWS (**4.5**) over the limitations of available capital for two purchases and their development within such a short time can be understood.

A satisfactory result of this impatience was to be realised within a few months with the purchase of the very substantial Institute Building, which now displays the Fresh Food Locale façade, while No 2

4.5 Mr Booth, the CWS director whose guiding hand was to be so influential in the development of the Society for over 25 years (photo courtesy of Mr Booth)

4.6 The old Groceteria of MacMillan days had seen many changes before it finally became a licensed premises beside the Clifton Steps. Betty Bishop and Monty Preece, the Manager, photographed at the shop in 2001 (photo George Symons)

is now The Vineyard – with the licence – the two properties being divided only by the Clifton Steps (**4.6**).

The frequent mention of John Morris in these Minutes is a measure of the responsibilities accepted by him now as a de facto leader of the new Society throughout this testing time towards consolidation and expansion, and development for the future. He was watching over the opportunities, presented in both Islands for the acquisition of properties, which would allow that essential expansion and redevelopment particularly necessary in Guernsey. As a part of this policy he would be in frequent contact with Mr Booth of CWS, as the CWS was the final arbiter in every case. He had to attend the half-yearly meetings in each Island alternately, fully briefed to meet committee and members' queries and questions and, no doubt on a daily basis to deal with staff matters and the inevitable administrative demands of a growing Society. No mean task for that young man who had, so unexpectedly, found himself in charge in 1939 and had steered the Jersey Society through the Occupation.

As an example of these additional routine tasks was the passing of contract before the Royal Court in Jersey for the purchase of No 6 Georgetown Park Estate from Mrs Joan Barnard, née Luxon, and the

Extinction of Seigneurial Rights on the property, which was to be used as a private dwelling for staff. It was an addition to the five such staff houses already purchased, Mr V Howells to be tenant of No 6, and made a modest beginning to the future practice of providing a limited amount of staff accommodation in Society properties.

As a welcome relief at this time was a letter from the CWS Directors agreeing to increase the limit of the bank overdraft from £30,000 to £60,000 in order to assist future developments.

Coincidentally with this good news came the information that two shops, Nos 22 and 23 Charing Cross, were up for sale at £20,000. These properties offered the considerable advantage of being attached to the existing main premises at the rear, and were being surveyed to see if they had sufficient floor area for a grocery and a butchery department. All must have proved satisfactory – particularly the final purchase price – for again John Morris appeared before the Royal Court in Jersey to pass contract for the purchase of 22 and 23 Charing Cross from Mrs Daisy Dupré née Bolton, and Mrs Joan Fauvel née Dupré, together with stores at the rear for the sum of £16,000.

No time was lost in developing these premises and the architects' plans were quickly approved. This was an early move towards the present integral frontage of the Co-op along the whole of the north side of Charing Cross.

However, criticism was soon to follow from Mr Booth, who spoke out at the September 1958 meeting on the issue of the costs of the proposed redevelopments in St Helier and St Peter Port. The Minutes of this meeting record a lively exchange of views:

> Artisans Institute – Mr Booth spoke on the capital commitments which would arise for the proposed alterations at Charing Cross and Rectory House and stated that the present overdraft limit of £60,000 would be insufficient to meet even these developments. Members were however still of the opinion that the Artisans' Institute should be purchased if the price was reasonable, as the present grocery shop was inadequate. No: 2 Market Street, the original grocery shop of 1947, was rented from the CWS Limited at an approximate rental of £4 per week, and if new grocery premises could

4.7 The Artisans Institute in St Helier when first opened in 1959 as the new Food Hall with the original Co-operative fascia

be obtained, it was suggested that the present shop could be used for Men's wear. The meeting resolved that we ask Mr Booth to put our problem to the CWS Directors to see if they would either purchase the property and rent to the Society, or make available additional credit to enable the Society to purchase. In the event of the Society being able to bid for the property, the question of price would be left to Mr J Mills, Mr Booth, Mr Morris and the CWS.

This difference of opinion appears to have been quickly and amicably resolved for very soon after this minor, but no doubt annoying delay, we read in the October Minutes that the tender price of £419 for the demolition of 22 and 23 Charing Cross, received from Le Quesne Limited, had been accepted and that the Manager was authorised to invite and accept a tender for the rebuilding so as to complete the new work as soon as possible.

By the New Year this minor contretemps between Mr Booth and the Committee was overcome to the advantage of both Islands. In the January 1959 Minutes appears the brief but telling entry 'that the tender of the CWS Limited, Building Department, of £24,911 for the rebuilding of Nos: 22 and 23 Charing Cross be accepted, this being the lowest of five tenders'.

This was quickly followed by a Special Management Committee Meeting held in Jersey at the Registered Office in Don Road on 19 February 1959, when with reference to the purchase of the property, The Artisans Institute, Guernsey, the Manager informed the meeting that he had signed an agreement with the auctioneer to purchase the property, and had paid a deposit of one thousand pounds, being ten per cent of the purchase price.

The Minutes confirmed this:

that the Society purchases from the Trustees of the Guille-Allez Trust, the property known as 'The Artisans' Institute situate at Market Street, St Peter Port, Guernsey, for the price and sum of Ten Thousand Pounds sterling (£10,000) free of Rentes.

That Mr Eric John Andrews, the Society's Manager in Guernsey, be and is hereby authorised to appear on behalf of the Society before the Royal Court of the said Island of Guernsey in order to consent to the above mentioned conveyance of purchase from the Trustees of the Guille-Allez Trust.

Matters were moving easily now that the differences of opinion between CWS and the Management Committee were resolved; several items occur in succession to show amicable progress. In April 1959 we read that CWS Limited had submitted the lowest tenders for the alterations to the Artisans' Institute – £7,607 for the building alterations and £1,784 for the shop front (**4.7, 4.8**).

Parallel with this was the long-anticipated improvement to the original shop, No 2 Market Street. Minutes of May 1959 record that:

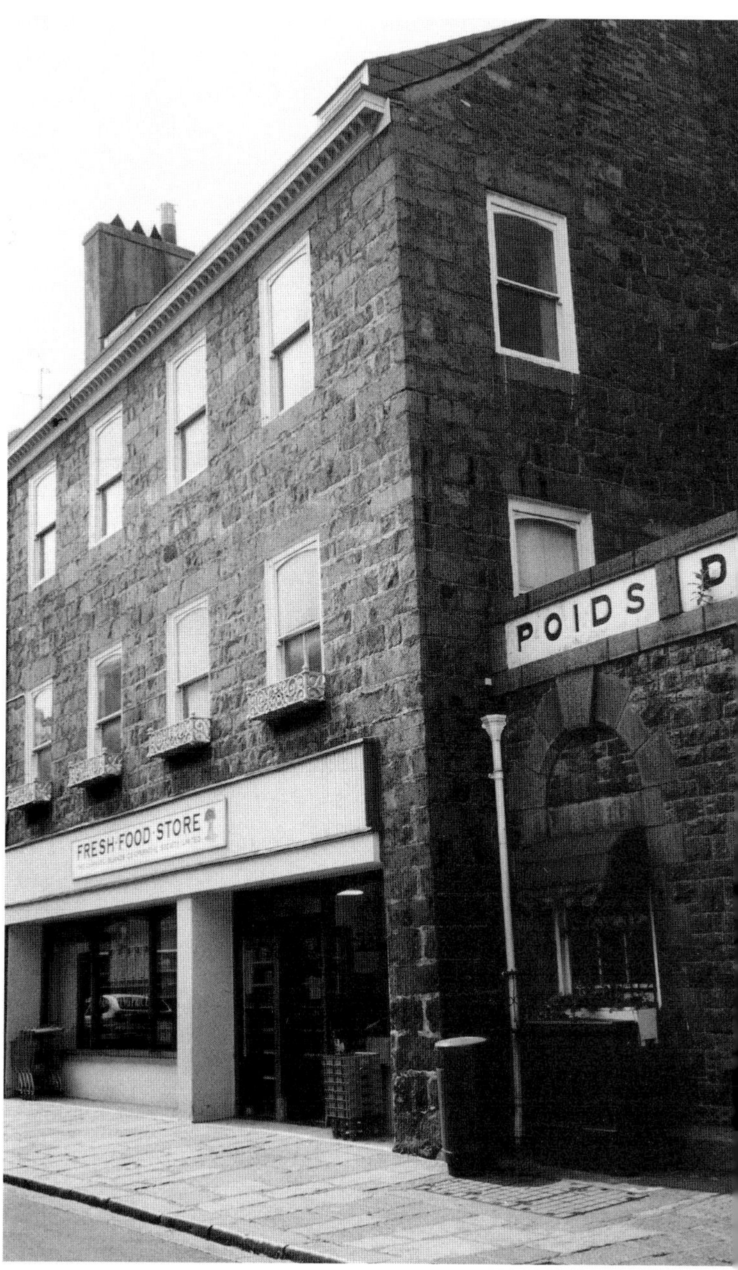

4.8 A view of the Artisans Institute in 2000 with the fascia of a Fresh Food Store. The French Halles adjoin it, where a produce stall was run for a number of years by the shop staff (photo Ken Renault)

> When the grocery department has moved out, the CWS, who own the property, have agreed to put in a new shop front and adapt it for the use of the Society as a Men's Wear Shop but until Rectory House is completed, this shop would be used for general drapery and clothing with furniture on the first floor. This alteration will cause a small increase in the rent paid to the CWS.

As we have read before, there had been several abortive attempts, even in the years before the Occupation, to establish the dry goods trade in Jersey. These attempts had generally failed, mainly because of lack of suitable accommodation and space, as drapery, clothing and footwear obviously need greater space and facility for display and to allow movement of customer and staff. There may also have been, in the early attempts, a certain reaction from the buying public, even from members, that the Co-op was basically a working family's food shop; the Fifty Shilling Tailors and similar stores with branches everywhere were likely to have had a greater attraction for them. This was borne out by the occasional reference to poor sales figures in the Drapery and Menswear department.

But circumstances within the Society were changing, and here was a more positive attempt to promote sales other than groceries and liquor by devoting a whole redesigned shop to the non-food trade. The success or otherwise of these attempts will be revealed later.

Looking back for a moment to the Half-Yearly Meeting of Jersey members on 2 December 1958 it can be noted that when an election was held for one Jersey member to the Management Committee the scrutineers were Mr N Le Brocq and Mr A Baird, whose duty it was to collect and count the voting papers. The name of Le Brocq was to feature more prominently in the years ahead.

Purchase having been completed and contract passed, the work on the old Artisans' Institute was moving ahead rapidly. In the May 1959 Committee Minutes an interesting item appears:

> Opening of New Food Hall – The CWS Publicity Department had been asked to provide a layout for window posters, handbills, and press advertisements. It was proposed to give free grocery parcels value five shillings to the first 750 personal shoppers spending £1 or over, and also one pound of pork sausages free to every purchaser of fresh meat of 7s 6d and over. In addition there will be special reduced price offers of twenty various commodities [see **4.1**].

This was followed by a routine note on the Market Street wine licence. The Manager informed the meeting that he had instructed Advocate Randall to apply for a provisional wine licence for the Artisans' Institute.

In July a brief note states that the Manager outlined to the meeting the publicity arrangements for the opening of the new Guernsey Food Store. Concurrent with Guernsey's intentions was the proposal to publicise the opening of the new Drapery and Furnishing departments at Charing Cross with appropriate advertisements in the *Evening Post.*

While the term Food Hall may sound a little presumptuous for the newly fledged Channel Islands Society when compared to its use by the new supermarkets then rising in prominence and size on the mainland, it was nevertheless a sign of things to come in the Islands. It made a fitting symbol of the considerable advances in the Market Street area since MacMillan's shop was taken over in 1947, just 12 years previously.

Along with all this activity was the necessity for management to travel frequently in and around the Island. The meeting of May 1959 in Guernsey records approval for the purchase of a car for the use of the Committee and the Manager, the choice to be left to Mr Booth and Mr Morris. No car ferry was in service then so presumably this car was for use in Guernsey only, for John Morris and visiting committee members attending half-yearly meetings, and for local management to visit their stores.

The late 1950s were certainly a period of expansion for the Society, with emphasis on development and modernisation of the Guernsey properties, which had suffered some considerable but understandable neglect. The unavoidable delays in implementing such a programme may have contributed to the slower pick-up of membership there, which remained around 1,500 or so. However, the September 1959 Report showed a figure of 2,050 and by March 1960 it had risen to 2,144, a welcome sign for the future.

In Jersey the two new shops, Nos 22 and 23, now merged with the old-established corner premises, were about to open accompanied by new-style publicity in the *Evening Post.*

The Half-Yearly Report of September 1959 could justifiably expand its usual review of the previous six months and enlarge upon the successes achieved in both Islands with a forecast of things yet to come. It is worth recording here the cheerful, optimistic account of those successes as set out in the Committee's Report.

> Trading Result – The percentage increase is less than has been recorded for the past few years, but this has been adversely affected by the rebuilding at Charing Cross, St Helier, and also at Market Street, St Peter Port, and we apologise for the inconvenience caused whilst rebuilding was in progress. The Gross Profit for the Half-Year was £59,272, as against £57,709. Expenses are above normal, due partly to special circumstances and items of non-recurring nature. Wages have increased by £1,909, repairs by £1,773, and Architect's fees by £870. Dividend is down by £759 due to a reduction in the rate. Taking all things into consideration, the Half-Year has again produced a satisfactory result, and we thank the 145 Employees and Officials for their good service.
>
> Developments – During the Half Year we have opened two new Food Shops, one at Charing Cross, St Helier, and the other at Market Street, St Peter Port. We think that the CWS Architect and Building Department have done a fine job, and have enabled us to set a new standard in hygienic food retailing in the Islands. The new Men's Outfitting Shop at Charing Cross was opened at the beginning of October, and sales have been encouraging. It is expected that the new Drapery, Footwear and Furnishing Store at Charing Cross will be opened by the end of November. The Registered Offices will also be moved to Charing Cross, and the Don Road Offices closed. The Men's Outfitting Shop at Market Street, St Peter Port, should also be completed by the end of November. Alterations at Don Road, providing for a small Grocery Shop and increased Grocery Warehouse accommodation, should be completed early in the New Year.
>
> New Appointments – Mr LM Jones, who has been Dry Goods Manager since the department was opened, has been appointed Manager of the Furnishing, Men's Outfitting and Footwear Departments. Mr HB Cook, formerly with Alcester Society, has been appointed Drapery Manager. Mr M Galway has been promoted to Manager of the Meat Department at Jersey.

Though not detailed in this Report there had been some criticism expressed at intervals on the disappointing sales of the Meat Shops, particularly in Guernsey. It was hoped that the installation of refrigerated counters in all shops selling meat would eliminate this loss of confidence and encourage members and the public to patronise the Co-op for their meat products. In this respect it was pleasing to note that Mr Michael Galway had been congratulated on his work as acting Manager, and was recommended for the post of Manager of the Jersey Meat Department. This took effect from November 1959.

During 1959 suggestions had been made that the Society should adopt a colour scheme for its properties and vehicles with an emblem or monogram, or a logo to use the modern term. This would give the Society in both Islands an immediately identifiable image. The idea was taken up by the Advertising Section of CWS who submitted designs and colours, resulting after some delays in the adoption of the universal Co-op symbol, which were used for many years.

Yes, the 1950s had been a really exciting and formative decade for the new Society; there was an impetus throughout which would continue into the future. The 1960s were just ahead!

5.1 Not a happy new year! The morning after the Charing Cross fire of 1 January 1964, which was apparently caused by an electrical fault. There was extensive internal damage to the building, but no injuries. The corner shop, Pitt Street, on the right, had been rebuilt in 1937/38 but now had the new Co-operative fascia of the late 1950s (© Jersey Evening Post)

Chapter 5

The Sixties

The previous chapter has covered a critical period in the Society's history – the post-Occupation recovery of the original Jersey Society from the tremendous difficulties thrust upon it by the War and the Occupation, followed by the ten exciting if hesitant years of rebuilding and consolidation, and eventually the amalgamation of the two Societies to form The Channel Islands Co-operative Society Limited.

All this naturally demanded initiative and considerable effort from those at the helm, the members of the Management Committee, the Manager, John Morris, John Peach, the Grocery Manager, and indeed from all the staff. As the 1959 Report, numbered 145, commented:

> Throughout this period the CWS remained active and always ready on the Society's behalf offering advice and assistance both practical and financial, whenever necessary, or by referring the Society to the Department most appropriate to the needs of the moment, for example to the Building Department, their Architects or to their Advertising Section.

As the 1960s dawned the Management Committee continued in office virtually unchanged – Mr J Mills in the Chair, supported by Mrs L de Ste George and Messrs W Foley, JG Dunstan, E Brouard-Munford, WJ Balshaw, RW Clark and HR Graham. At the Annual General Meeting on 29 November 1960, two names were put forward, Mr EG Bewhay and Mr N Le Brocq. The result of the ballot could not have been closer, 27 votes cast for each! Special Rule VII applied, and the election was determined by lot. Under this rule of the Industrial & Provident Society the final decision was reached by chance-draw from the two names, Mr N Le Brocq being the one pulled out – and a very fortunate chance this was to prove for the success of the Society through the next 35 years.

A rather puzzling change of terminology occurred at this time on the half-yearly reports. The September 1959 Report gave the usual group of committee members by name under the heading 'Committee of Management'. The Report for March 1960, just six months later, gives the same group of names but describes them as 'Directors', under the overall title of Officers of the Society.

The term 'Directors' continues on all subsequent Reports though the minutes of meetings continue with 'Management Committee members'. In January 1964 there is a sudden change on the minute heading to read 'Meeting of the Board of Directors'. No explanation of this immediate change of title occurs in the minutes, but was it a sign of a new era for the Society, that such a more accurate, businesslike title should be adopted to coincide with the move of the Registered Office from Don Road to the new building at 27 Charing Cross on 7 December 1959? In fact, the indecision over the correct form of title had caused confusion for some time but, as would be determined later by a more detailed reference to the Rules, the term 'Director' had been correctly adopted and would continue to be used.

The next ten years or so was to become a period of yet more optimistic development, matching and keeping pace with the commercial quickening of the times. Perhaps a modest symbol in this direction was the adoption of a new front page to the March 1960 Report and Accounts, which showed a photograph of the Drapery department at Charing Cross. A more formal change was the note that the Society's Auditor, Mr LC Field, was no longer with CWS and was now incorporated with the firm of English and Partners.

Before this period of optimism could really get under way it would be necessary to clear one or two outstanding matters, a particularly important one being that of rates of pay. This had been raised by the Transport & General Workers Union in October 1959, the first such formal approach to the Society. Application had been made by the Union for a revision of all rates within the present Agreement. The Manager and Mr Booth had discussed this with the Union, pointing out that the additional expenses caused by the development programme would not allow any additional expense that might jeopardise the dividend rate. The discussion closed with the suggestion that another meeting be held in a year's time when results of the half-year performance would be available.

In fact, the Union must have pressed the case for an earlier decision for in February 1960 a formal meeting was held between the Union and the Management Committee to follow up that of the previous November.

To set out the negotiating basis of the two parties and to show the firm decision reached by the Society it is worth repeating the substance of the minutes of that meeting:

> The delegation from the Union consisted of Mr Hyman, Mr Saunders and Mr Purse, Officials of T&GW Union attending in person, to pursue their claim for increased rates of pay. Their letter of October 27th had asked for rates comparable with Provincial 'B' as applicable to mainland societies.
>
> The Chairman welcomed the Union officials, and stated right away that the Society was not prepared to negotiate increased rates of pay, but after this meeting would give consideration to its case, and notify the Union of its decision.
>
> The three Union officials then in turn addressed the meeting. Mr Hyman stated that if no agreement could be reached, the matter would have to be referred to the Arbitration Tribunal in Jersey. There was virtually no discussion, and the brief meeting ended.
>
> After the delegation had left, the question of increased rates of pay was fully discussed by the Committee. It was claimed by the Union that the rate for adult males is only 3/- over the rate paid by our competitors. This is only partly correct because the Jersey rate is 8/- above the Guernsey rate, and furthermore, during the busy six months of the holiday season our competitors work a 48 hour week against our 44 hours, and if we work our staff this extra four hours, and this is often necessary, they receive six hours pay of £1 2s. 6d. The Union also stated that as officials were paid mainland rates, this should apply to all staff, but departmental managers were only paid the rate agreed with the Union of which they are members, the National Association of Co-operative Officials.
>
> The Society could not agree to be tied to mainland rates, as we were not affiliated to any district wages board, and consequently have no say or representation in any wages negotiations. The mainland rates for Co-operative Societies apply to members of the Union of Shop, Distributive & Allied Workers, and our employees are not members of this Union. Although the Society is showing an increase in sales of 9.3% for the 20 weeks of this period, wages have increased from £21,289 to £24,239, a percentage of 13.8, and the total wages rate has increased from 2s 3d to 2s 4½d, per £1 sales. Other advantages enjoyed by employees of the Society are as follows:
>
> Many employees are paid merit increases over the minimum rate and some employees are paid commission. A half-yearly bonus is paid and the Society maintains a Superannuation Scheme. We have a Sickness Agreement and protective clothing is provided where necessary.
>
> In view of these facts the Committee decided – that the Union be informed that we are not prepared to reconsider our previous decision, as conveyed to the Union in our letter of November 1959, for the reasons as mentioned above.

These minutes, detailed as they are, show not only the criteria by which wage rates and differentials were calculated at the time, based on sales figures, but the firm attitude adopted by the Society and the rebuttal of the Union's approach come across clearly. This firm but friendly relationship with the Union was of particular value at a time of change and expansion.

More telling is the follow-up of a few months later when, in June 1960, Mr Saunders of the Union wrote asking the Society to agree 'to an increase of 6/- for adult males and 4/- for adult females with a proportionate increase for juniors' – this presumably being per week, and the adult rate to be payable at 22 years instead of 23 years. In response the Society offered an increase of 4/- and 2/- respectively, payable at 22 years. This offer was accepted by the Union, apparently without further discussion.

While the negotiations were going on another difficulty in financial terms was being raised by Mr Booth, who reminded members of the urgent need for more capital, in order to reduce the large overdraft at the bank and provide for the development of Rectory House. He said: 'We hoped shortly to obtain a mortgage of £30,000 on our Guernsey properties, and it was also possible to obtain a mortgage of £10,000 yearly without States' permission on Jersey properties, but we should also consider offering 5% Development Bonds to members, either for our own use or on behalf of the CWS.'

Following Mr Booth's warning the Secretary gave the following review, informing the meeting 'that our Bank Overdraft was now approximately £40,000, but the Bond of £10,000 on the Don Road property had now been registered, and we should receive payment on September 20th. The mortgage on Guernsey properties was being negotiated. A decision regarding increasing Share & Loan Interest rates would have to be taken at our next meeting in October.'

It appears that the opening of the shop at Rectory House was only the first stage of the development of that building, and we shall read more of this later. Obviously, the capital position was becoming more serious, and the CWS was concerned.

It is also apparent that about this time some difficulties were being felt over the staffing of several departments: the Butchery, Bakery and Drapery all attract criticism over stocks, sales and the lack of experience of the staff, which changed more frequently than was desirable.

Mr Booth spoke of the Drapery department in particular, as a result of the Auditor's report, which criticised the high level of Drapery stock. His remarks centred on the seriousness of holding such high stocks in relation to sales and stressed the need to exercise tighter control over future buying to avoid stock depreciation. The Manager was advised to institute greater control over buying.

In view of this criticism it was becoming necessary to reconsider the Society's position in the non-food departments, which had in previous years been built up so patiently in response to members' wishes during the 1920s and 1930s. But circumstances were changing. In addition to the existing town shops, particularly the departmental stores of De Gruchy, Voisin & Creasey, which were already catering for local needs in footwear and drapery, the chain stores of the UK were beginning to move into the Islands. These offered a wider range of specialist styles and enjoyed a stock base on the mainland that was immediately responsive and available to local demand from public and members alike.

A rather amusing reference to the situation came up at the April 1961 Committee Meeting. Not only was there another Drapery Manager resignation to report, but the Manager's Report on the departments and branches was considered and discussed, and there were criticisms of a minor nature. It was agreed that there was a marked difference of taste between the Jersey and Guernsey people, particularly in dress, Guernsey people being of a conservative nature, and less fashion-conscious. To a lesser extent, perhaps, but also susceptible to existing established businesses were the Butchery and Bakery departments of the Society, though these would hold their own for the foreseeable future.

An indication of yet another lack of judgement in drapery buying was recorded in May 1961, when members were reminded that 'last year we tried to cater for the gift trade, but owing to such competition it was not successful. It is considered that this type of trade cheapens the store, and is not in the best interests of the members and the Committee quite correctly resolved that no more gift stock be bought.'

Meanwhile Mr Peach, the Grocery Manager and Buyer, was able in September 1960 to write a friendly letter to offer customers a new grocery order service at the Don Road branch, including orders for the delivery of coal and coke (**5.2**). Later on in the decade the Board, with reluctance, had to react to rapidly rising transport costs by imposing a charge of 6d for each grocery order delivered (**5.3**).

Also at this time of heart-searching a discussion took place regarding the desirability of providing members with a properly stocked Footwear department. This department was not included in the new Guernsey store, yet the Jersey store, which was much smaller, was trying, though not very successfully, to offer this service. It was suggested that the space then taken up by the Footwear department would be better utilised in allowing the dress section adequate space for stock and display.

Channel Islands **CO-OPERATIVE Society Limited**

Telephone: GUERNSEY Central 3757 Telephone: JERSEY Central 31221

Branch Office:
Market Street, St. Peter Port.

Registered Office:
27 Charing Cross,
St. Helier, JERSEY.

26th September, 1960.

Dear Madam,

Your local Co-operative Society has for some years operated a Grocery Order Department at No. 26 Don Road, next door to the Berkeley Court Flats. Recently it has been made possible to extend this branch in order to provide a further service to shoppers, and we have now opened a small counter service shop where it will be possible to buy all your groceries. A full range of commodities is stocked, similar to that kept in our larger stores at Charing Cross and Georgetown. This will include wines and spirits, cigarettes and tobacco, bacon and cooked meats, frozen foods, bread and cakes produced at our own Bakery, and in fact all the thousand and one items one is used to find in a Grocery Store.

The Manager of our Grocery Order Department, Mr. W.E. Ellis and his staff will be pleased to attend to all your normal requirements and will in addition be able to accept orders for the delivery of coal and coke, "Phurnacite" and Anthracite.

I may say that you will find the facilities for parking at this shop considerably easier than in other places anywhere near the town centre.

You will I am sure be delighted with the new service we are providing in this district and I should like to extend a personal invitation to you to utilise the shop and its facilities. Dividend will of course be paid in the usual manner on all purchases.

Yours faithfully,

J. Peach

J. Peach
Grocery Manager & Buyer.

5.2 A letter dated 26 September 1960 from Mr Peach, the Grocery Manager, promoting the Don Road Grocery Order Department with its well-stocked retail counter. He conveys a personal message, addressing the individual member, through the reference to easier parking seems a little naïve

TEL: JERSEY CENTRAL 31221

THE CHANNEL ISLANDS CO-OPERATIVE SOCIETY LIMITED

REGISTERED OFFICE
27 CHARING CROSS
ST HELIER · JERSEY · C.I

22nd. February, 1967.

Dear Customer,

Grocery Department.

For some time we have been concerned over the increase in transport costs. These have risen considerably over the past few years, making the delivery of grocery parcels a very expensive service.

We think that you will agree that our prices are very competitive, even when compared with self-service stores, but the difference in expenses between cash and carry trade, and a delivery service giving credit facilities, is considerable.

We have decided that from 6th. March there will be a nominal charge of sixpence for each grocery order that is delivered. This does not pay for the service, but it will assist in making it more economic, and we hope that you will not consider the charge to be unreasonable.

Yours faithfully,

p.p. THE BOARD OF DIRECTORS,

General Manager and Secretary.

5.3 The inflation of the 1960s rendered continuation of this personal grocery delivery service ever more costly, and in 1967, almost apologetically, the Board authorised a charge of 6d (about 3p)

Following on this discussion there was general agreement by the committee that there was a clear choice: provide good facilities or none at all. It was felt that the present Footwear department would never be successful. When at some future time it was convenient to do so, this department should either be closed down or transferred to a specialist shop with adequate facilities. This was done – the department was finally closed in September 1961, the stock to be disposed of to best advantage.

This was another recurring embarrassment for the Society over its unsuccessful attempts to run certain non-food departments, the Dry Goods, as they were called. A paradox continued to confuse the issue: that though the Co-operative movement was aimed at providing the working man and his family with all their basic needs at lower prices, certain items never claimed their allegiance. This position continued into the 1960s, which were beginning to witness a broadening financial ability among members for such purchases as footwear.

Rising wages and salaries were encouraging people to look around at the old-established stores like Freeman Hardy & Willis, and Dolcis, among well-known names, which offered a wider range and choice of style than the Co-op. As we shall read later, the dilemma over footwear would not go away, but some thirty years ahead a satisfactory solution would be found by which to bring footwear into the Society's orbit again – though without the direct responsibility that is causing difficulty here in the 1960s. Shoefayre was to be the answer.

No doubt this situation arose and continued to embarrass because the Co-op could not obtain goods from those established quality manufacturers to sell at lower prices, and could only offer a limited range and choice of style that did not attract the members. This echoed an item of interest that came up at Management Committee in March 1959 when the Manager reported that he had been asked if the Society would become members of the Jersey Chamber of Commerce.

The Jersey Society had been members but had not paid subscriptions since 1947, while the Guernsey Society had resigned from the Guernsey Chamber in 1958. Discussion suggested that no benefit could be anticipated by rejoining the two Chambers, and in addition the price-maintenance policy of Chamber members was contrary to the pricing policy of the Co-operative Society. This decision, after due discussion, endorsed the independent line followed by the Society on such issues that might prejudice the Co-operative spirit.

However, this matter came up again four years later, in July 1963, when the Manager was approached by a Chamber committee member, again inviting the Society to become a member. It was mentioned that matters affecting Society business were often considered by the Chamber – for instance, there was consultation with States committees, and membership would give the Society opportunity to express its opinions on such matters as stamp trading, early closing, proposed bankruptcy laws, etc. On this occasion the Committee members agreed to apply for membership but reserved the right to take independent action if in the interests of the Society and its members.

An interesting item came up in October 1961 that was to have important results for the Society and local members and shoppers in the northern end of town. A Mr FG Le Huquet, the owner of Ferbrache's general grocery store in Val Plaisant, informed the Society that he was intending to sell the property and that Mr Ferbrache had offered £5,000.

This property was adjacent to the Le Riche motor garage and workshops that the Society had purchased in 1951 and which had continued in that useful role for the Society's growing fleet of vehicles. Very quickly the Society offered £5,500, which was accepted, and the purchase was effected under mortgage, the details of which make interesting reading forty-five years later.

> Mortgage of £10,000 – A letter from Dr E Neumann was read, regarding a 'Simple conventional Hypothique' for a term of five years with extension if mutually agreed at 2% interest yearly. All legal fees, procuration fees and valuation fees to be paid by the Society but to be borne by Dr Neumann, and to be deducted from the first two years' interest. It was stated that there was very little money on offer, and we may have to wait some months before obtaining a mortgage through the Royal Trust Co.

The Committee agreed to take up the mortgage from Dr Neumann on the terms and conditions stated. This was an opportunity not to be missed, and the Manager reported that our offer to purchase this property for £5,500 had been accepted by Mr Le Huquet:

1 The usual legal formalities quickly followed and Mr John Russell Morris be and is hereby named mandatory and representative of the Society, in order to pass before the Royal Court of Jersey on behalf of the Society, the Contract or Deed of Purchase of the grocery shop together with store at the rear, tenanted by Mr H.C. Ferbrache, situate number 59½ Val Plaisant in the Parish of St Helier from Mr F.G. Le Huquet for the gross price and sum of five thousand five hundred pounds sterling (£5,500)
2 and also to pass the Contract for the Extinction of the Seigniorial Rights on the same shop at the usual rate.

Although it would be some years before the Society could realise its hopes of opening up a Co-op store in this populous and extending residential area, the site at least was there. All would depend on an alternative property suitable for garage and workshops becoming available, which was to prove a considerable difficulty, as we shall read later.

With the growth of tourism and the hotel and entertainment business, and the social life of the Island demanding a greater choice of wines and spirits, thus serving to expand the drinks trade to the Society's advantage, application had been made for membership of the Jersey Wholesale Wine and Spirit Trade Association. Eventually, after restrictions by the Association on the payment of dividend had been heard, the idea was dropped.

But it came up again in 1962. In addition to publicising the 'six years' progress' since amalgamation and payment of the general dividend (**5.4**), a fresh application for membership was submitted, which drew the even more rigid restriction of an undertaking not to pay dividend on retail trade. However, the Manager appears to have talked around the issue of dividend payment informally with the Association, with the result that the application was finally accepted.

The following extracts from the Minutes give the story, and indicate the amount of time taken up with administration and negotiation over simple matters – no doubt because of an ongoing suspicion of the Co-op principles on payment of dividend:

> Wholesale Wine Business – A further application had been made for membership of the Jersey Wholesale Wine & Spirit Trade Association. There was the possibility that the application may be successful, if we give an undertaking not to pay dividend on wholesale trade. The Grocery Manager submitted a report on the advantages of setting up a separate Wholesale Wine and Spirit Department, should this application for membership be accepted.
>
> The Committee agreed:
> 1 That we would give an undertaking to the Jersey Wholesale Wine and Spirit Merchants' Association not to pay any dividend on wholesale trade, and to sell at prices agreed by them, if the Society is accepted as a member of the Association.
> 2 That we do not approve the suggestion of setting up a separate Wholesale Department for Wines & Spirits, as the object of the Society is primarily to supply our members.

SIX YEARS' PROGRESS

	1956		1962
Membership	6,162	-	**9,366**
Share Capital	£75,839	-	**£182,583**
Reserves	£10,861	-	**£57,000**
Sales	£403,173	-	**£751,645**
Capital Expenditure for past six years		-	£178,662
Depreciation		-	£91,851
Dividends		-	£148,866

PAYMENT OF DIVIDEND

Dividend will be paid at the Jersey Office, 27, Charing Cross, and also at the Guernsey Office, Market Place, from Monday, December 10th, to Friday, December 14th, from 10 a.m. to 12–30 p.m., and from 2 to 5 p.m., except on Thursday afternoon.

C.W.S. Printing Works, Reading.

5.4 The increasing consolidation of the new Society during the six years since amalgamation was publicised in bold and impressive figures from 1962

This seemed a reasonable compromise but a further letter from this Association was received, asking the Society to give an undertaking not to pay dividend on retail trade. The Manager stated that he had informed the Secretary of the Association that the Society could not entertain this unreasonable request, but that it would agree not to pay National Members Dividend on wine and spirit sales. The Manager stated that it had been mentioned to him unofficially that the Society's application had been accepted on these conditions.

An unusual item appeared in the minutes when discussing staff matters, suggesting that the position of a Co-op Manager was a much-desired post. It was stated that in the case of one vacancy 70 application forms had been sent out, presumably in response to applicants having read an advertisement of the vacancy. Of these 61 had been returned, from which Mr Booth and the Manager would make the appointment and fix the salary. However, past events suggest that there were occasions when the 'right man for the right job' was not always found or that the department to which the successful applicant was appointed did not satisfy his hopes or ambitions.

This seemed to be the more frequently experienced situation in the Dry Goods sphere; the changes of Manager were certainly more frequently seen in Drapery and Footwear than in the traditional grocery and provision trade. It is not difficult to see the reason: whatever ambitions or loyalty the post-holder may possess or display, the Society's drapery and footwear were not the most exciting merchandise to handle. The difficulties in footwear, for example, already touched upon, and slow-moving custom, did not inspire the greatest enthusiasm or compare with the changing scene and the commercial bustle and business of the retail food trade, which the, perhaps unhappy, Manager upstairs could hear going on downstairs. He seemed destined merely to wait for the next customer while down below they were passing through all day long!

This scene is companion to the ongoing discussions with the T&GWU over a wages agreement. In February 1962 negotiations were being conducted over the scales for Managers. Although the figures shown are obviously irrelevant to today's situation it indicates the strong position the Society was prepared to take up.

A letter from the T&GWU was read, informing the Society that its suggested scale for Branch Managers was not acceptable. It was noted that the Society's suggested new scale would mean an increase of approximately 15/- weekly to Mobile Shop Managers, and the rate would be considerably higher in other cases. It was also mentioned that it was proposed to double the bonus, and this would amount to over six shillings weekly. The Manager considered that the suggested new scale was generous, and was as much as the Society could afford at this stage, bearing in mind that although the scale was higher on the mainland, Society wages rate per £1 sales were above the mainland average, as the Society had no self-service shops. It was noticed that the scale suggested by the Union was 5/- less than the Provincial 'B' mainland scale.

The Committee took a firm stand, and informed the Union that

> we consider our proposed increases to be fair and reasonable together with the increased bonus, for this year, but we would give an undertaking to pay Grocery Branch Managers the rates suggested, within the next two or three years, according to our ability to absorb them, and in reference to the bonus payments it was suggested that this should be made more of an incentive bonus, related to turnover.

Following this spirited discussion the meeting resolved

> that in future the bonus of two weeks' pay due at December would be increased or reduced by the same percentage as the difference in sales for the previous year. For example, if the Net Sales increase for this year is 5%, the bonus due to all staff would be 105% of two weeks wages if employed for the whole of the financial year, or one fifty-second part for each week of service, if still employed at the time the bonus is approved for payment.

In view of the continuing discussions with the T&GWU and the national trend of inflation with its effect on the economy generally, an interesting item occurs in April 1962. A Mr SJ Chaffey, the chosen candidate of the 61 applicants mentioned previously, was appointed Store Manager in Guernsey at a salary of £950 per annum, with a flat provided at St Sampson on an agreed rental of 30/- per week.

As a nostalgic reminder of the many changes in the towns of both Islands, during the early 1960s an offer was made to the Society of the Fairview Dairy on the corner of Bath Street and Phillips Street. The members responded with an inclination towards the setting up of a milk round, but were reminded that the States were at that time, July 1962, considering the establishment of a central milk processing plant, which would render independent dairy businesses redundant.

Though not yet fully realised by business interests of the time, the 1960s were to herald great changes in Island life, one of the most far-reaching being publication of the Island Development Plan for Jersey. The proposals outlined in the Plan were discussed at some length as they would affect

Co-op development prospects particularly in the Georgetown area and in Val Plaisant, where the old Le Riche garage business had just been purchased with the intention of building a new store.

In fact, events were moving quickly now and, despite doubts over the future of these two areas, other possibilities of equal merit were appearing. It was rumoured that the CWS store in Kensington Place might become redundant; parallel with the hopes of the new store in Val Plaisant was the possibility of converting Kensington Place to workshops to take the vehicles and equipment then at Val Plaisant and releasing that property for rebuilding if the Society could persuade, indeed convince, the planners that that area of town needed a new store.

Still more exciting for the future expansion of the Society was the knowledge that the site of Pool's Garage on the corner of Burrard Street and Don Street was vacant and now on the market for purchase. Mr Booth and the CWS architect were to inspect the site; but it was to be some years yet before the Homemaker store made headlines in the press.

The expansion of the Charing Cross area to form a cohesive whole also became a practical possibility with the news that Dot Traders of No 21 was being advertised for sale at £12,000, with a lease still to run. Although the Committee realised that it was considered desirable to own the whole of the Charing Cross block eventually, it was felt that the lease and the high price being asked made it an unattractive proposition at the time.

This was a rather surprising view to take for only four months later, in February 1963, it was reported that Bichards at 24 and 25 Charing Cross was to be approached by Society solicitors with an offer of £25,000 for the freehold. 'We need this property in order to expand and it is no use waiting for it to come on the market.'

Following upon this apparent change of heart came the obvious change of direction, and No 21 became the centre of attraction:

> With reference to 21 Charing Cross, it was suggested that we approach the owner of this shop adjoining our food store, Mr B. Cane, and offer £10,000 for the freehold. It is understood that the existing lease with Dot Traders had some years to run. The Manager had been informed by the States Planning Officer that the Café and Ladies' Hairdressing salon also along the same frontage were scheduled for demolition, and this would leave us with a corner site on the proposed wider road. There was hope that we would be offered the remainder of this island site by the States when demolition had taken place.

Naturally these opportunities raised considerable discussion and, eager not to lose this opportunity, the Committee resolved that an offer of £10,000 be made as suggested.

In the meantime the anticipation of taking over the CWS Store in Kensington Place for garage and workshops was quickly dashed for the relevant minute stated that the Manager had been informed that the CWS Greenfruit Department had not considered giving up the local depot, as had been rumoured, so there would be no hope of this store being available in the near future.

However, we shall see how events turned in the Society's favour, and how hope, anticipation and practicality merged in time to produce the results so longed for by members and management alike. This enthusiasm for growth and redevelopment was to a large extent pressed upon the Society in both Islands to enable it to take advantage of the changing social conditions that were soon to revolutionise public attitudes towards shopping.

The main rivals in food and drink, Orviss and Le Riche, already well established in their field, were themselves also undergoing a similar self-analysis. Orviss, still very much a family firm, had become lethargic in outlook and eventually succumbed to the more vigorous understanding of the situation by Le Riche, which not only took over Orviss in 1961 but was itself dedicated to expansion, not only in town but in the west.

This growing affluence and the birth of the full supermarket ideas of the early 1960s led to a levelling off and up of shopping habits by customers of widely varying social standards. Very soon now we would all be pushing those ubiquitous trolleys around the aisles regardless of what the lady next door might think! With the exception of the many corner shops that continued to serve the particular local needs, this changing pattern of shopping threatened to leave the Society behind unless it could expand to keep pace.

No doubt this was discussed at length by members of the committee and among management. While adhering to the Co-operative principles and the 'divi', the cloth cap image was fading and the Society was compelled to take a wider view of its future and to plan for wide-ranging expansion and improvement to its stores. The main store, Charing Cross, needed rebuilding rather then mere expansion so that it could cope with the growing support of custom by the general public as well as by members, a sure indication of social change.

We see this taking shape in the minutes of the period, with an urgency becoming apparent based on a good deal of personal intervention to ensure success. To have adjacent properties available for purchase at the same time was too good a prize to miss. No 21 was eventually purchased at £10,250 – a very reasonable increase over the initial price, which was at first thought to be too high!

Progress on Bichard's was more protracted, but the persistence of the Society in conducting negotiations led to several reports in the minutes. When the question of making another offer for this property was discussed it was stated that there was little to be gained by waiting, as the lease would shortly expire and in all possibility the rent would be increased. It was suggested that Mr Booth and the Secretary could meet Mr EJ Becquet, who acted for two of the joint owners.

And again in May 1963, 'Mr Booth and the Secretary reported on the meeting with Mr EJ Becquet, solicitor to the owners. It was considered vital to our future development to purchase before the present lease was renewed.' The Committee decided 'that we make a further offer to purchase the freehold for £40,000' rather than 'to remain silent and possibly lose the opportunity'.

However, this offer apparently was not accepted, and some months went by without further progress, though subsequent minutes indicated a continuing determination to purchase.

In the meantime disaster struck! On New Year's Day 1964 fire broke out in the main store on the corner of Pitt Street (**5.1**). Damage from fire and water was considerable, although the flames were confined to the first floor. But smoke and water on that floor and the lower floor as the water seeped through ceilings and ran down the stairs damaged the stock in the showroom below, where furniture and bedding and electrical goods were displayed.

An interesting and unexplained departure from the normal heading of the Management Report covering the fire indicates a 'Meeting of the Board of Directors' and continues in the otherwise usual form and layout to mention relevant details of the damage to the Drapery, Furnishing, Menswear and the Offices, putting the stock loss at £20,194. No factual or material cause for the fire could be established, but it was thought likely to have been caused by the overheating of an electrical plug or appliance left switched on from the night before.

As a continuing thread of planning for the future the Reports of the time speak of improvement and development within the existing store and also envisage further property purchase. Regrettable though the fire was, it provided a timely opportunity for the extensions and improvements spoken of during the previous year as well as those essential repairs brought about as a result of fire.

At the meeting of the Board of Directors held at Jersey on 26 January 1964 members present were Mr J Mills in the chair, Mrs L de Ste George and Messrs RW Clark, W Horrod, W Foley and N Le Brocq. JR Morris as Manager was also present while apologies were received from Mr Ferguson and Mr Tucker.

> The Manager reported on the extent of the damage by fire, heat and smoke to the Furnishing, Drapery, Men's Wear and Offices. As we were fully covered under our Fire Policy, it was not expected that the results for the half-year would be adversely affected. We had no cover for Loss of Profits, and this should be considered in the future. Messrs S Balcombe & Co (Fire Assessors) had been appointed to make our claim, and the stock loss has been agreed at £20,194, the claim for fixtures and fittings and buildings would be agreed later. Mr Booth had been a great help in organising the Drapery salvage sale. The work of re-instating the Drapery and Furnishing Departments was proceeding, and should be finished by the end of March. Consideration was given to the building of a second floor over the Furnishing and Men's Wear premises, the present offices to be used as additional furnishing showroom. If we could purchase the premises Maison Burton at 20 Charing Cross, build a new self-service food hall at Nos: 20 and 21 on the new corner, we could move the Drapery Department to the present food store, and utilise the ground floor for a separate Electrical Department.

But this report, necessary and detailed though it is, was only the bare, factual account. The personal reaction and response of the staff was another matter. In retrospect we can visualise the circumstances: New Year's Day, a Bank holiday, first day of the New Year and the staff, from management down, were in a relaxed mood after the previous evening's parties, anticipating a quiet day ahead before the shop opened again on 2 January. They were to be jolted into action when the calls for assistance came round. Accompanied, no doubt, by 'the shop's on fire' after John Morris was alerted by the police, who had first noticed smoke issuing from the upper windows at about 3.45 am, and had called the Fire Brigade.

The Fire Brigade was quickly on the scene. Within an hour and a half firemen had succeeded in bringing the fire under control, though dense, acrid smoke from the bedding, mattresses and similar materials hampered their movements. The danger was over, but much remained to be done. When the staff began to arrive around dawn they were faced with the daunting task of attempting to salvage what they could and arranging transport to the store in Kensington Place for those items still in a reasonable condition.

While firemen continued the damping down staff were rescuing ledgers, papers and other valuable documents from the office – fortunately these had not suffered serious damage – but filing cabinets, safes and other metal surfaces were hot from the effect of the flames. Colin Davies, later to become Society Secretary, recalls the efforts of several of the staff in carrying buckets of water from a hydrant near the Town Hall to the shop, to do their own damping down before some very hot items could be handled.

Fortunately, the Food shop was not directly affected by the fire, though the lingering smell of smoke and charred timber and the sight of the devastation next door were a disturbing feature of the corner for some weeks to come.

There is no doubt that the fire, disturbing though it was, gave an additional impetus to those plans and purchases that had occupied the minds of Directors and Management throughout 1963. And, as we see in the protracted negotiations over Bichard's, eventually it could be said that the fire and its after-effects had been a catalyst in bringing these varied plans together.

The Committee, eager to take advantage of the opportunity to expand if only upward for the moment, resolved 'that we agree in principle to the suggested extensions over 26/8 Charing Cross for new General Offices'.

Concurrent with these plans was the continuing delay in obtaining a decision on Bichard's property, of which, obviously, the Society was now even more anxious to obtain possession. This property and No 21, which was now the Society's property, would be a great step towards incorporation into the rebuilding of the whole block, but nothing more was heard until March 1963. At that time it was stated that 'private discussions had taken place with the local manager, regarding the acquisition of the lease. Any further development would be reported at the next meeting.'

These discussions obviously led nowhere for no further report appears until September, when it seemed that the Society was indeed back to square one. At the 6 September meeting we read:

> It was reported that this property would shortly be offered for sale. We made an offer of £40,000 in May 1963, and we should no doubt have to pay more than this. It was suggested that Messrs. Bernard Thorpe and Partners of London be asked to negotiate the purchase on our behalf.

Several months passed again, with no positive information to hand, until in April 1965 the members heard yet another negative report. This indicated little, if any, progress on the hoped-for Bichard purchase, but it did detail how management were planning in anticipation to integrate it into the overall plan for the whole block:

> There is still no information regarding the sale of the shop property 24/5 Charing Cross. It was agreed not to fix a limit on the price we would pay. We had offered £40,000 in May 1963, but we may have to pay more than this. If we buy the property, it was suggested that we should consider moving the Electrical Section to the Ground floor at present occupied by the Drapery, and move the Drapery Department to Bichard's, without making any structural alterations. It was not recommended that we enlarge the present grocery by taking part of Bichard's, but that we wait until Dumaresq Street is widened, and build a new self-service food hall adjoining the present grocery shop.

At last, in September 1965, we read the Minutes of a Special Meeting, which finally ended the Bichard saga in favour of the Society, though no details are given of any protracted negotiations that may have taken place in the intervening five months. Possibly the fact that three parties and two lawyers were involved had a great deal to do with the delays!

> Minutes of Special Meeting of the Board, held on 15 September 1965
> It was resolved that Mr John Morris, Secretary and Manager of the Society, be and is hereby named mandatory and representative of the Society, in order to pass before the Royal Court of Jersey on behalf of the Society, the Contract or Deed of Purchase of a shop known as 'Bichard's', situate 24/25 Charing Cross in the Parish of St Helier from the Attorney of Mrs Elsie Louise Veale and of Miss Joan Morish Le Boutillier, and from the Attorney of Mrs Joan Cordingley, for the gross price and sum of forty-three thousand pounds sterling (£43,000).

Holding a special meeting was a clear indication of the importance attached to this acquisition. Having obtained possession the Society lost no time in pursuing its plans for integrating Bichard's within the existing premises. Acquiring the property for only £3,000 more than the offer of £40,000 two years previously must have been of great satisfaction to the Board. Without further delay Mr Booth, just four days after the Special Meeting, reported that the CWS Architect 'could survey the property tomorrow in order that alterations could be started as soon as possible'.

Later the same month – the architect must have moved very quickly indeed, a measure of the urgency – the members heard the welcome news of a considerable rearrangement of departments and accommodation, including a public office counter:

> At the subsequent meeting the Architect's plan was considered, showing a new shop front, and removing the stairs leading to the flat to give more space. Application had been made to the IDC and it would be at least four weeks before planning permission was received. It was agreed that the new shop be used for general drapery on the ground floor, with fashions on the first floor, and stockrooms above. There would be access on the ground floor between Men's Wear and drapery, and also on First Floor. New stairs in Drapery to be sited on wall adjoining Men's Wear, moved to new position at bottom of stairs leading to General Office. At our previous meeting it was suggested that the Electrical Section be moved to the ground floor, but after discussion it was decided that the carpet section be moved to the ground floor, together with upholstery.

These detailed accounts of the proposed rearrangement of the interior are a sign of the determination of management and staff to begin work on the restoration and upgrading of 27 and 28 as soon as possible. They also suggest the difficulties when moving, or planning to move, the several different departments into areas thought to be more suitable or more convenient and all in close proximity to the food store. And it appears that previously there was no public access to the office for members to discuss matters with the office staff or to seek advice. Such an essential access was now being planned for the first time.

By contrast, the purchase of No 21 had been a simple matter but now, the Bichard's acquisition being completed, the Society was well advanced towards showing a complete Co-op frontage to Charing Cross, enabling a future programme of rebuilding to be envisaged with confidence. During this determined effort of acquisition in a particularly prominent area, other issues were being discussed. The pressing question of warehouse accommodation in Guernsey was brought into focus by the offer from J&S Norman Limited, Merchants, to build a large store at St Sampson.

From the Minutes of 10 February 1963 we read the details:

> Regarding the possibility of obtaining extensive storage in Guernsey ready-made as it were, a letter from J. & S. Norman Limited was read, offering to build a warehouse on Bulwer Avenue of approximate measurements 200 ft by 60 ft and rent on a long lease at between 2s. 6d and 2s. 9d per square foot (approximately £30 weekly). Warehouse accommodation is badly needed, in Guernsey and if we preferred to build our own store, a convenient site is almost unobtainable, and interest and depreciation charges would certainly be no less than the rental asked. There was also the problem of finding the capital. Grocery Warehouse would require 5,000 sq. ft., Furnishing Warehouse 4,000 sq. ft., and Garage and Mobile Stores 3,000 sq. ft. Apart from the convenience of handling, saving could be made to offset the rental by letting or selling Longue Rue Warehouse, giving up the lease of Braye Road, sell our premises at Nocq road, open a ladies' hairdressing establishment over the Men's Wear shop at 2, Market Street, or lease the premises. It would also enable us to have the old ballroom on the top floor of Rectory House as an

additional showroom for furniture. The Manager stated that we should also require a petrol tank and pump to service the vehicles. It is understood that the building could be ready for Christmas of this year.

This would be a major step forward and the Society informed Messrs. J. & S. Norman Limited that we accept in principle their offer, and ask them to submit a detailed drawing for our approval.

The amount of detailed planning ahead – in the event of such an offer materialising – is an example, parallel to Bichard's, of the serious work undertaken by the committee members and the management staff in analysing the needs of the Society as the pressure grew to expand, always within capital limits. But the offer was sufficiently encouraging for members to request details for a full consideration.

As an indication of the continuing growth of business in both Islands the minutes refer to a similar problem already present in Jersey, when it was reported that the Furnishing department was seriously lacking storage space, and might have to consider a large warehouse similar to the one proposed for Guernsey. If given planning permission to build a food hall at Val Plaisant, that would also call for a new garage. It was considered that a site adjoining the Bakery at Beaumont would be suitable. This was eventually achieved as a part of the new warehouse when this was finally built some years later.

Again we read from the minutes of the forward planning that exercised the minds of management and members in anticipation of the moment when a suitable property might become available.

In Guernsey one solution to the increasing pressure on space within the Market Street store was renting a shop in the French Halles. This was eventually done during the 1960s for the sale of greengrocery and it certainly eased the congestion in the main store, particularly on Saturdays. The welcome growth in membership and sales here was causing considerable difficulty in the old Market Street stores, which were still in their original form and unable to expand because of steeply rising ground behind.

The St Sampson area also was, so far, not well provided for in respect of a good grocery store, and the Society was frequently looking out for another property on the Bridge. In June 1963 two adjacent shops on the Bridge were noted and enquiries made as to possible purchase.

Another opportunity occurred in Guernsey at about the same time, when it was believed that the States might be offering the Poids de Roi for sale. The Committee considered this as a possible wines, spirits and tobacco specialist shop with access to the Artisan's Institute, now the Fresh Food Store, thus relieving congestion in the store. However, this offer did not materialise.

On a more serious and personal matter – that of staff – it was noted briefly in July 1963 that staff difficulties had arisen. This was enlarged upon later to disclose that the main issue was that of obtaining staff, particularly juniors, and that it might be advisable to increase the wages of juniors.

Certainly, a number of complaints had been reported of deficiencies in stocking of shelves and cabinets in stores, which was attributed to shortage of responsible staff, and of embarrassments over the conduct of individual members of staff resulting in the occasional dismissal. It was therefore surprising that the Committee should report under 'Duties of Personnel' that 'the Society was too small to justify a Personnel or Public Relations Officer though it was suggested that someone should be responsible for those duties'. It would be some years yet before the Society fully realised the need for the appointment of an officer to be solely responsible for dealing with issues of general discipline, petty pilfering, training to common standards, overcharging and general courtesy to members and the public – in short, the upgrading of all staff to their full potential to the advantage of the Society and the customer.

This was obviously a continuing problem for it came up again in May 1964, when reports showed that complaints had been made of the service at the Bakery and Provision counters. Again the reason given was that of experienced staff leaving and the lack of suitable replacements.

Meanwhile the continuing problem of updating the Georgetown store came up again with further consideration of the recently produced Jersey Development Plan. It was discussed at length at the meeting held on 15 July 1962:

It was noted that the proposed new road at Georgetown would go right through the Coal Store, and other arrangements would have to be made for this department. One centralised storage and bagging depot for the Island had been mooted, and there appeared to be no reason why we should not join with other merchants in

> such a scheme. The new road at Georgetown would enable us to rebuild the food store, with possibly a frontage on both roads, and it was agreed that we would inspect the Georgetown site next time we have a meeting in Jersey. Development proposals for Charing Cross would not adversely affect us, but it would appear that we would not be permitted to develop our shop and garage property at Val Plaisant as planned, if the present proposals for Springfield are eventually agreed by the States.

Obviously, the Society was concerned at the effect the Development Plan would have on the proposed future developments in that area and at Val Plaisant, where the interrelated needs of moving the garage and workshops were also affected.

The Committee wrote to the Islands Development Committee of the time, but with apparently little result. Almost two years later, in 1964, we read of considerable loss of trade at the Georgetown shop and 'that one of the reasons for this decrease in trade was the dilapidated state of the premises. We should discuss if it was practical to rebuild without waiting for the proposed new road.'

Following this rather damning report, which was no credit to the Society, it was discussed again at the next meeting. Here the Manager reported that the Architect had advised that it was unlikely that the States would agree to any piecemeal development in the area. Once again the matter of a new store at Georgetown had to be held in abeyance.

As the 1960s progressed the Society found itself in a frustrating situation: plans for future continuing development in both Islands were very much in their minds, but delayed by the now more dominant IDC and the Jersey Development Plan. The advisory influence of the old Comité des Beautés Naturelle had been replaced by the legal status of the IDC. In one respect this was a necessary advance in legislation for the benefit of the Island but, of course, there were snags: approval for schemes, proposals and the plans themselves were now more likely to suffer delays.

However, one item of good news received in September 1963 was a letter from J&S Norman Limited in Guernsey informing the Society that the new warehouse off Bulwer Avenue, which had been discussed and agreed in principle in January, would be ready by January 1964 as promised. This would be of great relief to those managers who had difficulty in allocating space for stock in their already congested shops.

At the same time we read of an additional mobile shop being ordered, with the comment that it would work in conjunction with the new Bulwer Road warehouse, taking its stock from there instead of from the shops. This was borne out by the plan of the new warehouse, discussed at the February 1964 meeting, which indicated the extensive range of goods that needed storage space away from the shops, particularly Furnishing and Electrical, which required adequate space.

A suggested layout plan of the new warehouse was presented for discussion by the committee, showing the layout for Furnishing & Electrical Warehouse, Grocery Warehouse, Grocery Despatch Department and three Mobile Stores. A staff room was to be provided with cooking facilities.

It has been noted that the Minutes of January 1964, following the fire, had been headed 'Board of Directors' instead of the usual 'Management Committee'. This was taken up in March with the explanation that 'under Society rules we were Directors and not Managers and that when there was to be a revision of the Rules approval should be sought for this amendment to be noted'. From March 1964 the more dignified and more appropriate title of Directors was adopted.

Throughout this period of sometimes frustrating but often exciting, progress following the Occupation years, the name of the young John Morris, who had been thrust into the limelight in 1939, has often been mentioned. His dedicated service to the Society did not go unnoticed beyond the Society. It was acknowledged by the community when the Constable of St Helier invited him to stand for the office of Centenier. Mr Morris stated that he would accept the invitation if he had the permission and support of the Society. This was readily given, and it can be seen that indirectly this would be further support and quiet but welcome publicity for the Society itself.

The 1960s were certainly a growing-up period for the Society in both Islands. Now as the decade drew to a close we see a maturity manifesting itself in a growing confidence in the future, engendered no doubt by the number of projects in hand all demanding an integrated approach.

The Annual Report & Accounts for 1963 speaks of a mild optimism for the future despite the poor season for the Jersey growers but with confident hopes for a good tourist season. Net sales had increased by 15% over the year from £762,505 to £897,057. Membership also increased from 9,366 to 10,885.

This was the centenary year of the CWS, so special mention was recorded of the help and guidance given by that body. Congratulations and appreciation were offered for the support given by its Directors and Officers during the life of the original Jersey and Guernsey Societies, and later the amalgamated Society, and the future was anticipated with confidence. It was clear that the partnership over the years between CWS and the Society had become softer and more amenable, more advisory than supervisory.

One rather less cheerful feature of the sales figures for 1964 is the slight decrease in sales total, caused by the fire of January 1964, which obviously closed several departments for some time until restoration was completed. Mention is made of the competition from new supermarkets elsewhere and the Society's intention to counter this by introducing self-service as soon as possible, to reduce wage costs and to encourage more custom from members and public.

The 1965 Report refers to the continuing increase in trade, and notes that membership and sales had more than doubled over the previous seven years. The new developments were outlined, with the self-service Food Shop at The Bridge, St Sampson, nearing completion. Similar plans were also agreed to convert the recently purchased store at Castel to self-service. The delay in the rebuilding of the Georgetown branch was continuing, because of the apparent procrastination of the IDC, which required demolition of the Coal Store to enable the new road to be built. This possibility of demolition precipitated the decision that the Society should give up coal sales and distribution to members and participate in the central coal storage and distribution proposals now being put forward. These proposals, noted briefly as far back as 1962, were far-reaching in their effect on both Society and members but, as the details outlined in the Minutes of July 1965 indicate, there was no alternative. Georgetown was rebuilt.

On the proposed Island solid fuel depot,

> The Manager stated that all Coal Merchants who were members of the Jersey Coal Importers Board were now in favour of a Central Storage and bagging depot. A suitable site was available to the north of the Bellozanne Sewerage Works, and application had been made for planning permission in principle. The scheme suggested was to form a limited liability company of the present seven members of the Board who would take out shares in proportion to retail purchases over the past two or three years. The new organisation would buy and sell all solid fuels, and the seven coal merchants would close down their separate businesses. A capital of approximately £100,000 would be needed of which the Society would have to contribute £14,000. The Manager stated that he was in favour of the scheme, as we would soon have to find another store owing to development of the new road at Georgetown, and it would also expedite the building of a supermarket there. A discussion took place and it was stated we should have only 14% of the votes in this monopoly and it was questioned if we should have the same restraining influence over prices. It was intended that the shareholders would receive about the same in business, and as the new organisation would be able to operate more economically there should be no need to increase prices. One objection was the loss of sales and the good service given to members, who in future would receive no dividend on coal. Whilst the profits on coal would not be returned as dividends on these purchases, they would be for the general benefit of the Society and the members. Considering all circumstances, there was no practical alternative, and it was resolved that we become shareholding members of the proposed new organisation.

This decision may have been somewhat reluctantly reached by the Board and members, in that coal, one of the necessities of the ordinary working family of fifty years previously and therefore contributing to the dividend, was no longer so central in people's lives: modern housing was increasingly being equipped with various forms of central heating and coal was no longer rated so highly for domestic purposes.

Another major item in the Society's future planning was the development of the Beaumont site, which was also subject to planning permission, and following from this, the progressive movement of departments, stores and equipment between designated sites or stores. Again the minutes tell the story.

On the development of the Beaumont site the Board discussed the immediate needs, the emphasis of capital letters serving to indicate the urgency of the situation:

> In the event of Planning Permission being granted by the Island Development Committee, we should immediately instruct our Architect as to the size and type of building required, so that plans may be submitted without delay. It was agreed that the MOTOR REPAIR WORKSHOP, GARAGE AND THREE MOBILE STORES be transferred from Val Plaisant, the GROCERY WAREHOUSE and DESPATCH DEPT. to be transferred from Don Road, and the FURNISHING and ELECTRICAL STORE be transferred from C.W.S. Kensington Place. We should then be able to sell Don Road property to offset the capital cost. The manager was asked to find out the floor area required for each department.
>
> Later Mr Mather of CRS [Co-operative Retail Services] led a general discussion on the future development of this vital site. It was suggested that the first move in Jersey would be to build the garage at Beaumont, so that work could be started on a new Food-hall at Val Plaisant, with flats over, before the expiration of Mr Ferbrache's lease in June 1966. The re-building of Georgetown shop was also most urgent, as soon as the States had decided on the proposed new road. It was suggested that a large Warehouse be built on the new Beaumont site, similar to the one in Guernsey, for a Furnishing store, Grocery Warehouse, Mobile Shops Stores, and Grocery Order Despatch Department. Don Road was not a good trading street, and this property should be sold.

This last remark on Don Road, when read with the accompanying illustration, is indicative of changing times; the Don Road Store had served its purpose for many years, but no longer could it attract custom. No longer was that area of Don Road a 'walking street' either, unless you happened to live in it.

It has been a theme of this chapter that over the ten years since amalgamation, contacts had improved between the Society and its management and the CWS. More cordial relationships had also developed on a personal level. Good as its word, CWS had continued to give advice and practical assistance, in the rebuilding and the likely costs to be incurred, for example, in an easier manner, Mr Booth being the principal facilitator in this.

However, feathers were ruffled again in June 1964 when a rather surprising situation arose, the dismay stemming from the apparently sudden decision of CWS to propose a change of overall liaison to the CWS Retail Trading Group. The Society took a firm opposition stance on this, and again the minutes tell the story:

> Liaison with CRS or CWS – A letter from Mr E Mather of the CRS Limited and correspondence from Mr DH Lewis of CWS informed us that the CWS had decided that the liaison with this Society would be taken over by the CWS Retail Trading Group.
>
> Disapproval was expressed with the proposal, and also the discourteous manner of approach. Over the years we have received invaluable help and assistance from the CRS and particularly from Mr Booth, who had intimate knowledge of our problems and the personnel, and once again we would record our appreciation of Mr Booth's services. We now have to face intense competition from Supermarkets, resulting in lower profit margins, a decrease in sales and an increase in wage rates, and during this difficult period we would miss the advice of CRS Officers.

The Board was obviously very disturbed at the prospect, particularly with the sudden decision without reference to the Society, and it responded sharply: 'That Mr Mather be informed that we see no reason for any change in the liaison with CWS, and that we do not agree to the proposal.'

Mr Mather was obviously invited to attend a Directors' meeting to explain the reasons for the change, which are not detailed here; neither is the reason for a concern over intense competition from supermarkets. But this anxiety over competition was an obvious reference to the progress being made by Le Riche, led by Dick Riches in the mid-1960s, towards the rebuilding of their older shops as early supermarkets and the intention to command the Red Houses crossroads and the growing Quennevais area with their greatest venture so far, a purpose-designed supermarket.

The Co-op was only just self-service in the early 1960s (**5.5, 5.6**), and the necessary checks on expenditure for any ambitious expansion beyond Georgetown and Val Plaisant already suffering seemingly interminable delays were a restraining factor. We shall read later of the Society's moves towards the west, which would enable the Co-op to take on that Le Riches competition on equal terms.

In response to the invitation Mr E Mather, the Chief Executive Officer of Co-operative Retail Services, addressed the meeting, giving the background and circumstance leading to the request by CWS Retail Trading Group to take over the liaison from CRS. Mr Mather had discussed the position with Mr WT Welch [CWS Director]. The Board informed Mr Mather that they were very happy with the services so readily given by officials of CRS, and that we were not prepared to accept the proposed change, as it would not be in the best interests of the Society. Mr Mather informed members that the CRS were charging the CWS for expenses of supervision.

Following the meeting the Board's thanks were extended to the Officers of CRS for their excellent advisory services, and we agree to pay for these services, should we be called upon to do so.

This unexpected distraction being overcome, the search for more suitable premises for a Society store in Guernsey was rewarded when Mr Collas of the Bridge, St Sampson finally agreed to sell, and his shop, building and yard were purchased for £13,250. This opportunity was quickly taken up with the Architect, and plans prepared for modifications and tenders invited. By early 1966 the store was open and trading, though this would prove to be only a brief interim stage; the Society was after a more prominent and permanent presence in St Sampson, an objective still a few years ahead.

For some time now the Society had endured patiently the need for additional warehouse storage space, in Jersey particularly. No doubt rumours were again circulating that CWS was at last considering giving up its Kensington Place Merchants store, which it was realised would be a valuable asset to the Society. Used for many years by CWS as a store for export, it had now decided to close the business on 9 July 1966. Correspondence with Mr Templeman of CWS Estates and Property Department led to negotiations on the price, which was quickly agreed at £25,000. This happy transaction quickly led to planning for its use; the CWS Architects were called in, with their Structural Engineer, to advise on the adaptation for Society use. These adaptations were considerable to enable the full use of the space for the several differing purposes required. After the previous rebuff

5.5 Discussions at Board level on the merits of self-service very soon led to its practical application. Charing Cross was transformed in 1961, with the wines and spirits, tobacco and cosmetics department strongly promoted

By Courtesy of H.M. Customs visitors are allowed to take into the United Kingdom free of U.K. duty:—

1 bottle of Wine
½ bottle of Spirits or Liqueur
½ lb. Cigarettes (200 Standard Size), **Tobacco or Cigars**
5 oz. Toilet Water
5 oz. Perfume

Price List

CHAMPAGNE	*Vintage*	*Bott.*
Charles Heidsieck	1953	28/6
Lanson, Black Label	N.V.	25/6
Moet et Chandon	1953	30/9

SPARKLING WINES	*Bott.*
Duc d'Albares	7/9
Sparkling Muscatel, Ackerman-Laurance	12/9
Dry Royal, Ackerman-Laurance	13/6
Golden Guinea, Muscatel	15/9
Baby-Cham	(1/3 each)

PORT	*½-Bott.*	*Bott.*
Dow's, No. 1., Ruby	–	9/6
Warre's, Cardinal Red or White	–	9/6
Warre's, Full Dark	–	9/6
Duval	–	5/–
***Ruby, Sandeman's	6/6	11/9
***White, Sandeman's	6/6	11/9
Partners' Finest Rich Ruby, Sandeman's	–	14/9
Picador, Finest Old Tawny, Sandeman's	–	12/6
Vintage 1950 Sandeman's	–	17/–
Commendador, Feuerheerd	–	14/9

SHERRY	*½-Bott.*	*Bott.*
Duval	–	5/–
Amontillado, Sandeman's	–	12/6
Apitiv, Extra Dry Pale Fino, Sandeman's	–	12/6
***Brown, Sandeman's	6/6	11/9
Brown Bang, Golden Oloroso, Sandeman's	–	14/9
***Dry Pale, Sandeman's	6/6	11/9
Pemartin, Choicest Oloroso, Sandeman's	–	16/9
Amontillado, Carlito, Williams & Humbert	–	11/6
Dry Sack, Williams & Humbert	–	17/6
Walnut Brown, Williams & Humbert	7/6	14/–
As You Like It, Williams & Humbert	–	18/–
Canasta Cream, Williams & Humbert	9/3	17/–
Crema, Gonzalez Byass	–	16/–
Royal Amontillado, Gonzalez Byass	–	11/3
Tio Pepe, Gonzalez Byass	–	16/9
Dry Fly, Findlater's	–	11/6
Bristol Milk, Phillips	–	17/6
Bristol Cream, Phillips	–	23/–
Celebration Cream, Pedro Domecq	7/9	14/6
Double Century, Pedro Domecq	–	11/3
Bristol Milk, Harvey's	–	20/3
Bristol Cream, Harvey's	–	23/9

APERITIFS & TONIC WINES		
Sanatogen		7/6
Byrrh O.B.	–	8/9
Dubonnet	7/3	13/9
St. Raphael, White and Red	7/–	12/9
Wincarnis	–	12/6
Lillet	–	13/6
Pernod 45°	15/9	29/6

VERMOUTH		
Brega Rossi, (Sweet)	–	9/9
Cinzano Red (Sweet)	7/6	12/9
Cinzano White (Sweet)	–	12/9
Cinzano Dry	–	13/6
Martini Sweet	7/6	12/9
Martini Dry	–	13/9
Noilly Prat (Dry)	7/6	14/–
Votrix, Sweet and Dry	–	6/9

WHISKY—(as available)	*½-Bott.*
Vat "69"	12/6
Teacher's	12/6
John Haig	12/6
White Label	12/6
Johnny Walker	12/6

Tobacco—*continued*	*per 2 oz.*
Sweet Cut	4/6
Wayside Mixture	4/5
White Ox, Dark Shag	3/1
Will's Golden Virginia	4/3

and all other well known brands.

CIGARETTES		*Pack*	*200*
Astorias (American)	20s	1/8½	17/1
Bristol	20s	1/7	15/10
Chings No. 5 Plain or Cork	20s	1/5½	14/7
Chings Filter	25s	2/–	16/–
Consulate, King Size Mentholated	20s	1/9	17/6
De Luxe Medium Blue	20s	1/8½	17/1
Essex, King Size Filter	20s	1/6	15/–
Flag	20s	1/1½	11/3
Gladstone	20s	1/6	15/–
Grosvenor	20s	1/8½	17/1
Joy Sticks (Double Length)	10s	1/9½	35/10
Kensitas, Extra Size	20s	1/8½	17/1
Black and White	20s	2/3	22/6
Benson and Hedges	20s	2/3	22/6
Ching's Silk Cut	20s	1/6½	15/5
Craven "A"	20s	1/8½	17/1
Capstan	20s	1/8½	17/1
Churchman No. 1	20s	2/–	20/–
Du Maurier	20s	1/8½	17/1
Gold Flake	20s	1/8½	17/1
John Cotton	20s	1/8½	17/1
Players Navy Cut	20s	1/8½	17/1
Piccadilly	20s	1/9	17/6
Senior Service	20s	1/8½	17/1
State Express 333, Filter tip	20s	1/6½	15/5
State Express 555	20s	2/1½	21/3
Waverley	20s	1/4½	13/9
Lucky Strike	20s	2/–	20/–
Palette	20s	2/6	25/–
Park Drive Plain	20s	1/5½	14/7
Passing Clouds	20s	2/1½	21/3
Peter Stuyvesant	20s	1/9	17/6
Piccadilly No. 1	20s	1/9	17/6
Player's Gold Leaf	24s	2/8 (240)	26/8
Player's No. 3	20s	2/1½	21/3
Player's Perfectos Finos	50s	9/–	36/–

Cigarettes—*continued*		*Pack*	*200*
Player's Batchelor	20s	1/7½	16/3
Regent	20s	1/5	14/2
Rothman's King Size Filter	20s	1/10	18/4
Rothman's King Size Plain	20s	1/11	19/2
Sobranie Black and Gold Virginia	20s	3/1½	31/3
Sobranie Black Russian Gold Tipped	25s	4/5	35/4
Sobranie Cocktail Virginia	10s	1/8½	33/8
Sobranie Cocktail Virginia	20s	3/4½	33/8
Wild Woodbines	20s	1/4½	13/9
Export Woodbines	20s	1/9	17/6

and all other well known brands

CIGARS .. .. Popular Selection.

LIGHTERS at Channel Islands prices—RONSON, ROLSTAR, MOZDA, COLIBRI, Etc.

CHOCOLATE LIQUEURS			
French	Gonnet	4 oz Plexiglass	6/6 each
	Gonnet	8 oz Cabinet	13/6 each
	Gonnet	16 oz Cabinet	22/6 each
Dutch	Rademaker	¼ lb. Wood Casket	5/6 each
	Rademaker	½ lb. Wood Casket	11/– each
	Rademaker	1 lb. Wood Casket	20/– each
	De Beukelaer	Singles	5d each
	Ringers	From 4/6 to 20/– per box.	

PERFUMES			*London Price*	*Jersey*
Marquay	Le-Lu	⅛ oz.	18/6	**8/6**
	Le-Lu	¼ oz.	28/6	**15/3**
	Le-Lu	½ oz.	53/6	**28/9**
	Prince Douka	⅛ oz.	18/6	**8/6**
	Prince Douka	¼ oz.	28/6	**15/3**
	Coup-de-Feu	⅛ oz.	18/6	**11/6**

COSMETICS			
Max Factor	Hi-Fi Lipsticks	6/6	**4/11**
	„ Refills	4/3	**3/3**
	Creme Puff	6/9	**5/1**
	„ Refills	5/–	**3/10**
	Panstik	4/9	**3/7**
	Top Secret	10/–	**7/7**

that No 60 was not to be given up by CWS this decision was a great relief to the Board.

Concurrent with this welcome development was the continued planning of the new Georgetown and Val Plaisant stores, both to be supermarkets. Both were to suffer further delays caused by IDC requests for fresh revised plans prepared by the architect to show modifications by the Society and by management. Getting these two new shops opened, one in a new area, must have seemed a tedious and frustrating task but exciting too, as they were to be completely new stores on the supermarket pattern.

One of the snags to this development of Val Plaisant was the necessity of vacating the site completely by the move of the vehicles and their garage, the motor repairs workshop and the three mobile stores to 60 Kensington Place – would that be ready in time? It seems that a successful juggling act was achieved and that transfer was made on a temporary basis, for work was also in progress at No 60, but at least it was not necessary to rent premises elsewhere, which could have made it an expensive move.

All this activity was proving costly anyway. An inside view of this appeared in a Minute of July 1966:

> On the issue of capital required for this major development a letter from the Architect was read and discussed, giving an estimated cost for Georgetown premises of £38,000 based on £4 per square foot. With interior fittings the total cost would be £50,000, and a similar amount would be required for Val Plaisant. At the moment we had an overdraft of £10,000, and we had overdraft facilities up to £100,000. Although our interest rate on Loans had been increased to 6%, this had attracted little new money, as Merchant Banks were offering higher rates. The position would have to be watched closely, as finance could become a problem within the next twelve months.

In addition, there were costs of £15,000 for the first structural changes to Kensington Place. It was altogether a demanding period financially, but the Society was much more stable in money terms than it had been just a few years previously. But vigilance and care would still be necessary, for here we see the beginning of the inflationary effect resulting from the abolition of the interest limit in our Code of 1771 and the influx of new banks and merchant houses into the Island. After enjoying a reasonably settled period the hire purchase rates to members also had to be increased in line with the trend.

In April 1965 it was reported that

> we increased the hire purchase interest charge from 2½% to 3½%. There were no complaints from members, and we were still charging much less than our competitors, who usually charged a minimum of 10% per annum. Now that the Bank Rate had gone up from 6% to 7%, charges on Bank Overdraft would cost us more, and we would be justified in increasing HP Interest to 5% as at the moment the charges did not cover the costs of finance, labour, stationery and bad debts.

In view of the continuing inflationary trend upward the Board resolved in advance 'that as and from 1st August 1966 the interest charges on all new HP business be increased from 3½% to 5% per annum', which for the period was a quite considerable increase.

The Annual Report of 1967 refers to the now expected annual increase in membership and trading figures, and the latest progress on developments and also pertinent comments on the possible effect on the Islands of the expected admission of the United Kingdom into the Common Market. So even nearly forty years ago this possibility was in the news, though no one could have forecast the difficulties and confusion that are being experienced now under the Brussels jurisdiction.

In January 1967 we read again of the change of title from Manager to Director, and now see the reason – it had been thought to be in accordance with amendments to the General Rules received from the Co-operative Union. But this was not necessary, as it was permissible already under General Rule 3. So the apparently sudden change of title in January 1964 was quite in order. Many members may not be aware of the extent to which all Co-op Societies are required to conduct their business in conformity with the General Rules.

Opposite page **5.6** Two samples of the Society's price list from 1961: perhaps surprisingly, a great many of the brands have survived into the twenty-first century. At the back of the list came the friendly advice: 'Are you a Member of a Co-operative Society? ... If so, give your Society Share Number when purchasing. Full dividend on all purchases'

The following minute gives the latest view of the position.

> A letter was received from the General Secretary of the Co-operative Union Limited with reference to their latest form of Model Rules. It stated that:
>
> As your Society is currently using Model Rules Form 6 I see no reason for changing at the present time. When, however, you feel there are fundamental changes to be made in your Society's rules it would then be opportune to consider the adoption of our more up to date Model Rules which, of course, contain most of the recent statutory provisions.
>
> The Channel Islands Society responded with the reply that they did not foresee any change to the Rules at present.

Meanwhile, in 1966 future redevelopment of the Charing Cross area was still actively in mind. The Society was now on the verge of tempting opportunities. It had become a possibility that the whole of the block bounded by Pitt Street and Dumaresq Street might become available through the States Development plan for Dumaresq Street. Under this plan they would be purchasing all the properties adjacent to the Charing Cross store with the exception of No 4 Pitt Street. The Society's view that it was desirable to acquire all remaining properties in this area prompted the immediate approach to Mr HA Cabot offering up to £5,000 for No 4.

With this came also the opportunity to purchase No 6 Dumaresq Street as a result of the States purchase of a length of the street for widening. Being adjacent to the main store, it would have been a desirable addition possibly for use as a loading bay in the future. However, the Society's offer to the States of £5,500 was turned down.

On No 4 Pitt Street, Mr Cabot was very elusive, and declined to reply to the offer for his property or even to discuss the proposition. He was approached again with the offer of an exchange of either St Paul's Vicarage or one of the Society's bungalows for No 4. Mention of St Paul's Vicarage is a recall of the purchase of the Le Riche garage and workshops in Val Plaisant in 1951. It appears that the house that went with the garage contract had remained in Society ownership and had been used by St Paul's Church as accommodation for the incumbent. But Mr Cabot knew his value, and while accepting the idea of an exchange stated that he would expect some additional cash as well.

There the matter rested until in December 1968 it was noted that No 4 was up for sale with a local agent for £20,000, a high price for a property only 18 ft x 20 ft. Acquisition came a step nearer when after discussions with the IDC, who were purchasing properties along Dumaresq Street for road widening, stated that they would agree to sell No 4 and odd pieces of land for £40,000, thus giving the Society ownership of the whole of the block. However, so near yet so far. The IDC proposals for the continuation of the Dumaresq Street widening did not materialise fully at that time, and this would lead to an interesting sequel to be revealed later. And £40,000 was a considerable sum for the Society at that period.

At the same time the pressure was still on for additional grocery warehouse space to replace the storage that would be lost when Georgetown and Val Plaisant were operating fully as supermarkets. Kensington Place when available would be fully occupied with vehicles, workshops and bulky equipment. Thought turned to the Royal Crescent Methodist Chapel, which had been for sale for a while with the price now down to £10,000, but nothing more was heard of this possibility. Doubtless the work involved in adaptation was too formidable to contemplate.

Difficulties and delays were persisting with the Georgetown and Val Plaisant stores, small scraps of odd-shaped land needed to be acquired to regularise the overall shape of the stores and the IDC insisted on fresh plans being prepared for these changes. The IDC would also not accept the idea of the main shop frontage on a clearway, but did ultimately accept a secondary entrance. This entrance was little used and was closed in the 1970s.

An interesting link with the past occurs here for this panelled wall was originally a shop frontage when a well-known Jersey family, the Boucherés, occupied the present Georgetown Co-op site. Named the George-town Lighthouse, this was a general ironmongery business selling lamp oil and all manner of domestic and household goods – hardware, as such a business was called (see **3.6** above). One of their later delivery vans featured a miniature Corbiere Lighthouse on its roof. It was this property that eventually became the grocery business, which the Society bought in April 1947. It had a useful yard at the back extending to Elizabeth Street, which is now the rather restricted but necessary car park, and an outbuilding in Elizabeth Street, which became the coal store. This enabled the coal store operating from the CWS premises in Anley Street to be vacated.

After the Boucheré family gave up its business the shop became a grocery for a while, but at the time of purchase by the Society it was empty and easily prepared and adapted for similar use by the Co-op. This original grocery shop, rather like No 2 Market Street, in its turn, could continue with little interior alteration for the moment though obviously the Society had plans for rebuilding. No doubt for reasons of financial restraints on capital expenditure mentioned in that minute of July 1966, these plans were to be delayed for some years. The Annual Report for March 1958 had referred to it – 'and it is hoped that the rebuilding of the Georgetown shop will be completed during the present period'. In fact, because of difficulties with the IDC it was not rebuilt and opened in its present supermarket form until 1969, 22 years after its purchase.

So urgently was the pressure being felt for grocery warehousing that Kensington Place came into the picture again. Members were reminded that

> It will be essential to provide better warehouse facilities before Georgetown Supermarket opens at the end of this year; the floor area used at present was 5,000 sq. ft. Kensington Place would be an improvement, having a floor area of 8,000 sq. ft if we could find alternative accommodation for the motor repair workshop and Mobile Stores, but the ideal solution would be a new warehouse at Beaumont, if permission could be obtained. The Rediffusion store at La Pouquelaye was for sale but not considered suitable.

Just a few months later, this came up yet again when it was emphasised that present accommodation was most unsuitable, and it was essential to have better facilities by the time Georgetown was operating. This problem had been discussed with the Assistant Planning Officer:

> There was no prospect of obtaining permission to build at Goose Green Marsh in the near future. There was a site adjoining our Garage at Kensington Place owned by the estate of T Wilson, but this would be costly to buy, demolish and rebuild. Messrs Sidney Horman Limited owned a store at 6 Patriotic Place that would be ideal, and it was agreed that they be approached to see if they would consider selling.

This frequent vacillation over possible alternatives, and Kensington Place in particular, are an indication of the pressure being experienced in practical terms and in the minds of Board and management, who were obviously concerned at this seemingly intractable problem. It was resolved to discuss it again at the next meeting.

When further discussed this urgency became centred on the original proposal to build a warehouse at Beaumont on the edge of Goose Green Marsh, but this plan had been long delayed by several considerations – drainage problems, consultation with the Commoners and the inevitable applications to IDC for discussions on the several alternatives and, it was hoped, the satisfactory solutions. But so far, the final solution seemed as far away as ever.

Similar progress was being pursued in Guernsey during this same period, with similar frustrating results, or lack of them. It was hoped to find suitable sites in the country parishes, but several recommended options were turned down, often on the criteria of size of the area or its layout, for the Society had now to think more seriously of supermarket designs and layout. The supermarket philosophy had come to stay as counter service, even self-service, was becoming uneconomic, and even the more modest designs now needed car parking space. Although the mobile shops were still on the road car ownership was increasing and, as we have seen in recent years, car parks now need to be as large and extensive as the store itself. In fact, in November 1968, while considering the practical options of sites on main roads, it was stated that such sites would need parking for 100 cars to anticipate the increasing, and welcome, surge of custom.

In mid-1968 it was also suggested that the Board should, at last, seriously consider converting the Charing Cross store to self-service. This would obviously cause considerable disturbance to existing business while any conversion was carried out, and eventually it was thought better to wait until the Dumaresq Street redevelopment plans at the rear were more clearly known.

In fact, a more positive discussion took place in December 1969 about future planning of Charing Cross, when Dumaresq Street was widened. The grocery area was in need of a facelift, the shop was dull, and counter service out of date. It was suggested that if the wines and tobacco section could be moved to other premises, it would be possible to convert to self-service: 'The Menswear shop also needed attention, it was too small to give a full service, and if we could find other premises, this shop would be ideal for Wines and Tobacco.' Obviously, the limitations of the restricted area available for any rearrangement of departments were difficult to resolve, so it was decided at this stage that Mr Young, the CWS Architect, be given a plan of the central premises, and be asked to submit suggestions on the future planning of the departments.

As we shall see later, the road widening plans were never completed, and it would be many years yet before tentative plans for the Charing Cross area could be more positively discussed.

It is not difficult to imagine the amount of travelling between and within the Islands when pursuing these plans and the problems that must have devolved upon John Morris, the CWS and Directors and senior managers. One of the most interesting and satisfactory of these changeovers was that of 2 Market Street, where the Manager himself was recommending a conversion to self-service. He had studied the possibilities within his shop, which was now, twenty years since first opening, considered a small shop. The Board were convinced of the practicalities and agreed that the CWS architect and shopfitters be called as quickly as possible to ensure reopening before the visitor season started. One feature mentioned was the introduction of a frozen food cabinet and a dairy cabinet, both now common features in all new stores.

Parallel with these many proposals and developments ran the issue of capital expenditure, which, just a few years previously, would have been brought to notice as a warning by Mr Booth to exercise caution. It is a telling feature of the growing success of the Society and its ventures that the matter of finance and expenditure no longer feature in the minutes by way of warning. The Annual Report and Accounts of the mid- to late 1960s tell us why: trading sales figures increasing every year had enabled reserves to be built up, and the continuing support and advice of CWS in various ways ensured that capital in hand had increased and expansion could be planned with confidence.

This is shown by a telling Minute on Investments in November 1967:

> We had a large credit balance on current bank account with the CWS on which we received interest of ½%. £100,000 had been placed with Kleinwort Benson (CI) Limited at 5½% on seven days call. The rate from 16th November would be 6%, owing to increase in the Bank rate. £25,000 had also been placed with Westminster Foreign Bank Limited, for three months certain at a fixed rate of 6%.
>
> Loan Interest – Local Savings Banks were now paying 6½%. Rates offered by merchant banks and finance houses remained high, and were unlikely to fall in the near future. We had £50,000 on 7-day deposit, but more capital would be required for development, and in order to attract this, the Loan Interest rate would have to be increased from the present 6%. It was resolved 'that the rate of interest paid on Loan Accounts be increased from 6% to 7% from 7th July 1969'.
>
> Investment of Superannuation Funds – A letter from Mr A. Duval, CIS Actuary, was read, recommending that £15,000 be invested in 8½% Treasury Stock 1997, and that £10,000 be invested in 5½% Treasury Stock 2008/12. He agreed that it would be advisable to consider a suitable Unit Trust for any further investment. It was resolved 'that as Trustees of the Employees' Superannuation Scheme, the Society should purchase the sum of £25,000 in Treasury Stock as recommended, through the Jersey Savings Bank'.

Obviously, now that the financial concerns were virtually at an end the Society could afford to expand at just the right moment. Shoppers were becoming more discriminating in their tastes, more demanding in choice, the car was becoming less of a luxury, and the supermarket, though not yet sophisticated, as we know it today, was becoming a force in the Islands. Above all, the previously prevailing image of the Co-op as a different sort of shop was no longer valid. The Society was indeed on the threshold of active competition with Le Riche, the firm of Orviss having been taken over by them just a few years previously.

It was an opportunity that went some way to satisfy the Society's hopes of consolidation and competition on equal terms and justified the efforts that were now beginning to show results. In Guernsey, for example, the Longstore property on St George's Esplanade (**5.7**) and Colyton House in the Bouet had just been purchased, the former already earmarked for a supermarket with flats over. Within weeks of the purchase planning permission had been granted for demolition and rebuilding, subject to the provision of adequate car parking. The architect was quickly called in for the planning of the whole site.

5.7 Longstore House, Guernsey, as rebuilt in the 1960s, with the new Co-op logo displayed at the corner

In June 1969 a letter was received from Mr Booth informing the Society that he had relinquished his position as Regional Manager, and had been appointed manager of Swansea CRS. The Manager reminded the members that Mr Booth had been more than a good friend to the Channel Islands Society for many years, and much of its success was due to his help and guidance. The Manager said the Society had few problems these days, but if at all possible, it would be prudent to retain the benevolent interest of CRS in general, and Mr Booth in particular. Mr Fulker, Mr Mather and Mr Booth would be coming to Jersey on 19 June.

The meeting asked that Mr Fulker and Mr Mather should be informed that 'we appreciate the assistance given by Officials of CRS, and hope that our happy relationship will continue'.

The recent flurry of activity over the provision of increased grocery warehousing had been brought about by the IDC approval, at last, of redevelopment of the two town shops, Val Plaisant and Georgetown, which were now being rebuilt at the same time. The uncertainty over the final use of Kensington Place now brought Beaumont into prominence again.

Apart from the Bakery and a small vehicle workshop, little use had been made of the Society's land in that area. There were implications there that, owing to lack of urgency, had never been dealt with. In 1958 the Manager had reported 'that our land surrounding the Bakery at Beaumont was overgrown with weeds and is in a disgraceful state, and I suggest that the whole area should be tarmaced'. This had been done, but more detailed work lay ahead before the Beaumont Warehouse could take shape.

Little more was heard until 1963 when the States Lands Officer informed the Society that the States wished to provide a car park on Goose Green Marsh for which the States needed a right of way over the Society's land. This was agreed to subject to negotiation provided that the Society could purchase a strip of land from the Tenants of the Marsh, presumably to compensate for the loss to the car park. However, this idea was rejected by the Tenants, as there was an Act of the States prohibiting any further development on the Marsh until discussions on a proposed Trading Estate reached conclusion. This was conveyed by the Board to the Lands Office, which repeated its latest request of 1965 in greater detail, to which the Society responded with the suggestion that the Lands Office might be better able than the Society to obtain a satisfactory agreement with the Tenants.

Further discussion followed with the Tenants, mentioning for the first time the possibility of a Grocery Warehouse, Motor Repair workshop, three Mobile Stores with garaging, a Furnishing Store, a Grocery Order Despatch Department and possibly a Coal Store. This underlined the urgency of the situation and the continuing uncertainty over the Kensington Place allocation, though, as we have read, the necessity for a coal store was receding with the agreement of the Society to merge with the Coal Importers Board at Bellozanne.

Eventually, all was agreed, and the land exchange took place subject only to a restriction by the Tenants 'that only a store for storage purposes and a garage will be erected on the land, and that no sales shop or other commercial enterprise will be allowed and that the wire fence around the site will be maintained at all times'. There the Beaumont question rested for the time being; it came up again in 1969 with a greater degree of finality from the IDC.

But first the Society had to deal with the Tenants of the Marsh again over the flooding that apparently had become a nuisance. It was clearly a problem that needed a permanent solution before the Society could hope to build there. This came up in September 1969, and the matter appears to have been satisfactorily settled through the Court, for later that month we read of renewed contacts with IDC.

This issue came up yet again when the Manager reported that a complaint had been made to the Tenants of the Marsh about the flooding of Society land every winter, owing to the brook overflowing. It was suggested that in order to prevent this nuisance, another brook be made alongside the Society's north-eastern boundary, to take half of the water. In order to do this it would be necessary to sell to the Tenants a small triangle of land, and to purchase from them a larger area, and to pay them for the difference. The Society would also pay the legal charges, and half of the cost of making the brook. The Society's property would then be bounded on three sides by a brook and there should not be a flooding problem in the future. Was this wishful thinking?

Whatever was to happen in the future John Morris was authorised to represent the Society at the Royal Court in order to be a party to the necessary contracts.

The Beaumont Warehouse was still very much in view, and calls and informal meetings presaged a more or less final acceptance by IDC of the Society's proposals subject to the exchange of land at Georgetown, where road improvements were pressing. The following exchanges give the impression of a bit of friendly horse-trading, as it were, so that both the Society and IDC could achieve their objectives.

> Following a meeting the Manager had in September 1969 with Mr Woolmer on the proposed warehouse, a letter had been received from the IDC informing the Board that subject to certain technical considerations it would be minded to grant permission, but before doing so it would appreciate more definite information in regard to the future of our Don Road premises, and that we would be willing for these premises to be redeveloped for residential purposes [**5.8**].

The Board decided

> that the IDC be informed that provided permission is given for a Warehouse at Beaumont, we would agree that Don Road premises be developed for residential purposes. Permission could be conditional that we would demolish Don Road premises and clear the site, or that we would agree to sell to the States for housing development, or we would exchange for the remainder of the island site at Charing Cross.

By November the situation was firm, and preliminary planning permission was granted; the CWS chief architect was already at work on the plans, and by December the details of the interior were firm.

A formal letter was received from the IDC granting planning permission to construct a warehouse, in the light of the Society's undertaking that it would be willing for its Don Road premises to be redeveloped for residential purposes. It was stated that Mr RA Young, CWS Chief Architect at Bristol, was preparing plans for a 14,000 sq. ft building to accommodate grocery warehouse, two mobile stores and motor repair workshop on the ground floor, and furniture on the first floor. If approved, the Society would then be able to sell the

Kensington Place property. It was agreed that when the Society moved out of Don Road, the Order Despatch Service would be discontinued.

In December 1969 the Chief Architect wrote to the Society giving particulars of preliminary plans. These had been taken to the Assistant Planning Officer, and in the light of his observations, they had been returned to the Architect for amendment, before submitting for approval. Height of first floor was reduced from 20 ft to 15 ft, allowing for pallets three high instead of four. The present toilets and changing rooms would be used as a materials store, and new toilets for bakery staff were to be located in the new building. The estimated cost would be £150,000.

Throughout this busy three or four months a great deal was being accomplished to the benefit and satisfaction of both the Planning Department and the Society, for concurrent with the Beaumont activity we read of the negotiations going on over the island site, or the block, as it was now known.

On the Don Road property, the States Land Officer wrote to the Society in January 1970 stating that the States would like to negotiate the purchase of this property on behalf of the Housing Committee, who required the site for bedsitters. They would like to purchase as soon as possible, and then lease back to the Society until the Society was able to move to the new warehouse. The Land Officer was informed of the Society's interest in acquiring the remainder of the island site that would become available when the properties in Dumaresq Street were eventually demolished for road widening. He was told that the Society would like from the Island Development Committee a letter of intent, agreeing in principle to sell to the Society at a reasonable valuation.

Having read the Society minutes, extending over the period at least from 1963 to 1970, it is tempting to heave a sigh of relief that the objectives of the Society were at last being achieved. But the sheer time spent by the Manager and his staff in dealing with the simple need to build a warehouse on the Society's own land is a telling indication that there is more going on 'behind the counter' than the member or the customer imagine.

The October 1969 Annual Report of the Directors presents a satisfactory summary of the previous year's progress.

Membership was 11,126 in Jersey and 7,873 in Guernsey. Gross profit was £377,246, an increase of £60,225. Members' share balances were £205,943 and loan deposits totalled £290,495. The General Reserve Fund now stood at £190,000, an increase of £20,000 over the year.

5.8 The only known photograph of the Don Road Order and Despatch building, purchased in 1950 and demolished in 1969/70. The impression is of a more leisurely pace of life, particularly on the way to work in the mornings (© Jersey Evening Post)

Mention is made in this 1969 Report of the new supermarket at Georgetown and planning permission for the new warehouse at Beaumont. The Order Despatch service in Guernsey was to be discontinued but two additional mobile shops would continue to serve the country parishes. The search would continue for suitable sites for supermarkets in order to increase and improve service to the members.

The dividend was still 1s in the pound, with a bonus of 3d in the pound to be exchanged for goods in any department.

The Society was now recommending a complete amendment of the Rules, which had weathered several partial amendments in recent years. This would at last clarify that blurred distinction between Committee and Board of Directors. The Report closes with the announcement of wider powers of investment on behalf of the staff through the Employers' Superannuation Fund and records with pleasure the Board's appreciation of the efforts of the management and staff during the year.

The 1960s had been an exciting and progressive decade for the Society despite the delays and frustrations that seemed to be a necessary hurdle to that progress. Now for the surprises and successes of the 1970s.

6.1 The St Peter's Food Centre, with main façade to the left (before redevelopment)

Chapter 6

The Seventies

Following the fifteen years of successful amalgamation, now taken for granted, the Society was entering the 1970s in a confident mood. Modest progress had been made in the past, there was increasing activity in the present that could not have been contemplated just a few years before, and the future looked promising. This decade was to have its difficulties and disappointments but these would be overcome by the strength of unity and purpose that continued to flow from the top.

Several urgent items came up early in 1970. The views previously expressed by the Board that Charing Cross needed a facelift, and the provisional planning of departments already discussed, took a positive step in February when it was stated that there had been complaints for some time about the service in the Menswear and the Grocery. These complaints required prompt action. The Grocery Orders department was to be transferred to Don Road immediately, the Menswear to be closed in December and the shop converted to Wines and Tobacco; then the Green-Fruit Section was also to be closed and the area converted to Bread, Confectionery and Sweets. When closures and transfers were completed the main area of Grocery was to become a self-service shop. It was a wide-ranging plan of action – quite a major effort and to be subject later to further suggestions from CWS on the future planning of Charing Cross as a whole unit.

Giving an indication of the financial confidence now being experienced by the Society, when the Longstore development in Guernsey went out to tender in June, the successful firm was Troy Construction with a price of £81,435. Then in October 1970 the negotiated price from Farley & Son for the now-agreed Beaumont Warehouse was £210,862 – formidable sums for the time.

This situation had been recognised, and in February 1971 a Financial Statement was presented to the Board showing the financial commitments in respect of Beaumont and Longstore alone. The then-present overdraft facility of £200,000 would not be sufficient, and it was stated that about £100,000 more capital would be required by the end of the year.

This confidence was further borne out by the many references in the minutes to the necessity to open up more branches, particularly in the country parishes in both Islands. While the mobile shops were still on the road their range of goods was necessarily limited to the usual domestic needs and, useful though this service was, it could not satisfy the full range of shopping now being demanded by the average family and which would be readily available when self-service became the normal routine. And 'impulse buying', not being a feature of the mobile shop, was a great boost to custom in supermarkets and eventually of course to profits.

While the early years would have seen only modest numbers of staff in smaller shops, often taken on by the Manager and working for the Manager rather than the Society, this view could not be maintained indefinitely now that the Society was moving ahead to the prospect of larger shops and supermarkets, which are more demanding on both the staff and management.

Obviously this ideal of co-operation throughout all levels of staff had not yet become established, and the Board and management must have noted this from reports that came their way. Their concerns surfaced in the Minute of April 1970 and again in January 1971, but it would be some time before a satisfactory decision was reached.

In April 1970 the Board discussed the issue of staff relationships –

> particularly with regard to the need to educate members of the staff about the principles and ideals of the co-operative movement. Staff should be encouraged to participate in further education to this end by means of evening classes and correspondence courses; staff training sessions should be considered. Informal meetings could be held during the winter months for discussion. We should find out what interest and support these suggestions would receive.

It was resolved that Mr Norman Le Brocq and the Manager should draft a letter calling a meeting of the staff to discuss these suggestions, and this would be further considered at the next meeting.

Again in January 1971 concern was expressed regarding the difficulties in finding experienced shop managers. After some discussion it was suggested that Mr Pinel could undertake the training of suitable youths. This was brought up yet again by Mr Geall, who reported that

> Very few boys have been recruited over the years, mainly due to wages and conditions not comparing favourably with other trades. It was proposed to include in the revised Union Agreement, rates covering Trainee Managers, and with the assistance of States Careers Officers this should aid recruitment.

The importance of training was also stressed, and staff should be encouraged to join further education classes. It was suggested that there should be staff noticeboards in all shops, and any vacancies should in the first instance be advertised on the noticeboards.

This continuing concern over staffing at all levels was brought up for discussion on several occasions during the early 1970s, but no firm and positive decision appears to have been reached at Board level. It was compounded not only by the restrictions of the Housing Regulations but by the inevitable demand that would arise of additional staff for the new supermarkets and additions to warehousing that were now being envisaged. It could be said that the Society had become victim of its own success.

In January 1971 a 5 vergee field at Port Soif in Guernsey was offered. It was about the right size and about two miles from existing stores at Castel, St Sampson and Longstore – 'and was worth consideration if the price was reasonable, and if planning permission could be obtained'. The Board resolved that 'it should be inspected and further details obtained for consideration'. Among the many properties and sites scattered around the Islands under consideration were several in both Islands that would be discussed later with CWS.

It was very appropriate at this time of such activity and enquiry that a letter was received in April 1971 from the CWS Site Assessment Service offering advice on site opportunities, particularly in supermarket development, and guidance on the viability of proposed new outlets.

> At a Board Meeting the Directors agreed that the Society was in urgent need of new supermarkets in Jersey and Guernsey, this service could be of assistance in deciding how many were required to cover both Islands, where they should be sited, and what size. It may be a better proposition to build a large supermarket in St Sampson's area with parking for at least fifty cars, rather than do a costly extension on the Bridge, where parking facilities are restricted, when Collas' shop eventually becomes available. The meeting decided that we should ask for a survey covering both Islands. This offer was indicative of the continuing interest being shown by CWS and their offers to help and advise where and when appropriate.

In addition to the anticipated increased sales that would result from these proposed developments the Society was already enjoying some return in rentals from houses and flats let to senior members of staff. Now that the Society was building new stores with flats or offices over, there was the opportunity to let at commercial rates. The States of Guernsey for example had expressed a wish to negotiate a three-year lease for the Longstore Office suites, which did materialise in July 1971, when the Board of Administration took up a four-year lease over Longstore at £3,800 yearly with an option to renew. It was of considerable satisfaction that on the termination of this four-year period the States were happy to renew the lease despite the lack of adequate car parking space and some embarrassing deficiencies in design and workmanship of the building both of which took some time to remedy.

Parallel with the wish to develop further sites for new stores there arose the accompanying paradox of higher sales turnover, producing greater profits but also requiring ever more storage, which if not to be built by the Society would have to be leased at a commercial rental. This was brought out, unwittingly perhaps, at a meeting in May 1971 when a chance remark elicited 'by stocking broadloom carpets we could make an extra 10% profit estimated at about £1,000 per year ... but... the Furnishing Department is in urgent need of more space and the Grocery Department will also require more space when Longstore is operating.'

Ever watchful for fresh opportunities to expand the Society's interests still further, it is noticeable that several small sites or shops were being investigated in both Islands, with varying results as to commercial viability or planning opinion, the latter being of particular import. It is fortunate that during more recent years there has been less emphasis on the smaller sites, for obvious reasons, and greater concentration on the larger sites, which allow more scope for the general layout of the ancillary buildings and services and for the all-important and essential car parking.

Yet amid this flurry and excitement in the pursuit of suitable sites for yet more expansion – and the emphasis now was almost exclusively on supermarkets – an unhappy problem was becoming ever more evident in that a long-established department, the Bakery, was showing signs of decline to a serious level. Difficulties had shown themselves already at intervals – a new bakery area was needed at considerable cost, deliveries of flour were not always reliable and the unsociable hours were not readily accepted by the staff.

The Co-op Bakery was virtually a business in its own right, with eight vans on the road, delivering both wholesale and retail, but when it came under discussion in February 1973 it seemed that not one of the rounds was operating profitably. The Board was of the opinion that this decline could only be reversed by ensuring that the Society was producing a top-quality loaf to encourage sales. The Bakery Manager believed that everything that could be done to encourage more experienced staff to apply had been tried – but without success, the reluctance to work the night shifts being one reason.

It was suggested that one possible solution would be to combine the delivery rounds and employ the drivers on a franchise system, that is, working the rounds for themselves. However, the Board did not agree with this suggestion, reluctant, no doubt, to see the demise of one of the Co-op's staple items in the traditional weekly shopping basket. Perhaps the Board could not see, or were ignoring, the facts – that the supermarkets were themselves becoming largely responsible for this dilemma, with their wide-ranging stocks of breads and cakes on their shelves from which the shoppers could choose and help themselves. It was competition from within its own stores, and the Society could do little about it.

To be faced with such a problem must have caused much heart-searching by the Board and senior management. Up to the end the Society was issuing the usual circular letters to customers detailing the deliveries 'we offer a before breakfast daily delivery in all town areas and some country areas, and a daily delivery before lunch <u>everywhere</u>'. Enclosed were the detailed price lists of an impressive range of some 60 items – telephoned orders and enquiries began at 6.00 am; for enquiries on Sundays the Manager's private telephone number was given; and there were no tiresome answerphones in the 1970s.

It must obviously have been disappointing for the Board to have to consider closing down this personal contact with its members after over half a century, but a possible compromise solution was to present itself eventually.

In August 1973 the subject was aired again, this time with more positive action in mind. Obviously, informal enquiries had been made in a certain direction with the results set out in the minutes, which reported that in any event Mr Hedley, the Manager, would be leaving the employ of the Society on 22 September. A report from the Manager was discussed in which he gave his opinion that the department was unlikely to show a profit in the future, and recommending closure. It was known that Le Brun's Bakery was interested in taking over the business, and the President attended a meeting with Mr Brian Le Marquand when the following proposals were discussed:

Le Brun's Bakery would:

1 Take over production and delivery from 1st September
2 Buy at valuation the machinery and equipment (excluding ovens and vans)
3 Purchase stock of materials at cost
4 Take over retail debts, less 5% for collection
5 Offer employment to all staff
6 Pay rent of £100 weekly for bakery and vans, until 3rd November
7 Supply our shops at 25% discount.

It was suggested that the Bakery premises were suitable for conversion to a supermarket, with

Furnishing and an Electrical Discount Warehouse on the first floor.

The Board resolved that the Society should agree to the proposals, and transfer the bakery business to Le Brun's on 1 September. Ironic, wasn't it, that the Board should immediately think of the possible conversion of the Bakery to a Supermarket? Thinking ahead for a moment to the present IT Centre, now in the old bakery building, restored and adapted to modern standards, the Society can be grateful that no positive action resulted from those ideas!

Another area of trading that was to feel the wind of change was the Butchery, which had operated in both Islands on similar lines. Traditionally, the town markets have been the main centres for meat sales, and the Society had leased shops in both markets for many years. The markets allowed greater space for the display of meat and, more important, greater facility and space for the bulky freezer cabinets. These could not be accommodated in the earlier Co-op shops, which were smaller and intended primarily for groceries and provisions.

This arrangement for the regular supply of meats to members and public alike worked well until, in August 1970, the Board had to report to members –

> Under the heading of JERSEY MEAT MARKET SHOP it was reported that the Market Inspector had informed the Society that our stalls could not be brought up to the standard now required by the Public Health Law. The Public Works Committee would give permission for change of use, or would permit the tenant to_sell the lease. Two leases had been sold recently, for £3,000 and £2,5000. Seeing that the market shop does not operate profitably, and that we have three other shops in the town area giving this service, it was recommended that we close this shop and sell the lease.

Rather regretfully, no doubt, the Board decided 'that we keep the Meat Market shop open until the alterations at Charing Cross have been completed, then sell the lease'.

6.2 The impressive steelwork frame of the new Bridge supermarket in Nocq Road rising above the surrounding buildings immediately opposite the little Nocq Road shop, the Guernsey Society's first attempt to establish a store in St Sampson in 1950 (photo from 1988, © Guernsey Press Co.)

6.3 The Supermarket on Rue des Camps, St Martin, Guernsey, the back-to-front shop with the underpass entrance to the car park and store entrance, opened in 1979

In January 1971 a further report settled the matter when the Board stated that 'we are still awaiting a reply from the States Markets Committee. We have been unofficially informed that we shall have to sell to Mr Ireson, Butcher, who will then have to sell his stall to a person approved by the Committee.' The sale of fresh meat was then transferred to Charing Cross.

It seems from the several mentions in minutes during this period that the Society still intended to have a permanent and prominent store at the Bridge in Guernsey, that spot being central to an extensive urban and residential area. In July 1975 attention was drawn to a large derelict site just behind the Bridge at one time owned by Leale Limited. The Manager was authorised to follow up this possibility and report back. This idea eventually materialised though the site was to remain derelict and vacant for many years before development could take place (**6.2**).

While the Society's eyes were open to every further possibility, work was about to reach the final planning stage on Western Stores at St Peter's and Rue des Camps, St Martin in Guernsey (**6.3**), though there were some delays over land negotiations. However there was tacit approval by Planning in both cases, final approval being centred mainly on the issue of final boundaries and car parking areas and access. This involved exchanges with Mr Hefford, the Society's neighbour at St Peter and with Queen's Hotel in Guernsey.

This urge to expand, probably fuelled by the offer of the CWS Site Assessment Department in July 1971, resulted in a burst of enthusiasm, when twelve sites had been selected for discussion and consideration. Among them were field sites or shops scattered around the islands as far afield and as varied as Gorey, Pontac, Sion, Millbrook, Castel and even Glencoe. The CWS came into this situation at that time to offer advice and experience during the discussions. Prior to this, a report submitted by Mr E Allen, CWS Assessment Consultant, on a meeting with Mr J Beaty, Assistant Planning Officer, twelve sites were discussed, but for a variety of reasons only two of these sites had development possibilities within the short term, there being a reasonable availability to purchase and good chance of approval by the IDC.

Prior to receiving this report, in fact, as far back as November 1970 the Society had been working on the possible establishment of a new store in the Pontac area along the Coast Road. With a shrewd eye for an opening here in an extensive residential area with no traffic problems, and no doubt, with his ear to the ground, John Morris had discovered that Blandin's Store in the heart of the area was up for sale at £44,000 plus stock at valuation.

By January 1972 the Board could report that the deal was completed; Blandin's Stores had been purchased for £30,000 plus £2,000 for fixtures and £10,000 for goodwill. As a bonus, as it were, a vacant bungalow adjacent to the shop was also for sale at around £8,000.

Within a remarkably short time, compared to some of the Society's negotiations, the whole site was Society property and by November 1972 the

Architect had submitted detailed drawings to the IDC. Permission to demolish and rebuild was delayed a while, following some objections from local residents but these were amicably dealt with and the rebuilding was under way. So began the Co-op Fresh Food Store presence in a commercially desirable area in the East where Le Riche were unlikely to become rivals.

At about the same time an interesting possibility arose in town. Many of us, members and readers alike, will remember with a touch of nostalgia the names of George D Laurens and Frederick Baker, two well-loved shops in Queen Street, which in 1973 were about to be demolished and rebuilt as Queensway House. Not so well remembered perhaps, is the fact that CWS Property Development Service were aware of this and enquired if the Society would be interested. The Board discussed this possibility but thought that rents would have to be exceedingly high in view of the purchase price to be paid and the costs of any subsequent redevelopment. However, though the Board felt that it could not express positive interest it would ask CWS for further information. Apart from financial considerations the practical limitations would rule out any thoughts of even a modest store on such a restricted site, French Lane at the rear being the only access for unloading stock.

Of more immediate interest was the proposed sale of 60 Kensington Place, which had now served its purpose of relieving the pressure of storage, garaging and providing workshop facilities, these essential services now about to be taken over by the Beaumont Warehouse.

> No 60 would be vacant by the end of April 1972, when we moved out to Beaumont. Valued by Rumsey & Rumsey at £53,400 based on building replacement cost, but only at £40,000 on the basis of an investment showing 10% return. Purchased in July 1966 for £25,000, plus additions of £2,500. Mr CN Martland has made enquiries and would like to purchase. That Mr Martland was to be invited to make an offer for the property for consideration at the next meeting, when the best means of selling would be discussed. Mr Martland made an offer of £50,000. This was not accepted and the Board decided that the Store should be advertised in the *Evening Post.*

However, this decision was rescinded and No 60, having served the Society well during a critical period, was quickly sold to Langlois Limited for £60,000.

Looking back for a moment over the previous fifteen years or so and recalling the enthusiasm and effort displayed by the Management Committees of the time over the opportunities that fortuitously presented themselves for purchase – in Market Street for example and Charing Cross – it is worth remembering that any further expansion was merely of the 'add-on' variety or interior rearrangement of departments, the latter so often discussed in detail. What the Society was really searching for and hoping for was the big breakthrough to the West where, in Jersey, Le Riche, in partnership with the NatWest bank, was already well established at Red Houses.

The waiting proved worthwhile. During the early 1970s opportunities occurred in Jersey and Guernsey, as just mentioned, that were to prove the turning point in the Society's fortunes. Early in 1974 a possible site for another larger store in Guernsey came up, along Rue des Camps, St Martin, adjacent to the Queen's Hotel and for which preliminary approaches had already been made to the Planning Office. The owner of the hotel was very helpful with regard to the access to the proposed car park at the rear, and the Architect prepared plans for the whole area. This was followed up by several meetings and discussions with the Planning Office.

However, the expected Planning permission did not materialise at once and the Society faced delays and frustration while the project was discussed yet again. This time the Planning Committee was not happy with the parking access and with a shop front on the main road. Inevitably, further delays in obtaining planning agreement and acceptance prolonged the negotiations. Issues raised were the eventual use of the field at the rear not required for the car park, which, it was insisted, should revert to agricultural or horticultural use, or possibly be sold to the States for use as allotments. Planning also insisted on retaining the existing frontage of shops on Rue des Camps, which would entail designing the store so that the entrance was facing the car park, a little unusual in the mid-1970s perhaps, but fairly commonplace now. Planning also preferred a smaller store, a negation of the Society's purpose of the site. Agreement was reached, more amicably, with the owners of the Queen's Hotel for an exchange of land to enable a small extension to the hotel to be built by the Society. On the issue of

6.4 Les Woodcock (left) and Allan Smith at the Freezer Centre in 1976, with their awards of a Co-operative Certificate, Highly Commended, for General Advertising

access to the car park for the large refrigeration trucks and other Co-op vehicles, management was able to reassure Planning that agreement had also been reached with the hotel for such vehicles to travel over part of the hotel driveway to the store car park. It was altogether a lengthy and frustrating project but one that has proved its worth and which was later to be capable of extension and eventual rebuilding.

During this same period a major scheme was hatching in Jersey. Anxious to establish the Society more prominently in the west of the Island preliminary enquiries had been opened up in December 1975 with IDC concerning Vernon Villa at Beaumont, recently purchased at £17,000 with a view to demolishing and using the site for a food store. The IDC agreed to visit the site, which was situated adjacent to Goosegreen Marsh and between the St Aubins Road and Beaumont Hill, thought by the Society to be free of traffic problems. However, the IDC thought otherwise and rejected the proposals until further studies of the traffic flow and density in that area were completed. These studies resulted in the mini-roundabout at the junction which, as we all know, could not reduce the density but did at least ease the flow of vehicles and keep them moving.

Coincidentally, at the same time it was noted that Western Stores at St Peter's crossroads was coming up for sale, and this opportunity was not to be missed. It was reported to the Board, with great confidence, 'that Western Stores, St Peter, Jersey is offered for sale by tender. This shop although old is substantially built, and would not have to be demolished to provide a supermarket with parking for 30 cars. The Manager has made an offer of £75,000, but it would be worth paying more. The Manager was authorised to increase this offer if necessary.'

Suddenly aware of two possibilities coming up in the West at the same time the Board decided that 'If we are successful in buying Western Stores, we should not require another supermarket at Beaumont. It was suggested that the site would be suitable as a Freezer Centre.'

This was yet another example of the Society's determination to have a prominent presence in the west of the Island where for many years Le Riche had had predominance with their Red Houses corner. We shall read more of these two projects later.

6.5 Western Stores, St Peter, Jersey, the Brocq family store, in about 1976, when the Society bought it. Redeveloped in supermarket form, it was the Society's first major store

During this exciting period we note another and more personal decision of the Board that was to have far-reaching advantages for the future of the Society. On 1 February 1976 Allan Smith was appointed Grocery Manager and Buyer – a title that was to be changed, very shortly after his promotion, to Food Trades Officer – while Les Woodcock, the successful candidate from 260 applicants for the post, was designated Assistant Food Trades Officer (**6.4**). Such titles indicated the ever-widening extent and range of managerial coverage now required from the senior staff. We shall read more of Allan Smith in the years ahead, and in the near future of his adopting a more positive stance on the vexed issue of staff training. His promotion to Grocery Manager and Buyer followed the tragic death of the previous post-holder, John Peach, who had served the Society with distinction for over eighteen years.

The two new projects, just mentioned, were to progress side by side to establish the Co-op supermarket idea firmly in both Islands, each being in a strategic area for the attraction of custom.

The offer made for Western Stores was obviously not acceptable. The very much higher figure eventually paid is a measure of the importance of the site to the Society. It was indeed a prime site in a busy parish, adjacent to residential areas and with sufficient open area at the rear for a really adequate car park (**6.5**).

Events had obviously moved quickly for very shortly after, in February 1976, the Board was able to report:

> Western Stores: Following discussion, it was resolved that we purchase this shop at St Peter for the sum of £110,000, and authorise JR Morris to act on behalf of the Society in passing contract.

So for the first time the Society now possessed two sites, one in each Island, of proportions that would permit a new approach to their future plans; each site would allow the design of full supermarket potential, with space for expansion or rebuilding if necessary and with an adequate car parking area immediately adjacent. And each site was a focal point for shopping, each being central to an extensive residential area. The Society had good reason to be satisfied with future prospects.

Among the many other possibilities for expansion considered at the time were Maples in Minden Place and St Helier Garage on St Aubin's Road, the latter at £135,000. The Society's Board Minutes record a very wide range of sites and properties in both Islands that were investigated from time to time. An interesting and valuable asset that has built up with the new stores has been the accommodation above the stores, purpose-designed by the CWS Architect as flats or office suites to provide an income, some of the units being let to staff, others to various offices. It is a far cry from the earlier days of frequent movement of stock between the upper floors of the old original buildings in an effort to find adequate storage space.

In April 1977 a time when rising inflation was still to be reckoned with, an accounts report showed one instance of the sale of £100,000 14½% Treasury Loan realising £110,420, and of three other securities showing a profit of £23,512 on selling are pointers to the more aggressive, confident and positive policy now becoming apparent. With the current building programme in both Islands, the Society felt able to extend the overdraft facility and approached the Co-operative Bank with a request that the £200,000 limit be raised to £500,000. It was a very considerable increase but thought necessary to finance the costs of the current building programme and the future projects now about to be implemented.

It was not surprising that the Bank demurred at first and offered an alternative, a less attractive and rather restrictive alternative that the Board rejected with the Resolution 'that we inform the Bank that the offer does not interest us and is not acceptable'. It would be interesting to know just how the reply to the Bank was worded! However, the Bank relented, and we read later that the increased limit to £500,000 was granted.

These items from the minutes during 1977 and 1978 in particular prove the more confident, buoyant mood of the Board. In the late 1970s – recalling the 1960s and Mr Booth's frequent warnings against too great an enthusiasm for the rebuilding, even renovation, of existing stores and the accompanying search for new stores – we can see the progress made by the Society in a mere 15 years. One item of April 1978 indicates not only enthusiasm but also a determination to aim for the big league. At the Board meeting of 23 April Allan Smith reported that the hypermarket at Rohais in Guernsey might be coming up for sale in 1980. The owner, Mr Besant, would be prepared to sign an undertaking not to compete in future, but he would retain his four wine shops. The Directors agreed that this possibility deserved very serious consideration, and, if negotiations were successful, this could result in a big step forward.

The brief minute, previously quoted, on Vernon Villa at Beaumont was followed up and, planning permission being granted without aggravation, a complete rebuilding resulted in a unique project – a store designed to concentrate on frozen foods. Named the Freezer Centre, this was an innovation in sales practice. The building was very quickly completed, being of a simple walk-through design and layout, and by November 1977 it was ready to open its doors (**6.6**).

Among the several scattered sites previously mentioned that were being inspected with a view to possible development was the field between Rue de Trachy and Waterworks Valley, which was owned by the Pirouet family, and which was thought would be an ideal site for a supermarket. The manager agreed to make enquiries to see if it was for sale. This never materialised and, on reflection, it is very doubtful if the area would have proved suitable in the light of later policy and practice in supermarket design.

The site at Glencoe, St Lawrence was the field where the popular auction sales take place and was offered by Mr Liron on behalf of HP Davies Ltd. He was informed that the Society might be interested in buying one vergee for a Foodhall. There were not many houses in the immediate locality, but it was agreed that it was worth consideration, and would attract trade from St John and St Mary. Sites at Five Oaks and Sand Street could be investigated further. In the meantime it was decided that the Society should enter into negotiations to purchase Industria House, St Brelade, and Le Gros' Garage at St Peter subject to IDC approval being granted.

On possible supermarket sites in Guernsey, 'It was noted that a representative from the CWS Property Development Department would be over in about one month's time to carry out a survey of Guernsey.'

As 1978 dawned it was greeted with the continuing quest for out-of-town possibilities; no opportunities escaped the eyes of the Board, no

6.6 The Freezer Centre at Beaumont, opened in 1976. Left: George Gaudin (Refrigeration Installer); 4th left: Allan Smith (Food Trades Officer); 5th left: John Casselden (Architect)

doubt led by John Morris and Allan Smith. The Huelin premises at Five Oaks, an area that the Board had actively considered for some time as a site for a suburban supermarket, was a possibility. Events moved quickly then, and it was reported in March 1979 that the proposed meeting with the IDC had taken place and that the preliminary drawings for a two-storey building had been well received, leaving the architect clear to make the formal application with plans to include a caretaker's flat. However, the development was not approved by the IDC and the Society moved focus more fully on St Peter and St Martin, two of the larger projects that were beginning to take shape.

At the instigation of Allan Smith the Annual General Meetings were revised in content to become a much more interesting consumer evening. To encourage attendance the issuing invitations at the checkouts was introduced and also advertising the meeting on television and in the press. The success of this new format was dramatic, with attendance growing to around one hundred at each AGM, Jersey and Guernsey, from around twelve before the initiative.

As we read above, 1978 would bring more than the usual routine work and pressure on projects in hand. The indefatigable John Morris, now Secretary and Manager, was about to complete 40 years' service with the Society. Inevitably, as his retirement drew near, the Society was faced with the necessity to consider major changes in the upper levels of management, an exercise that had not been so fully met before in the Society's history. It is to the Society's credit and to that of the officers concerned that the situation was, within three months, settled to satisfaction.

It was a natural gesture to invite Mr Booth to express his views on the proposed structure for the immediate future – he had been intimately involved in the 'growing up' period following the Occupation and had been personally acquainted with many of the senior staff over a period of 25 years or more. The joint office of Secretary and Manager competently held by John Morris for some years was now to be divided, in view of mounting responsibilities reverting to the office of Secretary. Vernon Howells was proposed as Secretary-designate and Allan Smith as General

Manager-designate. Les Woodcock, who had been Assistant to Mr Smith for some time, was appointed as Food Marketing Officer; a further appointment of Food Officer, Buying, was to be made later. The successful applicant, Jim Hopley, was to have a profound effect on the Society.

This new team, already fully familiar with the Society and its structure and stores, had eighteen months in which to settle down before John Morris retired. Among the minor responsibilities that lay ahead for them were two pleasing and satisfying ceremonies: the opening of the St Peter's Food Centre in 1978 and of the St Martin Food Centre in March 1979.

The new Food Centre at St Peter (**6.1, 6.7**) was completed by September 1978, and Norman Le Brocq, the President, agreed to perform the opening ceremony. It was suggested that a reception be held at the shop on the previous evening, when the Directors, those concerned with the building and the Constable and Centeniers were to be invited. It was agreed that a presentation be made to the Constable for the elderly or the youth of the Parish. Mrs Cherry, Director, was to open the St Martin store, when completed the following March, in similar manner.

These two opening ceremonies could be looked on with great satisfaction, these stores being the first out-of-town Co-op supermarkets, one in each Island, symbolic perhaps of the intention of the Society to pursue its policy of expansion, of opening its doors as widely as possible to the Islands and its own members.

For the new management team there were several major items already demanding attention. Barely were their feet under their new desks than urgent consideration was needed on long-term future projects. Now that delegation of much routine or comparatively minor works was to be part of their brief it was possible to devote time and energy to the bigger issues. One such, mentioned briefly in April, came up again in July, namely Besants of Rohais.

This attracted the interest of the CWS Property Development Service and FB Williamson, the Manager, came over to discuss this with the Board, discussion that proved for the moment to be abortive though other matters of intent were also usefully talked over for action. Mr Williamson had been invited over to report on the viability of Besant's store. Mr Besant had been seen and agreed to discuss the sale. After the arrangements for the visit had been made, Mr Besant informed the Board that he had changed his mind and did not wish to sell. However, Mr Williamson and Mr Booth inspected Besant's store, and the Society's shops in Guernsey and Jersey. In reporting to the Board, Mr Williamson considered that the purchase of Besant's would be a good business proposition. He recommended that an approach be made to Advocate DWM Randall informing him of the Society's serious interest, before the Society made plans to develop the large site at Castel.

6.7 The main façade of the St Peter's Food Centre. The architects have successfully given a rural air to the design in keeping with the surrounding area

6.8 Anchor Market, St Sampson, remnant of the old Anchor Laundry in Nocq Road, purchased by the Society in 1979

The Board also felt that enquiries should be made about the Cabin Restaurant, 19 Charing Cross, owned by the States. If the Society purchased the lease it would be in a strong bargaining position when Dumaresq Street was widened, and this would assist in the eventual replanning of the central premises Nos 27 and 28, which had been under consideration. The Cabin Restaurant was the lower floor of an attractive French-style building (**11.5** below) that once stood on the corner of Dumaresq Street and Charing Cross, now demolished and leaving a rather untidy open area, in effect a vacant plot awaiting the final redevelopment of the whole block.

It is most telling at this stage to reflect on the quite remarkable change in Society affairs that had occurred during the previous 15 years. The Management Committee of the time began to feel the urge to expand to increase trade and income. The urge became an impetus as the committee, with John Morris in the lead, searched around St Sampsons and the parishes for sites. Modest sites though they were then, till on several occasions Mr Booth, ever watchful over the Society's finances, was compelled to warn the committee that there was not the capital available to expand so rapidly, for similar opportunities were opening up in Jersey too.

Still in Guernsey, a most interesting item came up in September 1978 when it was heard that the old Anchor Laundry site could be available (**6.8**). This property, owned by Jurat RA Kinnersly, had closed down and was for sale. It was suggested that it might be a better site than the one on Vale Avenue. The Manager was requested to investigate and report to the next Board Meeting. This was pursued with obvious intent and within a month the Board was able to report on verbal acceptance of the Society's offer. In October the President, together with JR Morris and the Architect, visited the site, which could provide premises similar in size to the St Peter's redevelopment in Jersey, and it was considered to be better for Society purposes than the site at Vale Avenue. The asking price was £150,000 and the Society had offered £130,000, which had received verbal acceptance.

It was resolved that the action taken be approved and the payment of a 10% deposit authorised, and that Mr JR Morris be authorised to represent the Society to pass contract at the Royal Court. It was Mrs Cherry, a Director, who had noticed the press announcement and perhaps knew Jurat Kinnesley personally, and she was thanked for bringing the property to the Board's attention.

The old laundry had closed down some time previously and the weekly Anchor Market was held in the office premises. Readers may remember this general public market. By 3 December 1978 the Board was able to report that contract was about to be passed and without delay a preliminary planning application was put in hand.

It was reported that the 10% deposit had been paid and it was expected that contract would be passed shortly. Discussion followed concerning the type of development desirable for this site, and it was resolved that the President and the Manager consult with the Architect in order to prepare plans for a preliminary approach to the IDC on the basis of providing a two-storey development. The possibility of rejection of this concept was to be borne in mind, and to avoid the delay that might result it would be advisable to prepare also, at the same time, for a single-storey development. There was little further delay, and it was reported in March 1979 that the preliminary drawings for a two-storey building had been well received, leaving the architect clear to make the formal application with plans to include one caretaker's flat. Contract was quickly passed and a preliminary planning application put in hand.

Back in Jersey, so soon it seemed, after the opening of the new Val Plaisant store it was considered necessary to increase accommodation and access, an indication of the value of the supermarket facility in that area. If further proof were needed, the car parking problem was a pointer to the support given to the new store; this too has been worsened in recent years by the replanning of the Springfield Stadium. Readers, and members in particular, will remember the parking on the roadways within the stadium behind the store, by permission of the RJA and the Society. The present area beside the store is barely sufficient on busy days. This is an inevitable result of the increasing use of the car in a residential area where in previous years the locals would have walked to the store; nowadays much of the shopping is done 'in passing' with the car. It was a telling indication of a concept to come – the convenience store.

For the Val Plaisant extension the quantity surveyor had negotiated a price of £115,286.46 with E Farley & Son Ltd, including the cost of lift and refrigeration. Work was to be completed in 22 weeks and the manager was authorised to sign the contract.

It was discussed at the time that when the alterations at Val Plaisant were completed the parking problem was likely to be greater than previously experienced, and Mr Smith suggested that double dividend at Val Plaisant could be allowed on Monday, Tuesday, Wednesday and Thursday each week in order to alleviate the particular difficulties of Tuesday and Wednesday (**6.9**).

It was no more than coincidence, but also relevant, that towards the end of 1978 the Jersey Model Laundry came on the market. This was taken up, quickly, purchased and opened as Besants, though shortly afterwards it became the present Safeway's Supermarket. Desirable though the site might have appeared at the time, the success of the competitor is tempered again by the success, if it can be called so, of the car, for, situated at the junction of Vallée des Vaux and Trinity Hill, the parking area is often inadequate and the entry and exit liable to cause traffic problems and inconvenience to nearby residents. Tenders to purchase this property had been submitted but the Society was informed that the property had been leased.

Colback's Garage, at the top of Queen's Road, was another property that presented itself at this time at a level of around £200,000 suggested by the agents. It was resolved that the tender be left in the hands of the General Manager at a level which, it was advised, should be in excess of £200,000 and that JR Morris be authorised to represent the Society, and in the event of our tender being successful, to pass contract at the Royal Court. This opportunity must have been considered very seriously by the Board for it to have reached this stage, but the purchase was not pursued.

Readers will remember, in fact most of Jersey will remember, Pool's Garage at the corner of Don Street and Burrard Street, a derelict site, boarded up for years, hardly suggestive of a promising store. So it would have appeared to the casual passer-by, even to a Co-op member, but to the Society it had more than promise, it had a future. This site had been noted and remarked upon several years previously and now had unexpectedly become available. The President reported that, in consultation with the Manager, the decision to purchase the site at £290,000 had been taken. Following discussion of the site, approximately of 10,500 square feet and the existing permit to develop to three floors on part and two floors on remainder, it was resolved that the Manager and the President be

6.9 Val Plaisant, in the middle of rebuilding work, February 1979

thanked for pursuing the matter to a successful conclusion and that the purchase be approved.

We can only surmise now how the acquisition of this site was so quickly brought to the stage of purchase. The personal note in the minutes suggests that the Society President and the Manager had engaged in useful spadework behind the scenes, as it were, to bring this forward without delay and the Board acknowledged this in its report.

Pausing for a moment to reflect on this seemingly continuous search for opportunities to expand, we have to admit to admiration for the amount of work undertaken by John Morris and his management and staff, latterly supported in this by the President, to achieve so much for the Society's commercial success and standing in the Islands' food and drink business. It could be said now, as was hinted in Chapter 3, that the Co-op was competing strongly with its rivals in both Islands. And there was still more to come.

In financial terms too, there were the occasional, and almost casual, reports of accounting success – the business was not only food and drink – the accountants were scoring points too on several such occasions. It had been necessary to sell £200,000 of 12½% Treasury Stock 1995. The sale showed a surplus of £26,938.70 over cost.

And there were the pleasing personal touches too, which indicated a continuing bond between the Society and those who had helped to build the reputation and success it now enjoyed. The Manager reported that the CWS Quantity Surveyor, Mr K Mayes, who had been involved in all the Society developments for many years, had decided to leave the CWS and would in future be operating privately, on his own account. It was agreed that Mr Mayes had an excellent knowledge of the Islands' building trade and that the Society had always been well satisfied with the manner in which he had represented its interests. It was resolved that Mr Mayes, following the severance of his connections with the CWS, be appointed to act for the Society as Quantity Surveyor.

And in January 1979 the Board decided upon a presentation to Mr Booth of a sterling silver tea or coffee service as a mark of the considerable advice, guidance and support he had given to the Society over some 25 years.

On the lighter side, a two-line minute in April suggested that the Society might be going into the Chinese takeaway business! However, this was merely a property purchase of 1 and 3 Craig Street, all within the extent of the proposed new store.

The old and recurring problem of warehousing came up rather seriously during the year, again a measure of the ever-increasing turnover in the stores. Obviously there was no easy answer to this, and it was a case of searching all avenues as the minutes pointed out. The growth in the volume of trade handled by the Grocery Department in Guernsey had, Mr Smith reported, brought the Society to a position where it would very shortly be unable to provide adequate servicing of the shops. Two properties had been investigated – Normans Store, alongside the existing Society warehouse, for which a firm rental had not yet been obtained; and a warehouse at Lowlands, St Sampson, available at £1.20 per square foot. It was resolved that negotiations be authorised with a view to obtaining the best possible solution to the problem.

For similar reasons, the Jersey Grocery Department had the same problem as in Guernsey, but without the same prospects for a solution. Mr Smith reported that should he be able to arrange the Society's wines and spirits business through the hands of local traders at properly advantageous terms then it would release one-third of the Grocery Warehouse space for general use. It was resolved that all avenues be explored to solve the problem and that every endeavour be made, particularly to find the means of releasing the space taken up by wines and spirits.

It became very noticeable during these years that car parking was frequently reported as a serious problem at all of the bigger stores and negotiations were continuing between the Society and the neighbouring property owners for additional land. It was a sign of the times that land now had to be purchased at high prices merely to park the cars of the shoppers during opening hours.

For example, in an effort to provide additional parking area at St Peter, Mr Smith had seen Mr Le Marquand, the owner of the land adjoining the Society's property. Tentative agreement had been reached for land, including some outbuildings, which would provide for 30 extra parking spaces. There were in all eight co-owners of this property and the arrangements might take some considerable time. It was resolved that the Board authorise continued negotiations, and very soon afterwards, at the meeting of 12 August, it was recorded that a letter from Bois and Bois had been received informing the Society that the Le Marquand family had agreed to sell the La Fosse farm outbuildings and land. Permission was also given for us to submit application to the IDC.

Similar problems arose at Rue des Camps, St Martin, where the Guernsey IDC had granted the Society a licence to construct the additional car park. Mr Mayes, the quantity surveyor, had checked the quantities and prices for additional parking submitted by Flouquet & Sons in the sum of £33,692. It was resolved that this price be accepted, and the work authorised. These minutes of the Board indicate the problem in time, legal fees, patience and cost incurred in seeking a solution! At least it can be said that the St Peter car park was a credit to the Society, with a spacious, well-laid-out, one-way system, trolley parks and every facility for the pedestrian with pavements and crossings. But note the number of properties involved in the transactions beforehand and the costs incurred! Car parking at the Society's stores had become a necessity, a situation that would have been ridiculed when Guernsey's first Food Hall was opened in 1960.

To close this chapter and to open up the 1980s in promising mood, the Manager reported in August 1981

> on the need for a Training Officer to be appointed. After lengthy discussion it was agreed that the services of a Training Officer be obtained. It was felt that a knowledge of the Islands was necessary and that the person appointed should be drawn from those persons available locally. If the need arose, the Officer, whether male or female, could receive training on the mainland.

Later we read:

> The Manager reported in March 1982 on his appointment of Mr Richard Le Brocq as Training Controller. Mr Le Brocq came with a most impressive list of qualifications and a record of achievement in the R.A.F., which he left as a Wing Commander. The need for the Training Controller to be aware of the fundamental differences between the Society and other retailers and of the necessity for imparting this to our staff was stressed.

7.1 John Cuthbertson with his mobile grocery shop, 1960s (photo John Cuthbertson)

Chapter 7

The Shops and the Staff

It has long been a characteristic of the Channel Islander to regret the changes that happen around him and sometimes resist them as far as he can by peaceful demonstration or by voicing his concern through his local paper. These concerns have been eased or mitigated to a degree by the Temps Passé features in the *Jersey Evening Post*, which allow him – and her – to recall the nostalgic images of the past. This tendency is the more poignant for those shops and businesses owned and run by Island families, sometimes for several generations, and within which other families or individuals have earned their livelihood and in doing so have felt an enduring bond of loyalty and friendship towards the business.

This has been the case in the staff of Voisin, for instance, now in its fifth generation of family ownership, and for De Gruchy, Le Gallais and other well-known and respected firms. Our own Co-op Society is already beating the drum, as it were, for while we read in these pages of the progress made since 1919 we also look mentally ahead to a centenary celebration, recalling as we do that the years go by all too quickly.

The Channel Islands Co-operative Society is an example of that feeling of nostalgia that has been evident among many of its staff who have served it so well for many years. In fact, its Island connections go back beyond its years in Jersey to its background of a prominent CWS presence, and in Guernsey through an interesting personal background to the first Society shop in St Peter Port over 50 years ago. This chapter will cover the story of those early shops and their staffs.

The early years of the Jersey Society from 1919 to 1939 saw only a limited acquisition of property, and that only with the financial backing of the CWS. Yet how fortunate it proved to be that the modest purchase of Nos 27 and 28 Charing Cross and the adjacent Pitt Street property was made early on in 1921, for by 1931 the Society was in serious financial difficulties. There was no possibility of further expansion at that time, although we see No 26 Don Road being purchased in 1932 for £2,500 (**1.18** above), no doubt with the financial help and support of CWS. That purchase also was to prove fortuitous for, as the general store and trading depot it would become, it served the Society well for many years until planning needs for road widening and housing necessitated demolition in 1969. In any event the essential rebuilding of the Charing Cross corner and the onset of the Occupation changed the Jersey scene completely. It was to be some years before the Jersey Society would see any further expansion.

The very first Co-op shop in Jersey, No 41 New Street, was well chosen by the Management Committee. Situated on the corner of Burrard Street, a busy intersection in mid-town, it would have been ideal for the fledgling Society to attract attention and custom – one can imagine the comments of the passers-by so soon after that momentous meeting in the Oddfellows Hall, saying 'the Co-op has actually opened'. The shop is still standing, an attractive one with window frontage on both streets – in recent years it has been a ladieswear shop, an antiques dealer's and until recently the Jersey Cancer Relief Centre. Now under the appropriate title of The Daily Grind it enjoys a daily customer support not all that far removed from the regular morning callers of 1919 looking for their bread and croissants (**7.2**).

No 41 had a comparatively short life with the Co-op, for being of small size internally, and lacking storage accommodation at the back, it quickly became too small for the increasing trade it

7.2 No 41 New Street, in modern times: The Daily Grind coffee bar, on opening day, 2001

was attracting. The move of the business to Charing Cross rendered it redundant. No longer able to draw on personal memories, we can imagine the interior, following the pattern of the day – wooden board floor (or tiled perhaps), mahogany counters at right angles at the back of the shop, shelving on the walls and confectionery displays in the windows. Stock was probably limited to the basic domestic items, most, if not all of it, shipped over from the CWS on the mainland, with an emphasis on butter, margarine, bacon, sugar, cheese and similar provisions. All of this was in bulk and would be broken down into the once-familiar blue bags or packed into greaseproof paper. The bakery and confectionery items would have been very evident for, having been a confectioner's under the previous tenant, no doubt there was a small bakery within the store. Confectionery was a strong point of the Co-op even in those early days, and several early photographs show window displays of bread and cakes.

As business consolidated and expanded at Nos 27 & 28 so the range of goods that could be stocked increased. We can see the beginnings of the dry goods trade that was being requested by members, though the rooms upstairs on that corner site were never intended as showrooms. Indeed, this lack of open accommodation may have accounted for the slow start and the continuing reticence of customers to climb the stairs for a pair of shoes.

The layout of the two shops at this corner block, Nos 27 & 28, would have been similar to No 41, and indeed to most similar stores of the time: wooden floors, probably linoleum-covered, heavy counters around the shop, simple window displays and probably the overhead wire cash carrier system that always intrigued little boys. Regrettably, it is now beyond the memories of members, customers or retired staff, to give us word pictures of that most interesting period in the story of the Jersey Society. However, in Guernsey, the story is different, for we have a lively picture of the beginning of that Society and a wealth of personal memories, with photographs of the early shops and their staffs, taking us back to the late 1940s, making it seem, as we say in the Islands, 'just the other day'!

We have mentioned already the first shop in Guernsey, discovered by Derek Falla and bought by CWS in March 1947 for the newly formed Guernsey Society. This store was known as the Guernsey Groceteria, bought by Duncan MacMillan and his wife in 1946 from John Richens, who also had run it as a grocery store for several years – in every way a going concern. It is interesting to note that the MacMillan family owned the shop for only a short period, a year perhaps, before Derek Falla came upon it, and in so doing enabled Duncan MacMillan to realise his hopes of starting a new life in Canada. Derek Falla's enquiries were made at just the right moment, the deal was struck and the shop changed hands. Having been a grocery store for several years little or no alteration was necessary before the budding Guernsey Co-operative Society could move in. One of the members of the small staff who ran the shop was Jimmy Batiste, the Manager, who was to continue working for the Society for many years.

For personal recollection of this early period we are indebted to Mrs Murphy of St Peter Port, who began her long connection with No 2 and the Society as Betty Bishop. She started working there as the 'Saturday girl' before the Occupation. This weekly job covered a variety of tasks, handling stock, with occasional spells behind the counter – in short, a thorough experience of the work involved in running a small grocery store. On return from their family evacuation during the Occupation Betty went back to the shop and the MacMillan family. She continued working there when the Society bought it and she remained until she left the Society's employ in the early 1950s.

On a recent visit to No 2, now the Vineyard (**7.3**), Betty remembered the shop in great detail, recalling the long counters either side right to the back of the shop and the stockroom above. Access to the stockroom was up the Clifton Steps outside and thence through an awkward doorway in the wall, which itself was up two additional steps at right angles, to the door into the store. When one recalls the size and the weight of the tea chests of the time, the bulk of the heavy butter and cheese blocks and the sugar sacks, one grows in appreciation of the staff when fresh supplies were delivered.

Here, the provisions, sugar, soft fruit, tea, butter, cheese etc were broken down, weighed and packed in the familiar blue bags – no pre-packaged items in those days. These were then lowered through a trapdoor in the floor to the shop below by means of a chain and pulley. One can imagine the occasional disturbance to customers when this had to be done, and the near misses that would create a moment of apprehension on the shop floor. Health and Safety legislation was yet to come!

Even in Society hands No 2 remained a family entity, for among the staff at the time were Ernest Vaudin, a nephew of Mrs MacMillan, and a friend, Mac Bundy. Together they continued their service

7.3 Betty Bishop at the Clifton Steps in 2001, showing the difficult access to the storeroom over the shop at No 2 Market Street, once the Groceteria, now the Vineyard (photo G Symons)

with the Co-op for many years, along with Betty, also a close friend of the family.

Betty remembers Jimmy Batiste very well, and also recalls his sister Doreen, who joined the staff about 1950, just as the first mobile shop was about to go on the road. In fact, Doreen really pioneered this thrust into the country parishes when she took over management of Mobile No 1. But this urge to take the business out of town was not without its trials, with the need to prepare, weigh and pack all the goods she needed, and then load them, before starting the journey, and all in that already over-crowded little shop. This was a tedious and time-consuming job, and it says much for Doreen's character and patience that she pursued it without complaint.

Doreen's fluency in French and patois and her knowledge of Island life and customs endeared her to her country customers, no doubt with advantage to Society membership, which was still growing in the early 1950s. An instance of the close contacts she enjoyed with her regulars was one occasion when a pregnant customer entered the shop, so far advanced that after a few exchanges Doreen took over. She hurried the customer back to the house, shopping unfinished, with words of friendly warning and encouragement, then took her shopping list and completed it for her.

By 1949 this situation of too little space for the increasing business was becoming intolerable. While welcoming the increase in trade the young Society was facing two possibilities. Obviously, No 2, with its dividend of 1s in the pound (5p), was becoming well known in town and no doubt around the Island. So it was decided to tap the semi-urban residential and business area of St Sampson, and at the same time to press for an additional shop in town or some additional accommodation for stores.

Betty Bishop was now, in the early 1950s, looking after the produce stall in the market, which was still a bustling centre for shoppers choosing their fruit and vegetables, meat and fish for the family. As further indication, if any were needed, of the decline in the status and the charm of the Guernsey Market, that corner, once the produce stall, is now a bicycle repair workshop! A little later the Co-op took up a stall in the French Halles for the produce. This remained a Co-op outlet for some twenty years.

7.4 This Shoefayre on the Bridge was originally the first Guernsey self-service store, opened and managed by John Cuthbertson in 1965. It was here that the midweek double-dividend idea began, and became accepted practice throughout the Islands' Co-op stores (photo G Symons)

The objective of opening a shop at St Sampson was quickly achieved – by 1949 in fact – with the purchase of a property in Nocq Road very near the corner of the Bridge. Desirable though this position was for custom and trade, the choice of site showed a lack of foresight as this property was really too small to be fully viable. It was hemmed in by the Salvation Army Citadel on one side and the Bridge corner properties on the other, thus limiting scope for expansion. Jimmy Batiste's sister Doreen came out to run Nocq Road, combining this with her job of organising the mobiles.

Though business was brisk Nocq Road was a difficult shop to manage, being situated in the narrowest length of the road, opposite the Anchor Laundry. It was also creating a traffic problem that was always destined to become acute. Within a year or so the decision was made to close and sell, but, as the minutes show, selling was to prove difficult. For a while the space continued to serve a useful role as a store for stocking the mobile shops but traffic problems soon rendered this impossible in the narrow roadway. To ease this difficulty a garage for the mobile vans and a store were built on the Braye Road.

So for the moment the Nocq Road idea lay dormant; but, like the mythical Phoenix, it was to rise from the ashes some 33 years later when the site of the Anchor Laundry was taken over and the new Nocq Road supermarket reared its head, as it were, above the surrounding buildings. It was ironic that the car park entrance was immediately opposite the little building where the idea was born all those years before.

Back in town the other obstacle to progress was being overcome: pressure on CWS from the Management Committee resulted eventually in the purchase of the Artisans Institute. The steps separating the Institute from No 2 no longer presented a difficulty, for the Institute could offer considerably more storage for bulk goods and also space for the office in one of the three floors above. This development was opened in 1960 with the name of 'Co-operative' on the fascia, and accompanying publicity naming it as Guernsey's first foodhall. This shop has remained a food store, the drapery having been moved to Rectory House when that was purchased and finally occupied, also in 1960.

Rectory House has seen many changes during its long life. It was, as the name suggests, the old Parish Rectory of St Peter Port Parish, ideally planned immediately opposite the Town Church. With an existing shop frontage it was well suited to cope with the overflow from No 2 until it, too, despite its five floors, became too restricted and further expansion was necessary. As the minutes show, it was during this period, in June 1959, that John Cuthbertson (**7.1**) only recently retired, after 40 years' service, joined the Society at the Market Street shop with Jimmy and Doreen Batiste.

John recalls his very early days there as 'bacon boy'. Within two weeks he was gaining experience first hand, helping to move into the adjoining Institute building. Within two years he was Manager of Mobile Shop No 5, working from the trading depot and store, which by then had been established on Braye Road. By 1963 he was managing the despatch department at the new grocery warehouse at Longue Hougue. In 1965 John enjoyed the opportunity of a two-week course at the Co-operative College at Stanford Hall, Loughborough, after which he returned to open the Society's first self-service store on the Bridge (**7.4**).

John recalls his long and varied service with the Society with obvious pleasure and satisfaction, for apart from the success he enjoyed in his chosen business career, he was well known and appreciated for his very active role as a volunteer, along with his fellow committee members, in organising the Guernsey Social Club events, particularly the Christmas party (**7.5**). It was inevitable during these early years of the Society's progress, following the lean years of the Occupation, that the staff, still few in number, would have quickly seized the opportunities for entertainment. By the early 1950s social events were becoming popular, prompted naturally by that bond of fellowship mentioned earlier. John remembers with a nostalgic smile the many and varied activities that were enjoyed – football, petanque, a trip to Herm, even shove-ha'penny.

In this social enterprise Guernsey seems to have led the way, for photographs of the early to mid-1950s show the happy spirit of party time, with staff and management enjoying their dinner dances together and giving the girls the opportunity to dress up for an occasion (**7.6, 7.7**). It took rather longer for this to materialise in Jersey, although there are mentions in the minutes of contributions, modest amounts of £10 or £20, towards the staff Christmas party (**7.8**).

Jean Macdonald is another of the retired staff whose experiences go back to about 1954, when she joined the group at No 2. At that time there was still the grocery store down below, but by then the old stock room above, once the scene of such frantic activity, had been taken over by footwear and general clothing, a quieter regime for the customers below. But access to that floor was still by

7.5 The good life at the Wayside Cheer Hotel, Guernsey: a Guernsey Social Club evening in the mid-1950s: John Cuthbertson on the left, Ray Jeffries and Manager Eric Andrews, nicknamed 'Charlie'. The story goes that when Eric was younger he worked in the Butchery. One day an inspector came round. The staff were made to line up, and the inspector stopped in front of Eric, who was a bit tongue-tied. The inspector asked him, 'What's your name, Charlie?' he mumbled that it was, and the name stuck

7.6 Eric Andrews with twin sisters Ann (left) and Shirley Le Moignan

the Clifton steps outside, so it is unlikely that trade up there was brisk! The back of the shop had become so cramped that with the old iron spiral staircase still in use as the only access to the office, now two floors above, Jean remembers the anxiety she felt when going up and down between shop and office. This unsatisfactory situation would continue until Rectory House was ready in 1960, and dry goods could then be accommodated more conveniently in that spacious building.

Jean also had a spell in the French Halles on the produce stall. She recalls, rather ruefully, that the wooden stalls, loaded with produce, had to be lifted and moved to and from the back of the building night and morning. It was rather heavy work for two young girls, and at times Mr Jennings would come along to see that all was in order, but never offer to help!

Customers' orders for delivery were made up at the warehouse near the Nelson's Eye at Longue Rue, where Jean worked for a while with Jim Marquis. She experienced there her first personal contact with Doreen Batiste, who quickly intervened for her when Mr Jennings once came in unexpectedly one Saturday morning and sacked her on the spot for laughing at something long since forgotten. Doreen heard of this and, after an interval, Jean was told to report back to Market Street on the following Monday, all forgiven.

7.7 Getting in the mood in Guernsey

7.8 A Society social from the 1962–64 period

It seems that Doreen could also be rather strict at times. Once, when Jean was working at the Bridge Avenue corner shop and rested for a moment from scrubbing the wooden counters and the floor, Doreen came in and called out 'come on, miss, you're not paid to look out of the windows'. But overall Jean had great respect for Doreen, agreeing that she had learned much from her.

Jean also enjoyed a spell on the mobile shops around 1960, loading up at the Braye Road store before setting off on a round with the driver, 'Rossie' Rosamund, a round that would include members at St Saviour, Forest and Torteval. Jean's many years of service with the early Guernsey Co-op gave her wide and varied experience in shops and stores. She looks back at this with a mix of pleasure and perhaps a little nostalgic distaste, as for example when recalling the floor scrubbing, or cleaning the great sides of bacon that were delivered to the Longue Hougue warehouse in big linen sacks – not a pleasant job during a hot summer! But this would have been typical of the grocery and provision trade a half-century ago (**7.9**).

In Jersey the acquisition of additional shops took rather longer than would have been wished by the Society, brought about no doubt by the period of recovery necessary after the Occupation and the need for financial prudence. But pressure on Charing Cross was building up and eventually, in 1947 – by coincidence the same year that No 2 Market Street was purchased – an existing grocery store was found at Georgetown. Also, as in Guernsey, the Jersey Society was eager to tap the suburban areas, and Georgetown, its first out-of-town venture, was ideal for that purpose. It was within an existing residential area, and the new Grasset Park estate going up nearby was an additional source of possible membership.

Several premises made up the block purchase that was to become the Georgetown supermarket we know today. Milton House, Lymington House and shop, and Tanguy's Garage in Elizabeth Street, which was to become the coal store, were purchased in April 1947 for £9,500.

Douglas Toop, who went on to serve 19 years with the Co-op, was the Manager there in 1948/49. He spoke of Georgetown as a dull shop with heavy counters and fittings and inadequate lighting. Tanguy's Garage in Elizabeth Street had been taken over to become the Co-op Coal Store, bordering on the yard at the back of the shop. This meant there was often a nuisance of noise and coal dust to contend with in and around the shop, not conducive to good customer relations, even if they ware members! In fact, protests were voiced on several occasions, and hosing down had to be resorted to in hot, dry weather.

It was a double-fronted shop, with the main half covering the usual groceries and provisions and the other half a strange combination of off-licence and greengrocery. Next door was Warren's newsagents, and nearer the corner was Guy's, a small general store. Sidney and Louise Guy ran their modest

7.9 A group of Guernsey shop girls, in dress typical of the 1950s and early 1960s, photographed in Market Street. From left: Thelma Pemberton, Jenny Bichard, Gwen Ayres, Edith Pengelly, Sylvia Simon, Olive Lovel, Sheila Bichop, Dot Povey

business in Georgetown Road almost next door to the old Boucheré shop. It was a small general grocery store, which also had a licence for alcohol sales. When the Co-op opened its first venture in the area there was inevitably rather intense competition between the two shops, which were offering the local residents much the same fare.

Valerie Guy of the David Place School of Dancing, daughter of the Guys, remembers well the rivalry, rather than competition, but also recalls that her mother and Doug Toop got on very well together. Valerie also comments on the nuisance of the coal dust and, with even more feeling, her regret at the loss of their extensive garden with fruit trees, which disappeared beneath the concrete of the shop car park.

Douglas recalls several memorable incidents in his shop, one perhaps more serious than most. On one occasion while serving a customer at the counter he noticed a rat running across the floor to the opposite counter, unseen by the customer. On the pretext of answering the telephone he called an assistant to attend to the customer's order while he hurried across the shop and fortunately was able to corner the rat and dispose of it. But as Jean Macdonald would have had to agree when opening up the sacks of vegetables in the Guernsey warehouse, which were often nibbled into by mice, these incidents were all part of the job 50 years ago.

The situation at Georgetown, regrettably, was to continue for the next 22 years. Despite the frequent appeals to the IDC for permission to rebuild owing to procrastination over road widening, which would never materialise, and irritating issues of exchanges of small areas of land, it was 1969 before the old Georgetown Lighthouse became the Co-op's first appearance in modern form at that end of town. It may not be realised by many, even by members, that the old shop frontage was not on Don Road. Don Road terminated at Elizabeth Street, and the continuation to the junction is Georgetown Road or, more familiarly, just Georgetown.

Returning to the Georgetown shop for a moment and Douglas Toop's long service with the Society, it is appropriate to note that Doug's second wife, Jean, also served the Society well for 16 years from 1974 to her retirement in 1990. She felt the urge to follow the family lead, as it were, and had a spell in the new Georgetown store.

Between that early start and retirement Jean had a spell of six and a half years in Guernsey, in time to work with and to phase out one of the two remaining mobiles and then to continue on No 2 for a while. Jean teamed up with 'Rossie' Rosamund, who had been driving the mobiles for many years, before she joined the staff at No 2 Market Street with Doreen Batiste. This was followed by promotion to Section Head, Fresh Foods, at the new St Martin's store when it opened in 1979.

The Toops returned to Jersey in 1980, and Jean then enjoyed a spell as Manageress of the Pontac store before a further promotion took her to the new Beaumont Fresh Food Centre for 18 months before retirement in 1990. Jean emphasises the pleasure and satisfaction she has always enjoyed throughout her service. That happy disposition towards her job must have been very evident at the retirement lunch with the Board, for at a later meeting the Directors referred to it and discussed further the opportunities available for women to pursue a managerial career with the Society, particularly when they wish to return after leaving temporarily to fulfil family commitments.

'The butcher, the baker, the candlestick maker', as the old nursery rhyme has it. Well, a candlestick maker never had a place in our Society but the butcher and the baker certainly had, throughout many years in the Islands, conforming to the true co-operative spirit of providing the family basics.

Little is remembered now of the butchery before the Occupation but its progress since is fully documented through the progress and dedicated service of one man who made it his career. It was in 1949 during this time of change at Georgetown that a young boy in town was earning a little pocket money as the 'Saturday boy' at Charing Cross. At 13 years of age Michael Galway was taken on by Mr Baird, the General Manager, to do general duties in the Butchery department for six shillings for the day (about 30p). Rationing was still in force and would remain so until 1954, so Michael's main job was delivering the weekly meat ration to local members. He would have been the typical delivery boy of the time, riding the usual heavy-duty bicycle with a small front wheel and a heavy wicker basket mounted over it.

The meat business must have been born in him for two years later, in 1951, and now 15, Michael joined the staff as trainee butcher. He remained in the butchery business for most of his 47 years' service (**7.10**). He obviously made the right impression on the Manager for only two years later, at 17, he was sent over by Baird to the Central Market to run the Co-op shop there. This he did very successfully with the help of the girl on the till and four staff, two of them being the drivers with their vans. The main tasks for the drivers were the collection of meat in bulk from the old abattoir on the Esplanade, and, when the rations had been prepared, to deliver them to the hospitals, the Little Sisters of the Poor and to the prison for which the Co-op had contracts, and also to a few of the hotels.

During the 1950s there were many butchers in the Central Market. When the irksome rationing finally ended the meat business became brisk, with all of them holding their own with favourite customers

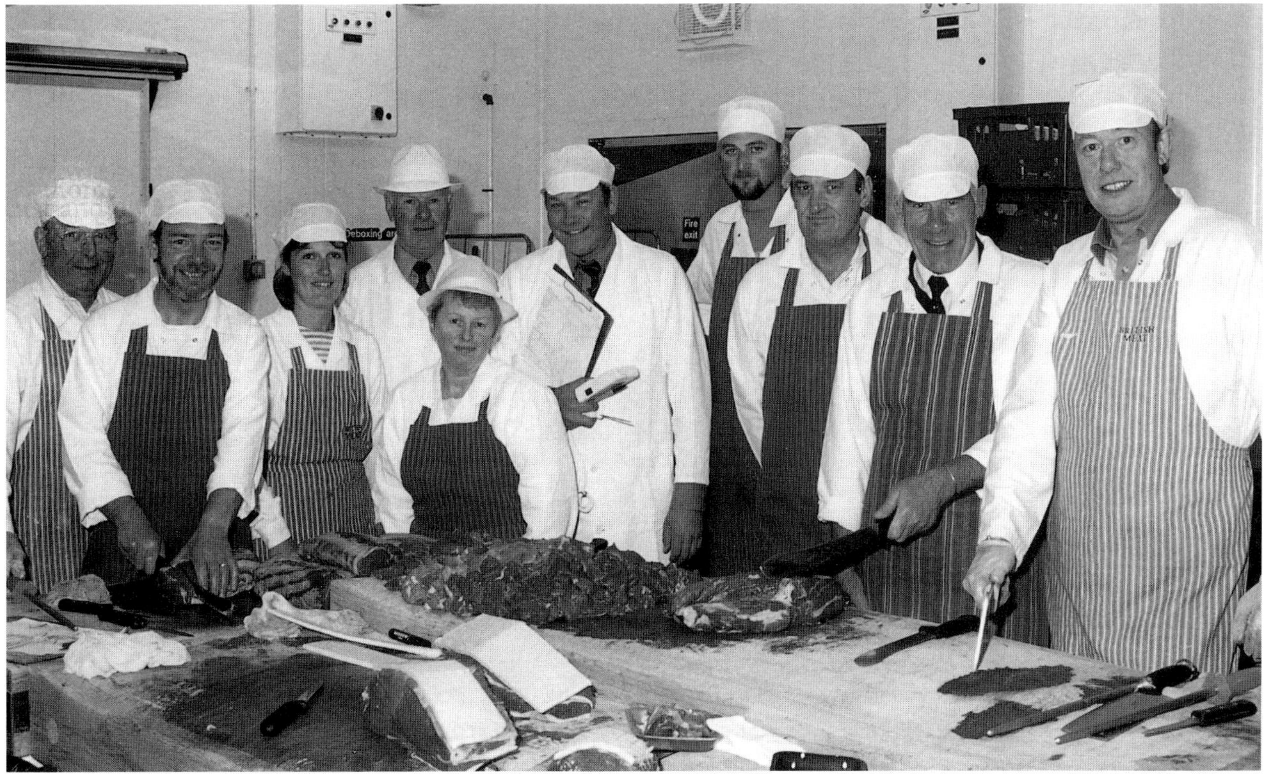

7.10 Michael Galway, fourth from left, with team at the St Peter's Butchery department, which supplied all the Jersey shops. Photo taken in 1997 (© Stuart McAlister Photographers)

7.11 Charing Cross on a wintry day, 1 February 1956, with Bichards Corner, Nos 24 and 25, on the left. The photo appeared in the Temps Passé feature, `Jersey Evening Post`, 20 December 2000

and the Co-op also welcoming and encouraging its members. But the system of handling the supplies of fresh meat coming in was not without its difficulties. Jersey pork was popular and easier to manage, but the meat prepared at the abattoir in the familiar large sides was taken to the old Minden Place cattle market, where the Society rented a large walk-in freezer store; from this store the meat was drawn as required for both the Market and the Charing Cross meat counter.

It was to Michael's credit that he realised the difficulties and the hazards of maintaining this store to the reasonable standards of hygiene for quality meat, and he abandoned this routine as soon as he could do so. His target was to build up the market shop and Charing Cross with modern cold cabinets and freezers as they became available (**7.11**), and, years later, achieved his goal of creating a modern-quality central butchery preparation department operating at the St Peter's store.

There has been a major revolution in the way that our meat is prepared and distributed to the several Co-op stores. It now arrives in boxes each containing joints or cuts of meat, wrapped in cellophane to prevent contamination or deterioration until such time as they are to be opened for use. Toni Rowles, the meat factory manager, and his staff prepare the individual requirements for each store, delivery being made in refrigerated lorries. As an indication of the care taken at this new Meat Department to maintain the highest standards of hygiene, Michael Galway, Toni Rowles, and many managers and staff have taken numerous Food Hygiene Certificates, successfully completing their courses at Highlands College run by the Chartered Institute of Environmental Health. As Michael Galway says, this is a more cost-effective way of preparing the meat than having butchers at every store.

Michael can reflect with justifiable satisfaction and pride on his 47-year career in meat with the Society. Thinking back with a smile, he recalls the only mishap that really upset his routine was the occasion when Baird the Manager, and three of his staff at the Central Market, had a good win on the Pools, gave the Society a week's notice and left!

Looking ahead, we see the acquisition of the old Western Stores at St Peter's crossroads as the first significant expansion in Jersey. This was towards the west, fulfilling that long-held desire of the Society to have a prominent presence in that area. The Western Stores had long-established family connections with the Society's President, Mr Norman Le Brocq. It was his grandfather, Albert Le Brocq, who founded the original Western Stores before the First World War; it was then a general country store selling food, general agricultural goods and clothing. Another branch of the family took it over in 1921, namely Stanley Edward Le Brocq, whose two sons, Edward and Stanford, continued to run it until it was bought by the Society in 1978. Throughout those years, as the only major store in the area, it had enjoyed a strong local support and custom from the village and latterly from the new housing areas, and this support was a strong incentive to the Society to purchase.

The accompanying photographs (**7.12, 7.13, 7.14, 7.15**) show the shop as many older members will remember, its inviting interior typical of numerous old Island shops that had served their customers so well before the self-service and the supermarket began to oust them in the 1960s.

This new store gave the Society the long-hoped-for opportunity to expand to a degree not previously possible. Here at a busy intersection, in an unfamiliar area perhaps, but surrounded by the old St Peter's village with a new residential area nearby, it brought the Co-op ideals to a local community, who may not have previously thought seriously about membership. Here at last the 'divi' was on their doorstep. And the splendid car park was an encouragement to members to vary their support between the town shops or perhaps even from Quennevais. Certainly the Society had other ideas in mind, still more expansive, to advance eventually into the rival camp, really out west. But that was still to come.

Here at St Peter, support for the new store was immediate. The Society's first really extensive supermarket was so successful that within a very short time plans were prepared for extension. Among the first of the new staff to settle in was Geraldine Garnier, who had previously been with Alliance nearby. When Alliance closed its St Peter branch, just as the Co-op was opening, Geraldine saw the right moment to make a convenient move for she lives within sight of the new store. That convenient move was the beginning of her 20 years' service with the Co-op.

Geraldine's first position was a spell on the tills at the checkouts – those cash registers that required the totting up of each purchase like the old cash registers. By present standards of EPOS this was a tedious job but Geraldine mastered it so well that, despite the slower pace, she became adept; but after

7.12 An interior view, typical of many old Jersey country stores, the brothers Le Brocq behind the counter

7.13 A young customer at the Le Brocqs' sweet counter: all very homespun!

7.14 Stanford Le Brocq in his office

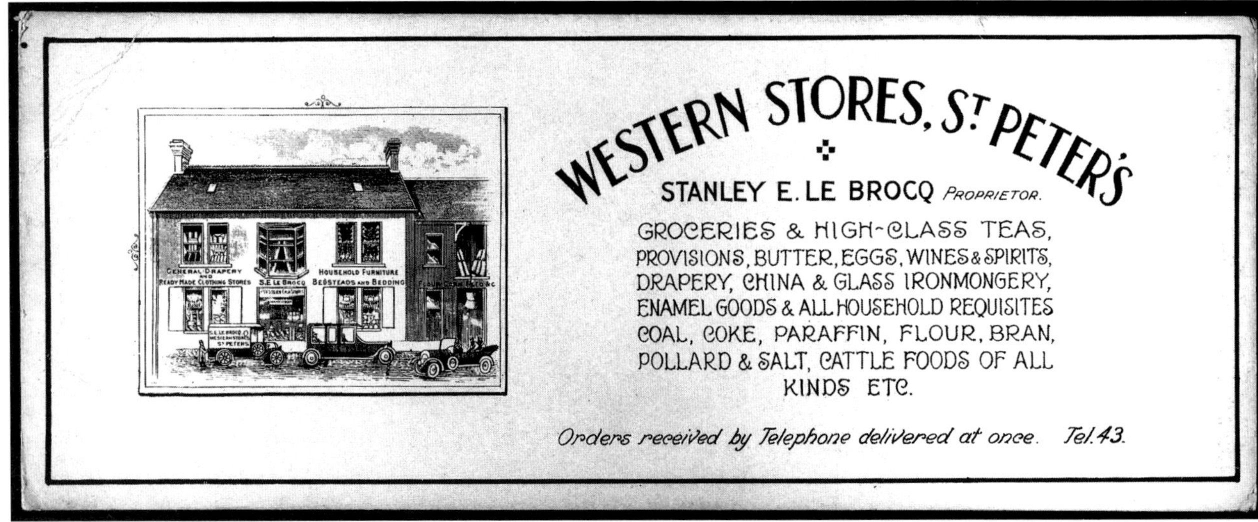

7.15 A desk blotter, a simple handout for regular customers, typical of a more personal era of country shopping

a year or so she was happy to take over Margaret Hall's job of cashing up in the office, Margaret having left Society employ.

Among those happy moments in the routine of cashing up were the occasions when the President, Norman Le Brocq and his wife Rosalie, would pay a shopping visit to St Peter's as an indication of their friendly interest in the shop and the staff. Norman was always approachable, and management knew that these were opportunities to voice any concerns they might have.

Geraldine recalls her years at St Peter, as do many of the old staff, as a very happy period of her life. Even the disruption and noise of the extension going on beside them, she dismisses as a minor disturbance. But disturbance of a different kind occasionally occurred when well-known personalities came in for their shopping – the success of the Co-op must have reached far and wide, for among the men remembered was Ian Lavender of the TV series 'Dad's Army'. Also seen were Barbara Windsor and the Three Degrees, the popular singing group of the 1980s. One wonders how the male staff reacted to such a wealth of talent; did they all rush for the tills? Their response is not recorded in the minutes!

When David Palmer came over from the mainland to join the Co-op in 1979, little knowing that he would later become the Manager, his introduction to the St Peter's store, just recently opened, was not exactly smooth and professional. He was due to start on the Monday following a particular weekend when the fog was so thick that flights were delayed. When at last the flight took off on Monday morning the plane had to turn back, the fog over Jersey being too dense to permit landing, so David found himself back in UK feeling a little concerned at thoughts of the embarrassing first impressions that would accompany his first meeting with the Manager.

At last on Tuesday afternoon he landed in Jersey, rushed to St Peter's store and introduced himself to Mr Hotton, who, after a brief exchange of greeting, said: 'I'm afraid I'm too busy to talk to you now, it's double divi day, but here you are, take this and take a walk around the store.' Mr Hotton then handed him a pricing book, the quick reference to every item on the shelves. Somewhat chastened, David did just that and found it to be a very useful introduction. As he says, then, nearly 30 years ago, there were about 2,000 lines of stock. Such an exercise now, with over 14,000 lines of stock, would not be so simple! His full introduction to the Manager and staff went off well on the Wednesday morning, and at the end of the day he was paid his week's wages. Unfamiliar with the Co-op practice of having payday on a Wednesday, he could only blink: 'I arrive a day late, do a day and a half's work and I'm paid for the week!'

Now, after service in most of the stores, including St Peters and now the Store Manager at Grand Marché, St Helier, David recalls the satisfaction felt at the extension of St Peter but also remembers the unseen difficulties that accompanied reopening. Office accommodation and other ancillary work at the back still remained to be done while the customers were busy in the front, no doubt admiring the results of the extension.

David remembers Geraldine Garnier with some admiration; in the early 1980s she was already highly adept at the daily cashing-up routine. Twenty-five years ago credit cards were not so frequently used by customers; most purchases were paid for in cash or by cheque. Geraldine, with the help of the team, was faced with mini-mountains of cash to count and check at the end of the day. David's occasional efforts to help were frustrated – as he says, 'I just couldn't keep up with her!'

One particular and popular feature of the St Peter's store is the in-store Bakery, where Annette Edwards is now Senior Assistant. Annette's first experiences with the Co-op began in 1965 when, like Betty Bishop in Guernsey, she began working as the 'Saturday Girl', cycling in from St John to town to work in the Don Road despatch section, making up the orders for delivery.

At the age of 15 she was taken on to the staff to work full time at Don Road on the orders routine. This was done rather like pushing your tray around the counter of a self-service restaurant: a basket progressed along the shelf of the store, picking up the customer's order piece by piece until it reached the checking point. It was a simple but effective means of bringing it all together. When checked and all in order the baskets were taken out to the van for delivery.

When the Don Road store closed in 1970, Annette joined the Charing Cross staff on the bakery side where, among many other duties, was that of taking in the daily deliveries from Le Brun's Bakery. While there she also had a spell on the bread delivery rounds driving a van on deliveries to the hotels. She remembers the friendly help of John Dart, who took her out a time or two to introduce her to her round and to her customers.

After closure of the Society bakery, Annette transferred to the mobiles, two of which were still running. She found this to be a very pleasant routine, giving her an even closer friendly contact with members in the parishes – one lady would even prepare a breakfast for the van crew on the morning they were due to call. Personally, she rather regretted the inevitable closing down of the mobile deliveries, though she was rather gratified to be running the last vehicle herself until it was finally phased out.

This break with the old tradition, maintained for so many years of delivery to the door, was an inevitable change towards the advantages of the supermarkets. These were still small in the 1970s but were gaining the support of the public. Car ownership was increasing, and the parishes were no longer isolated from the Co-op town shops, which, though only three in number, held a much wider range of provisions and produce than the mobile ever could. The mobile shop had maintained its role in both Islands for well over twenty years, but it was time for change.

It was during this mid-1970s period of change that Annette experienced a rather amusing episode, when a roving reporter of an American newspaper came to Jersey to look at the tourist aspect of the Island. This was just as the last mobile was about to come off the road. He was so intrigued with the Society's courtesy, as he saw it, of deliveries to the door in the 1970s that Annette had to demonstrate it all for him, for which she had her name and role well publicised in his report!

Annette is now working in the St Peter's in-store bakery, commenting on the changes she has seen and experienced in the traditional bakery and confectionery business of the Co-op during her 40 years' service with the Society. Not yet ready for retirement, she speaks with obvious pleasure of the occasion of lunch with the Board on completion of 25 years' service and the presentation of an inscribed wristwatch and a rather special fountain pen.

Another early Guernsey shop was that at Castel, which opened in 1964 (**7.16**). Remote from town, it enjoyed a good friendly support from the local members and residents, but its scope was limited because of its size and lack of adequate parking. While that may not have been a vital factor in the mid-1960s, with the continuing growth of car ownership in the 1970s and onward, this did begin to matter. With the opening of St Martin in 1978 some members, at least, might have transferred their loyalties. Reluctant to lose the shop altogether, management and architects worked on alternative plans to revitalise by expansion but, despite various schemes to increase the trading area, it became unprofitable to run and was closed in 1984.

7.16 An early Guernsey shop at Castel, purchased in 1964: a modern view, showing the garage next to the shop and the shared parking (© Guernsey Press Co)

One of the managers of Castel was Pat Le Tocq, who spent six years in charge there and built up a happy rapport with staff and customers (**7.17**). An advocate of customer care, he kept the shop going at a good level and might even have set the pattern for the L'Aumone of the future, some 25 years ahead, as his neighbour next door was a garage proprietor with a filling station who also lacked reasonable parking space on his frontage. Pat, being of a sociable nature, soon got on friendly terms with the garage proprietor. They made an agreement to share all the available parking area between their customers, a useful move for both of them.

Pat recalls with a smile a particular incident when his outgoing nature caused some embarrassment. He offered to take a customer's shopping out to her car, which she told him was a Morris Minor Traveller. Out went Pat and into the car went the shopping. A few moments later the lady came back into the shop to ask where her shopping was. He was nonplussed for the moment, but a brief discussion then revealed that there had been two Travellers outside of identical colour, and one had disappeared with the shopping! However, all ended in good humour when the other customer, on reaching home with twice as much as she had bought, realised the error and returned at once to the shop, much to Pat's relief.

Then there was the Birds Eye representative, who brought a supply of frozen foods out in his car, as they used to do in those days. As he unloaded he realised that one carton had been left behind. Quickly telling Pat he would go back and fetch it, he reversed his car to move off and crushed a carton he had left on the kerb behind him. Who said managing a country store would be a dull job!

There came a time when Pat would be moving to pastures new. Following a year or two at Market Street he was appointed Manager of the new St Martin's supermarket, where he continued working for 16 years before hanging up his apron for good in December 2001 after 23 years with the Society.

But Pat's 16 years with the St Martin's store were not without their memorable moments. Happy though they were, they presented him with experiences that put Castel in the shade. We have read of the difficulties encountered with the IDC over the site in general and the car park access in particular. To maximise the floor area of the store on that rather restricted site the building was extended to the boundary of the Queen's Hotel next door, leaving no room for a surface road. The access to the car park at the front of the store was taken under the floor of the extension as a miniature underpass.

7.17 Patrick Le Tocq, Manager at Castel for six years, with a friendly neighbour, the cat from next door

Innovative it could be said, a splendid idea perhaps. But, of course, heavy rain caused a build-up of water in the dip and the two automatic pumps, which were supposed to deal with this problem, would occasionally cease to work and irate motorists would get water up their cars' exhausts! More serious was the headroom, the clearance under the shop floor – or the lack of it at times. This was adequate for cars but tricky for the larger 4 x 4s or the bigger vans. Of course mishaps occurred, the more serious incident involving a car with a cycle rack on the roof complete with cycles, which added three or four feet to the height of the car. It didn't get through without damage!

And there was at least one occasion when a fully laden van delivering to the store, instead of using the delivery route, went through – just – but, having unloaded, the return journey wasn't so straightforward. The van now empty, the suspension and the tyres had returned to normal level and pressure, and, short of scraping through, it was no go – the only solution was to deflate the tyres!

Yes, Pat Le Tocq certainly had reason to smile – long afterwards – at the memory of a few incidents that caused him more then a little concern at the time. It is said that many rude words could be heard at times coming up from that underpass!

Perhaps IDC had not got it right after all.

What would you do to get your share of over £3 Million?

"You don't have to risk life and limb to earn a little extra... simply become a Co-op member.

This year Co-op members shared ***ver three million pounds*** in cash Dividend payout...

or converted their cash to Co-op vouchers*...
...worth an extra 15% at Homemaker Stores.

Join today and make sure you get your share in the next big payout. I know I will!"

THE CHANNEL ISLANDS CO-OPERATIVE SOCIETY

DIVIDEND

Get your share!

ouchers are not redeemable at Travelmaker
Food Stores. See vouchers for conditions.

Chapter 8

Advertising the Goods and Delivering Them

Advertising

As a glance through any local newspaper of the 1920s will reveal, and this is particularly so of the Jersey and Guernsey papers of the day, the advertising of goods and services was little more than a plain statement of fact, telling the public what was available and the price.

From the Co-op's point of view advertising was just that, merely a means of telling prospective customers and members the main items available, which items had just arrived, and their cost. In this practical approach the Management Committees were no doubt guided by the simple fact that advertising costs money, and in those early years there was little to spare for unnecessary frills. The buying public, the shoppers of Co-op goods, were still the ordinary men in the street and their families, seeking their basic needs of bread, milk, meat, coal and necessary domestic items, with a few luxury items of canned fruit, fish and the like for weekend visitors or treats. It was essential that the Co-op balanced the accounts at a level that enabled the dividend to be maintained year by year. The distribution of the dividend was one of the Co-operative Principles and not to be prejudiced by unnecessary expenses.

It was not until business began to recover after the Occupation that advertising became a necessary aspect of commercial life. The earlier years had relied to a greater degree on the static form of advertising by simple window displays and, of course, the colourful towers and columns of cans, tins and bottles stacked within the shop. Added to which was the fact that such displays could all be arranged and changed at intervals by a member of staff who showed a certain skill in colour and design – no additional wages and costs were involved!

In the 1950s period, the art of window dressing was the most effective, and least costly, means of telling the public what was available and the price. The expansive windows of the period invited a glance into the shop interior and perhaps persuaded a passer-by to enter – an early form of impulse buying. But, in any event for the Co-op, in the absence of available staff with a flair for window displays, the Society had never indulged in the art of window dressing as had been done by Orviss or Le Riche. Co-op windows of the time showed simple and practical displays, often supported by rather crude posters stuck to the windows or simple announcements written in white on the windows.

In some way regrettably, the modern supermarket has dispensed with window displays. No longer can tasteful arrangements of bottles, coloured boxes and cans tempt the passer-by. The need for maximum interior space illuminated throughout the day has rendered large windows superfluous for many stores. So, for the Society, simple advertising in the *Jersey Evening Post* sufficed for many years. This was practical and comparatively inexpensive. After the Occupation straightforward, factual advertising became rather more sophisticated, the illustrator was called on to convey the impression of a more personal aspect, the shopping housewife was pictured in line drawings as the modern young woman enjoying her trips to the shops, and her family were similarly shown as examples of the smartly dressed schoolchildren of the day (**8.2**).

Opposite page **8.1** This advertisement from 2002 has plenty of impact, supported by the reasonable proposition that becoming a Co-op member is a better way of getting your share than being a knife-thrower's assistant

CHANNEL ISLANDS
CO-OPERATIVE
SOCIETY LIMITED

OUTFITTING DEPARTMENT
CHARING CROSS

SOCIETY
AUTUMN BOYS' WEAR

AVAILABLE ON 20 WEEK CLUB AT NO EXTRA CHARGE, AND DIVIDEND IS ALSO ALLOWED

8.2 How it was done in the 1950s: a neat schoolboy being prepared for the new term, showing off his school uniform from the Outfitting Department

2lb. Sugar - - - - -	from 1/1½ to 1/-
1lb. Lard - - - - - -	from 1/6 to 1/3
Large Tins Pears - - -	from 3/- to 2/6
Large Tins Peaches - - -	from 3/2 to 2/8
Canned Cream, 6oz. - -	from 1/2½ to 1/1½
Red Salmon - - - - -	from 3/11 to 3/8
Pink Salmon - - - - -	from 2/6 to 2/3
Sardines in Oil - - -	from 11½d. to 10½d.
Stewed Steak in Gravy -	from 2/8½ to 2/5½
3lb. S.R. Flour - - -	from 1/8½ to 1/6½
16oz. Corn Flour - - - -	from 1/6 to 1/5
12oz. Custard Powder -	from 1/7½ to 1/5½
Large Size Stringless Beans -	from 1/8 to 1/6
16oz. Macaroni - - - -	from 1/4 to 1/3
Coffee and Chicory Essence -	from 2/6½ to 2/4
Toilet Rolls - - - - -	from 9d. to 8½d.
Bleach - - - - - -	from 1/3 to 1/-
Toilet Soaps - - - -	from 7½d. to 4½d.
Matches, doz. boxes - - -	from 7½d. to 6d.

FOR 2 WEEKS

ONLY

All varieties of C.W.S. Biscuits reduced by 3d. for every two packets

Kit-e-Kat .. 3 tins for 1/3

CWS READING

SPECIAL OPENING OFFERS *all at* REDUCED PRICES

You do not have to be a member to shop with us, but the *Dividend pays you* to be . . . Ask at the store or at any of our shops for details

8.3 Handouts like this were a popular approach to attract support and custom at special events, in this example the opening of a new store

But advertising was about to enter a new phase, and photography began to appear, first in simple black and white, then in colour, which quickly followed as rapid advances in printing techniques lowered costs.

One popular form of advertising, of the 1950s and 1960s in particular, was the simple leaflet or handout, available at the counters (**8.3**). These covered a variety of items or special events. One such was the Christmas wines price list, of several pages,

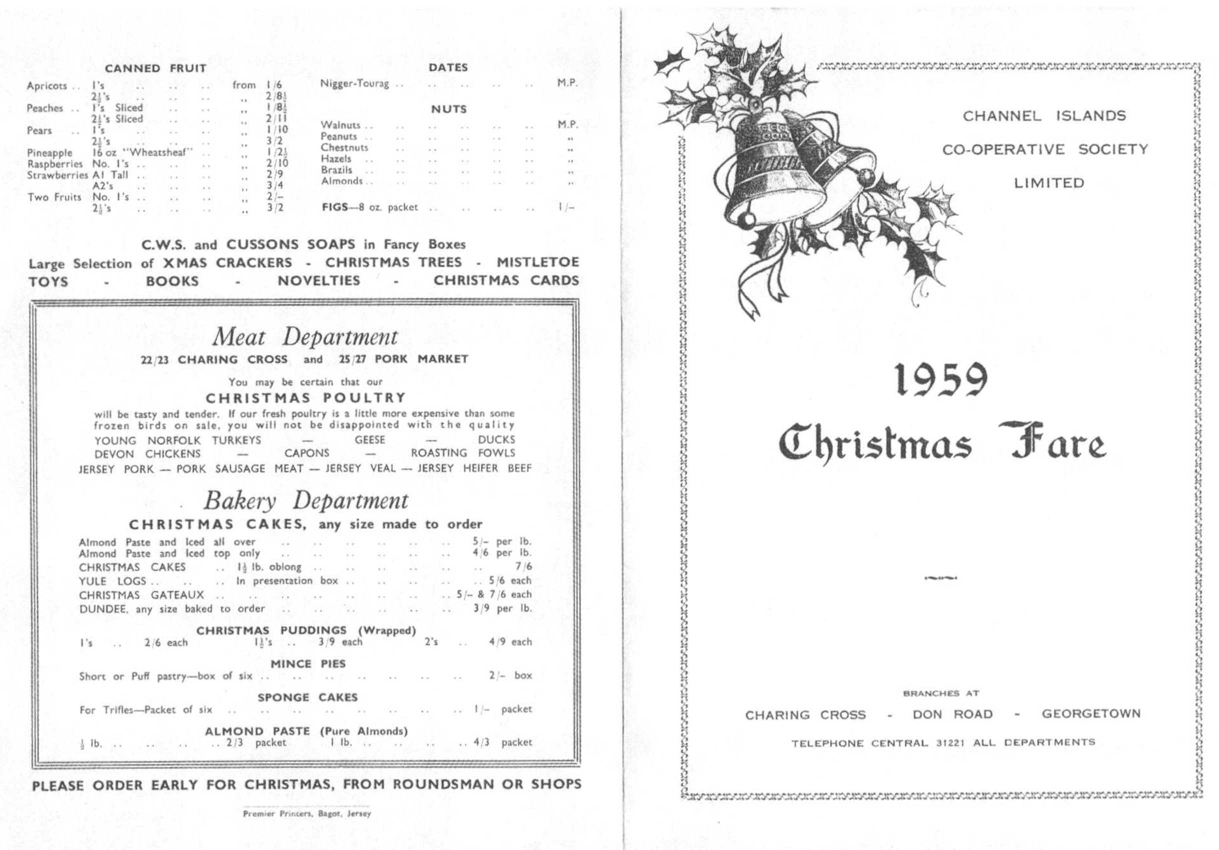

CANNED FRUIT

Apricots	1's	from	1/6
	2½'s	„	2/8½
Peaches	1's Sliced	„	1/8½
	2½'s Sliced	„	2/11
Pears	1's	„	1/10
	2½'s	„	3/2
Pineapple	16 oz "Wheatsheaf"	„	1/2½
Raspberries	No. 1's	„	2/10
Strawberries	A1 Tall	„	2/9
	A2's	„	3/4
Two Fruits	No. 1's	„	2/–
	2½'s	„	3/2

DATES

Nigger-Tourag	M.P.

NUTS

Walnuts	M.P.
Peanuts	„
Chestnuts	„
Hazels	„
Brazils	„
Almonds	„

FIGS—8 oz. packet .. 1/–

C.W.S. and CUSSONS SOAPS in Fancy Boxes
Large Selection of XMAS CRACKERS - CHRISTMAS TREES - MISTLETOE
TOYS - BOOKS - NOVELTIES - CHRISTMAS CARDS

Meat Department

22/23 CHARING CROSS and 25/27 PORK MARKET

You may be certain that our
CHRISTMAS POULTRY
will be tasty and tender. If our fresh poultry is a little more expensive than some frozen birds on sale, you will not be disappointed with the quality

YOUNG NORFOLK TURKEYS — GEESE — DUCKS
DEVON CHICKENS — CAPONS — ROASTING FOWLS
JERSEY PORK — PORK SAUSAGE MEAT — JERSEY VEAL — JERSEY HEIFER BEEF

Bakery Department

CHRISTMAS CAKES, any size made to order

Almond Paste and Iced all over		5/– per lb.
Almond Paste and Iced top only		4/6 per lb.
CHRISTMAS CAKES	1½ lb. oblong	7/6
YULE LOGS	In presentation box	5/6 each
CHRISTMAS GATEAUX		5/– & 7/6 each
DUNDEE, any size baked to order		3/9 per lb.

CHRISTMAS PUDDINGS (Wrapped)

1's .. 2/6 each 1½'s .. 3/9 each 2's .. 4/9 each

MINCE PIES

Short or Puff pastry—box of six .. 2/– box

SPONGE CAKES

For Trifles—Packet of six .. 1/– packet

ALMOND PASTE (Pure Almonds)

½ lb. .. 2/3 packet 1 lb. .. 4/3 packet

PLEASE ORDER EARLY FOR CHRISTMAS, FROM ROUNDSMAN OR SHOPS

Premier Printers, Bagot, Jersey

CHANNEL ISLANDS
CO-OPERATIVE SOCIETY
LIMITED

1959
Christmas Fare

BRANCHES AT
CHARING CROSS - DON ROAD - GEORGETOWN
TELEPHONE CENTRAL 31221 ALL DEPARTMENTS

8.4 Christmas came with its own special offers, as in this simple handout from 1959, with Gordons and other popular gins priced at 18s a bottle (90p) and biscuits, sweets and nuts sharing the billing, along with seasonal meat and bakery items

given a festive appearance, and detailing a comprehensive range of wines, spirits and similar items for the Christmas period. The 1959 issue, for example, listed among the whiskies Vat 69 and John Haig at 23s a bottle (£1.15), and many fancy tins and boxes of chocolates, fruit and nuts, the latter a great favourite at Christmastime. In that year Christmas cakes were on offer from the Bakery department, 'any size made to order', with a cake almond paste and iced all over at 5s per lb and almond paste and iced, top only, a little cheaper at 4s 6d a pound (**8.4**).

In more subtle guise, perhaps, the letters sent out to members from time to time, detailing the range of bakery products, for example, and their prices, were a persuasive invitation to order a little more than necessary as they could be delivered on request – no tiresome need to go back to the shop again. The samples shown, from 1966 (**8.5**) and 1970 (**8.6**), suggest a simplification in the approach, with wordage more than halved in the four years, and the new Co-op logo in evidence, although the same homely roneo look is maintained.

This practice of delivery to the door was yet another normal service and a form of advertising. Already well established by Le Riche and Orviss, and known throughout the trade, it could not be ignored by the Society. This facility became an essential feature of the grocery and provisions trade operating from Charing Cross and later from the Grocery Order Department in Don Road. As we have read, Charing Cross remained the principal shopping centre for members and, already by 1960, before Georgetown and Val Plaisant were rebuilt, it was necessary to relieve the pressure that occurred there from time to time. In 1960 members were told of new, additional services from the Don Road store; a small counter service shop was opened adjacent to the Grocery Order Department. Mr Peach issued a letter to members detailing the extent of the goods available, a surprisingly extensive range indeed.

But by then the shopping scene was changing. Already, in 1967, John Morris found it necessary to distribute an almost apologetic letter to members and customers advising them of a charge of 6d on every grocery order delivered (**5.3** above). Reluctant, no doubt, to lose custom by giving up the delivery service altogether, this was at least an

Wines and Spirits

all popular brands available

BRANDIES

	Bots.	½-Bots.
Logis Du May ***	22/–	11/–
Logis Du May V.S.O.P.	24/–	12/–
Logis Du May V.S.O.P. ¼'s 6/–		
Martell—Corvoisier, etc.	30/–	16/–
Pellisson ***	26/–	14/–
Pellisson 3 Crown—Golden Bell	16/6	9/–
Jules Belange ***	16/3	9/–

GINS

Gordons, etc.	18/–	9/9
Curtis—Nicholsons—Hill & Underwood	15/–	8/3
Rynbendes Pearl Gin	15/–	8/–

WHISKY

Vat 69—John Haig, etc.	23/–	12/6

RUMS

Nigger Head—Jamaican	15/–	8/3
Red Hart-Lemon Hart-Lambs Navy	20/3	10/9

PORTS

Cockburns Ruby	10/–	–
Sandemans Ruby*** & White	11/9	6/6
Sandemans Partner's Rich Ruby	14/9	–
Sandemans Picador Tawny	12/6	–
Sandemans Vintage 1947	17/–	–
Warres 1947	17/6	–
Hunt's Black Label	13/6	–
Hunt's Cream Port	15/–	8/–
V.P. Rich Ruby	5/9	–
Old Memory	4/9	–

TARRAGONA

Fine Old Darthez	5/9	–

LIQUEURS

Cointreau	27/6	14/6
Bols Advocaat	14/9	8/3
Bols Anisette	18/–	–
Bols Apricot Brandy	18/–	10/–
Bols Cherry Brandy	16/6	9/–
Bols Curacoa Orange	19/6	10/9
Bols Creme de Bananes	18/6	10/6
Bols Parfait Amour	18/–	10/–
Bols Peach Brandy	19/9	10/9
Marie Brizard Anisette	17/3	9/3
Marie Brizard Apry	21/–	–
Marie Brizard Cherry Brandy	19/–	10/6
Marie Brizard Creme de Cacao	17/3	9/3
Marie Brizard Kummel	21/6	11/6
Marie Brizard Peach Brandy	19/9	10/9
Benedictine	28/–	15/–

	Bots.	½-Bots.
Chartreuse Green	34/–	18/–
Chartreuse Yellow	26/6	14/–
Grants Cherry Brandy	18/6	10/–
Heering Cherry Brandy	21/6	11/3
Grand Marnier Rouge	27/–	14/3
Glayva Scotch Liqueur	28/–	14/9
Jamaican Tia-Maria	27/–	14/–
Van der Hum	18/3	10/–

SPARKLING WINES & CHAMPAGNES

POPULAR LINES IN STOCK

Baby Cham .. 1/3 plus 3d bottle (*Returnable*)

WHITE WINES

Graves Dry Select Calvet	10/9	6/3
Sauterne .. Calvet	8/9	5/–
St. Croix du Mont Jules Lafaure	9/6	–
Chateau Livran .. J. L. Denman	8/–	–
V. P. White	5/9	–
Spanish Sauterne	5/9	–

RED WINES

Vin Ordinaire .. Litre 5/3	4/3	–
Chateau Livran	8/–	–
St. Julien, Calvet	8/–	–
Beaujolais 1955	12/–	–

SHERRIES

Sandeman's Amontillado	12/6	–
Sandeman's Brown***	11/9	6/6
Sandeman's Dry Pale***	11/9	6/6
Sandeman's Pemartin	16/9	–
Sandeman's Armada Cream	15/3	8/3
Double Century	11/3	–
William & Humbert's Walnut Brown	14/–	7/6
Findlater's Dry Fly	14/–	–
William & Humbert's Dry Sack	17/6	–
Gonzalez Byass Tio-Pepe Dry	16/–	–
Gonzales Amontillado	11/3	–
Bristol Cream Harvey's	23/9	–
Bristol Milk Harvey's	20/9	–
Martins London Cream	19/9	–
Pedro-Domecq's Celebration Cream	14/6	–
V. P. Sherry	5/9	–

PIMMS

Pimm's No. 1	19/6	10/6

(Nos. 2, 3, 4 Pimms also stocked)

APERITIFS

Dubonnet	13/9	7/3
St. Raphael, Red & White	12/9	7/–
Byrrh Violet	8/9	–

VERMOUTHS

	Bots.	½-Bots.
Noilly Prat	14/–	7/6
Brega Rossi	12/9	–
Cinzano Red & White	12/9	7/6
Cinzano Dry	13/6	–
Martini Sweet	12/9	7/6
Martini Dry	13/9	–
Votrix Dry & Sweet	6/9	–

SQUASHES

Orange; Lemon; Lemon & Barley; Lime;
Blackcurrant; Grapefruit; Peppermint .. 3/– bottle
Ginger Cordial .. 2/9 bottle

GINGER WINES

Stones .. 8/6 V.P. .. 5/9

MINERALS

All kinds .. 8/– dozen including bottles

CIDER

Coates Flagons .. 2/2 plus 6d bottle

SYPHONS SODA WATER

10½d plus 3/– deposit

TONIC WATER & GINGER ALES

6/– dozen plus 3/– dozen deposit

SCHWEPPES

Bitter Lemon—Pineapple Juice—Tomato Juice

CIGARETTES

Packets of 50's obtainable in Christmas Packing.

CIGARS

La Fresca Whiffs 5's	2/3
La Fresca Whiffs 15's	6/9

CHOCOLATE LIQUEURS

Claret Filled	1/8
Gonnet 4 oz Plexiglass	6/9
Gonnet ½ lb. Cabinet	13/6

COCKTAIL CHERRIES

Special Offer 6/– & 3/–

COCKTAIL BISCUITS .. 2/– per packet

ALES—LAGERS—STOUTS

Local Ales etc., also Worthington; Bass; Guinness; Mackesons; Double Diamond etc.

Biscuits, Chocolates, Sweets, etc.

CHRISTMAS BISCUITS in FANCY TINS

C.W.S. 4 lb.	12/3
Rose Pompadour	8/6

Huntley & Palmer

"Christmas Assorted"	12/–
"Blue Wedgewood"	8/–
"Flower Tin"	3/9
"Golden Dragon"	8/6
"John O'Groats" Shortbread	5/–

Scribbans Kemp

Chocolate Fingers	2/6
Cheese Crisps	6/–

Cadbury

"Pastoral"	14/6
"Carnations"	6/8
Milk Wafer Tin	6/3

C.W.S. MINCEMEAT

1's .. 1/7½ 2's .. 2/9

CHOCOLATES

Cadburys

Various Prices .. from 2/6 to 26/–

Rowntrees

Various Prices .. from 2/– to 15/6

Frys

Various prices .. from 2/6 to 16/–

A WIDE RANGE OF **SWEETS**

C.W.S.

Teaching Clock	1/9
Nursery Tins	1/–
Sugared Almonds	2/6
Smokers' Outfit	1/11
Chocolate Cigars	7d.

Mackintosh

Quality Street 1 lb.	5/–
Quality Street 2 lb.	10/–
Quality Street 3 lb.	14/6

interim step towards the final termination of the service in the early 1970s. It was doubtful, anyway, if this personal service could have continued in the traditional manner. The ever-increasing traffic pressures in town and urban areas and even more importantly the escalating costs would have made the door-to-door service quite impracticable. The whole issue of delivery was taking on a new look; a subtle change was apparent, though perhaps not always appreciated by the customer.

One important change of this period was the introduction of commercial advertising to the Islands through Channel Television, which began its service in 1962. Very quickly local firms took advantage, the Society among them. A Board Minute of the early 1960s remarks upon the costs of advertising in the *Jersey Evening Post*, and it was resolved to try the new service. Co-op TV advertisements in various forms have appeared at intervals ever since and continue to do so.

The introduction of television was a turning point in advertising, which began to take on a new look; it became publicity in its fullest context. Unless it is really bold and informative an advert in a newspaper only fulfils its purpose once the paper is picked up and read, while television conveys the message immediately to the thousands who are viewing at any time. But despite the impact of television it did not take over completely. In fact, the national and international style of advertising, or publicity as it was becoming, took on a new, bold look with the ever-increasing range and perfection of information technology in the 1970s and, with a still cheaper form of colour printing now seen every day in the *Jersey Evening Post*, advertising took on a new look, a bolder confident look, almost brash at times.

A contributory factor in this new upward emphasis on publicity, or public relations, was the influx of money into Jersey's previously limited financial world. During the late 1970s and early 1980s, to meet the demands of the new finance houses and banks that were burgeoning in St Helier, many PR firms and marketing consultants opened up. These dealt in the newer styles of advertising by personally ascertaining a company's publicity and policy requirements, advising on the most effective way of catching the public eye and sometimes taking over the whole operation for its promotion in the press. And, though in no way connected with the financial world, such press promotions have been bold indeed on the Society's behalf.

TEL.: JERSEY CENTRAL 31221

THE CHANNEL ISLANDS CO-OPERATIVE SOCIETY LIMITED

REGISTERED OFFICE:
27 CHARING CROSS
ST HELIER · JERSEY C·I

WHOLESALE BAKERY DEPARTMENT. April, 1966.

Dear Sir/Madam,

It may be that we already have the pleasure of supplying your establishment with our bakery productions. If this is the case, we are pleased to attach our up to date price list for the coming season.

If, however, we have not as yet had the pleasure of supplying you with any of our goods, perhaps we may be permitted to put before you the main points of the service we offer. Our Bakery Manager will be pleased to call on you personally, at your convenience if you wish it, to discuss any aspect of our trading which may interest you.

We will deliver, free of charge, samples of bread or any other items we produce if you desire it. These samples are selected from normal productions so that the quality of our goods can be easily and fairly judged.

Wholesale terms are supplied and are normally the subject of agreement with our Bakery Manager.

We offer daily delivery, absolutely reliable and in time for breakfast. The time of serving breakfast varies of course, our method is to ask at what time delivery is required and should we be unable to meet this request precisely we say so, and then of course endeavour to offer an acceptable alternative time. We do not make rash promises that we are unable to keep.

Should any of our wholesale accounts find that they are in urgent need of a particular commodity, a call to our Bakery Office, Central 31221, Extension 23, will ensure that everything possible is done to meet their requirements. We really are prepared to go to a great deal of trouble on occasions of this sort to help our customers.

You will see on the attached list that we make a fairly comprehensive variety of "Cocktail" size goods. In this respect, if anyone has something "special" in mind, we do our utmost to meet the demand.

One feature of our price list worth special mention is SWEETS. You would find that the net price of a single portion is about 4d. to 5d. and these portions are not "mean in size".

If, after reading this letter you feel that you would like our Bakery Production and Sales Manager, Mr. J. Hedley to call upon you, please ring Central 31221, Extension 23, when arrangements for his visit to suit your convenience can be made.

Yours faithfully,

[signature]

Managing Secretary.

8.5 The Wholesale Bakery Department adopted the personal approach in the mid-1960s

The Channel Islands Co-operative Society Ltd.

Registered Office:

27, Charing Cross
St. Helier
Jersey, C.I.

Telephone: Jersey Central 31221

BAKERY DEPARTMENT
Wholesale Section

March, 1970.

Dear Sir or Madam,

We have pleasure in submitting our price list for the 1970 season.

We are installing modern travelling ovens in time for this season's trade to improve our quality and to bake our goods as late as possible up to delivery times. Consequently, we offer you a really good and FRESH product.

In all the town area and certain parts of the country, we offer a before breakfast delivery of bread and rolls, and in ALL areas a DAILY delivery. If, for some unforeseen or urgent reason, a second delivery is required, we are happy to oblige.

All discounts are personally arranged, generally by amounts purchased, by myself. A 'phone call to one of the following numbers will be sufficient to arrange for me to call at a time and date convenient to you.

Mornings	-	Central 33590
Afternoons	-	" 31221, Ext. 23.

Yours faithfully,

J. HEDLEY,

Bakery Manager.

8.6 In 1970 the key words 'fresh' and 'daily' are prominent in the service message, again from the Bakery

JERSEY EVENING POST, THURSDAY, JANUARY 18, 1968 9

Co-operative Society's first Jersey supermarket

Lots of room to combat 'shopping jams'

THE cheapest roasting chickens in the Island, guaranteed savings each week for everyone and plenty of room to park your car while you shop—this is the exciting news from the Co-operative's brand new Food Market which has just opened in Val Plaisant.

by JILL CHIDGEY

With over 200 cut-price items of well-known brands piled on the neatly stacked shelves, the bright and airy food hall has been designed to give plenty of room to shoppers and their loaded trolleys, so avoiding the usual "shopping jams". The actual hall size is 2,100 sq. ft. and apart from accommodating the central and side shelves, has about 50 ft. run of refrigerated counters, deep freezes and refrigerators for the meats and cooked food, a butchery, a greengrocery department and a large stockroom.

A special lift is installed at the rear so that unloading is quick and easy and goods are taken straight up to the stockroom, and to help all customers three economy check-outs have been brought over from the Co-operative's wholesale works at Dudley in Worcester. These check-outs are most efficient and are at present used all over Europe—the speed at which they can be operated prevents those awful delays when one has to stand waiting patiently with a heavy basket or has only bought one item and is in a hurry.

Store manager

Everything in the food hall has been clearly marked price-wise and is easy to find, but should anyone run into difficulties there is a very capable staff of 16 under the personal supervision of Mr. C. Pinel, the store manager. A Jerseyman, Mr. Pinel has been with the society for many years and has spent several of them as manager of the grocery shop in Charing Cross. His assistant manager, Mrs. Rouse, has also been with the "Co-op" for many years and for the past ten was manageress at the shop in Georgetown.

The well-stocked meat department with delicious local Springside chickens over 3 lb. in weight and costing only 8s. 6d., juicy legs of lamb, beef and pork, sausages and lard, is under the eagle eye of butcher Mervyn Stratford, who has five years' experience in this trade. Michael Burrell will also be there to help you choose your cooked meats, bacons and provisions and Mrs. Falle keeps an attractive greengrocery counter, with much of the fruit and many of the vegetables pre-packed so that they are easy to take home and free from unnecessary dirt.

Quite normal

In charge of all the buying is Mr. J. Peach, who today especially stressed the fact that all the cut-prices are normal procedure and not just special opening offers which will disappear after a week or two. Mr. Peach, as well as buying for this, the society's very first Food Market in Jersey, looks after the buying side of the stores in Guernsey and so his knowledge is obviously extensive.

Those who love fresh cakes, pastries and crispy bread will be pleased to know that Mr. J. Hedley, the bakery manager at Gosse Green Marsh, Beaumont will be delivering three times daily.

This is, of course, the very first supermarket to be opened in Jersey by the society and it will be able to supply a large number of people living in the Robin Hood, Val Plaisant, and Trinity Road area, as well as those who do not want to go into the crowded town and who want to do all their purchasing under one roof, and find a safe place to park their cars.

Apart from the many cut-price offers, especially for the young housewife needing baby foods, rusks or Paddi-pads, the store offers you a chance to become a member of the society.

Dividend

It only costs 2s. to join and then for every £1 of purchases you make, a 1s. dividend is paid into your account and can be claimed in a lump sum in December—ready for the Christmas turkey and all its trimmings! Last year the society paid £65,000 to shareholders in the Channel Islands as dividends on their purchases!

Certainly the way to cut your cost of living—four cherry fancies with every large loaf, 8 oz. Maxwell House and Nescafe 8s. 8d., Paddipads 1s. 6d., New Zealand butter 3s. 1d. per lb., Ovaltine 2s. 8d., rice puddings 10d., giant Branston pickle 2s. 10d., giant Chef tomato sauce 2s. 5d., self-raising flour 1s. 9d., Top Dog 1s. 6d., Kit-e-Kat three for 1s. 9d., Top Cat 8d., Heinz baby foods 7d., giant Kelloggs cornflakes 2s. 1d., Farleys rusks 1s. 6d., Brillo 1s. 9d., Dixcel rolls 1s. 4d., Lucozade 2s. 4d. and large Vaseline shampoo 2s. 4d. — plus free nylons with every £1 spent on groceries.

Prices on the well-stocked shelves are clearly marked and everything is very easy to find

The modern exterior is not easy to miss and at the rear of the store there is plenty of parking space

It is easy to join the Co-operative Society at the new food market and certainly worth it, as this new member will soon find out

Guernsey election to be re-run?

From Our Correspondent

GUERNSEY States members are to be asked to support a move to declare void last month's Douzeniers' election in St. Martin's. The required number of seven States members have signed a requête which is to be placed before the House at its next meeting asking for a change in the law to enable the election to be re-run.

The election on December 1 was to have been a three-cornered one for two seats on the Douzaine, but it was announced that the nomination of one of the candidates, former Senior Constable Mr. Roydon Lucas, was invalid because his seconder was not on the electoral rôle.

The other two candidates, Mr. Herbert Borne and Mr. Roger Berry, were automatically elected but parishioners are not satisfied and the Douzaine itself feels that the election should be held again.

Jersey soldier fined £9

AN 18-year-old Jerseyman, Brian John Pallot, who is on leave from the Royal Corps of Signals, was fined a total of £9 at the Police Court this morning on charges of being drunk and disorderly, refusing to leave licensed premises when ordered to do so by a policeman, and with using foul and disgusting language.

Centenier B. S. Medder told the Court that Pallot had been brought to the Police Station last night after the management of the First Tower Hotel had complained that he refused to leave the premises. Pallot had been in a very drunken condition and had resisted the police violently. A considerable amount of force had to be used to get the accused into the cells.

The Magistrate, Mr. Michael Newell, after Pallot said nothing in his defence, fined him £3 on each charge. Pallot offered to pay £5 of the fine this morning. The Magistrate agreed, ordering him to pay the remainder within one month, or he would serve seven days in prison.

8.7 The Jersey Evening Post of 18 January 1968 gave prominence as a news item to the opening of Jersey's first supermarket in Val Plaisant, with a half-page Co-op advertisement below

8.8 On the following evening, 19 January, the Co-op splashed out on a full page in the `Evening Post`, with bargain opening prices. The format was still simple and in black and white

8.9 A decade further on, in 1978, and again a full page in black and white, here announcing the rebuilding of the old Western Stores its reopening as the St Peter's Food Centre

This bolder trend in newspaper advertising brought the Society into full light and even if, as we noted above, it was only seen once when the paper was glanced through, a far greater impact was there to be remembered. The opening of Jersey's first supermarket at Val Plaisant in January 1968 is a case in point: the *Jersey Evening Post* gave its news report nearly half a page, while the Society took out a half-page black and white advertisement, its three photographs almost echoing those in the article (**8.7**). The next day, the first day of trading, the Society took a full page to advertise 'cut price money savers', with the neat slogan 'Every time you spend – you save!!' (**8.8**). A decade later, in 1978, the opening of the St Peter's Food Centre was advertised in a full page of the *Evening Post*, making do with one graphic and 12 words of text (**8.9**).

In 1998, the Society recognised the vital importance of 'marketing' by appointing Jim Plumley as Marketing Manager, the first such move to co-ordinate its marketing policies.

An example of using the news columns to support its claims was the two-page spread in the September 1999 *Jersey Evening Post* on grocery price comparisons between Jersey and UK, the Jersey column being, of course, of Co-op prices. Parallel with this trend comes the full-page spread extolling the values in food and domestic items to be obtained from the Fresh Food Stores (an example is shown in **8.10**). It is full circle from the

8.10 By 1998 food advertising had moved on considerably: here is half of a double-page spread in the *Jersey Evening Post* for a 'carnival of taste'

modest black and white panels in the *Evening Post* of the 1920s, but now bold and often with a touch of humour. Recruitment advertising in the press, too, has become fully up to date, with fewer but telling words, in both black and white, from 1999 (**8.11**) or colour (**8.12**); and Jersey buses promoting the Locale stores convey the message in the few seconds of attention time an onlooker might have (**8.13**).

Concurrent with this ever-changing trend in advertising is the return towards deliveries, not in quite the same personal manner as with the grocery

8.11 Simple graphics and a strong message made this an effective recruitment advertisement in the Jersey Evening Post from 1999

8.12 A more 'arty' approach was tried, in colour, to recruit for a coffee shop development in a Homemaker Store, again in the Evening Post

8.13 As a 'big player' in the local economy, the Co-op is a resourceful advertiser, taking advantage of every opportunity to keep its name in the public eye

order or the wide range of bakery products, but still delivery to the customer's home in vehicles specially built with freezer, cool and ambient compartments, a far cry from previous delivery vehicles.

Warehousing and Distribution

We have read of the ever-pressing need for warehousing in both Islands for both grocery stocks and the heavy and bulky electrical goods and furniture, which need careful handling and stacking. While customer demand was naturally concentrated on Charing Cross and Market Street it was possible to maintain stocks on the premises but, as we have read, this caused congestion and often difficult working conditions for the staff.

These difficulties are often referred to in the Board Minutes, and as the number of shops grew so did the burden of keeping them adequately stocked. This was more so in Guernsey, perhaps, where the two early shops were much smaller and where early expansion occurred.

Step by step this pressing issue of storage and warehousing would be kept in reasonable balance by the building of additional storage – the Beaumont Warehouse, for example, was erected after considerable delay and procrastination by the Island Development Committee – or by the leasing of existing covered storage space, which seems to have been more easily arranged in Guernsey than in Jersey. In fact, in the Guernsey operation, the stores at Lowlands on the Braye Road are serving the double purpose of combining the essential need for storage next to the retail showroom.

Over the years the growth in demand for all the many and varied products of the Co-op, now clearly designated Food and Non-Food, has led to a clear division between them in storage and delivery: no longer are they under the same roof. Food, being the more rapid in movement of stock and purchase, now boasts a computerised system of storage, ordering and delivery from the bulk food warehouse at Longue Hougue Lane, Guernsey (**8.14, 8.15**) and in Bellozanne Valley, Jersey (**8.16, 8.17**). Here Ron Morris controls all movements of food and liquor stocks and all orders and deliveries from the UK mainland and France (**8.18**). A comprehensive computer system keeps him in touch with all store managers and their demands. And non-food stock nowadays covers a very wide range of goods in electricals and furniture, far heavier and bulkier than was ever envisaged in the initial trading days (**8.19**). There is now storage and transport for non-food items based at St Peter's Technical Park, where stock is slower-moving than food at Bellozanne but it still needs specialised equipment.

Both Bellozanne and St Peter's have their needs in transport and deliveries watched over and maintained for many years by Mike Carter, a long-serving and versatile member of staff who, on a roving commission, cared for far more than he could have imagined when he joined the staff in 1954 (**8.20**). Mike began his service with the Society at the age of 15, earning £2 per week. He was inclined towards baking and confectionery so he started work at the old Todt Bakery at Beaumont. As the Society grew and developed its shops and delivery services so the motor vehicles multiplied and required regular servicing and maintenance, preferably on the spot. Mike became interested, and eventually involved, in transport, and for many years managed the vehicle maintenance workshop, which also has moved to Bellozanne from its previous location beside the old Beaumont Warehouse.

But this is only part of Mike's work, for he is also responsible for the maintenance of all forklift trucks, electric lighting and equipment throughout the shops and stores, much of it of a specialised nature, and for all vehicles of all types and sizes that make up the Co-op fleet (**8.21**).

All this is far removed from the early days of the Society when the little Ford vans would take bread and the grocery orders, previously given in and put up in the Don Road Despatch, to members around the town and the country parishes, almost invariably by the same drivers who knew all their customers as friends.

We read earlier of the seemingly interminable delays that beset the Society in its simple endeavour to build the new warehouse on its own land at Beaumont. It was not until the early 1970s that the Board could express some satisfaction at being, at last, established in its own purpose-built warehouse. But it would not be long before the Board was brought face to face with the unavoidable fact that its plans for future expansion through modernised shops and new supermarkets would place ever greater stress on the need for adequate and valid maintenance of stocks. The smartest and most up-to-date store will not hold its customers,

8.14 The Guernsey warehouse is interconnected to Bellozanne through the IT link (photo G Symons)

8.15 Nick Le Sauvage recently retired after over 37 years with the Co-op, most of it as a driver delivering from the warehouse to shops. Nick likes to keep moving even in his time off, having been a member of the Guernsey Walkers Club for more than 40 years and completing the Parish Church circuit practically every year (photo G Symons)

8.16 Interior at Bellozanne, where delivery to the customer begins from racking up to nine or ten pallets high

8.17 Forklift truck with storeman/driver at the top reaching out to a pallet for ticketing

or even its members, unless it can provide everything they need off the shelf. There had been occasional criticism in the past from customers who had remarked of empty spaces on the shelves, and management knew this as an occasional lapse by new and inexperienced staff but also as a weakness of the system for ordering stock and the means for delivering it.

Little could it be envisaged then that within a very few years the pressure for more storage, particularly for food, would render the new Beaumont store of 18,000 square feet less than adequate. In the mid-to-late 1970s Allan Smith was frequently and firmly reporting to the Board that in both Islands the need for adequate storage, with space for the future, was an urgent issue. He emphasised then that there seemed little hope for a permanent solution.

Beaumont did relieve the immediate pressure, but at a cost. It began life with limited racking, pallets stacked one upon another being the norm for bulk storage. In fact, the architect's design elevations, as required and approved eventually by

8.18 A younger Ron Morris, now Manager at Bellozanne Food Warehouse, loading his vehicle at Beaumont Food, Beaumont, the main warehouse prior to Bellozanne being purchased

8.19 All forklift drivers have to pass a proficiency test: the four drivers at the Non-Food Store at St Peter's Technical Park, 1997, from the left: Ernie Russell, Derek Herridge, Paul Dowinton and Ian Smith (© Stuart McAlister Photographers)

8.20 Mike Carter in the old Beaumont Vehicle Maintenance Workshop, now removed to Bellozanne

8.21 At the Non-Food Store a special fork lift truck with a long boom handles the carpet rolls with ease. Ernie Russell shows us how it's done

Planning, had of necessity lowered the stacking from four pallets high to three, thus reducing the total amount of usable storage space. Ted Tadier, who was Warehouse Manager at the time, describes the handling and the loading as difficult and awkward; while the forklift could bring the pallets out to the vehicle, they still had to be handled manually, to be pushed across the floor of the vehicle and into position to enable the correct unloading of each order at each store.

This was an untenable situation that demanded action. Eventually extensive steel racking was installed in 1977, and Unitainers were introduced to facilitate easier transfer of new stock from vehicle to the stock room at the store and around the aisles to the shelves and cabinets. Readers will have seen these Unitainers without realising their worth to the staff: tall, lightweight tubular frames on a wheeled platform being unloaded in the aisles just where you want to reach for a bottle of your favourite sauce! But how useful they have proved to be in keeping the shelves and cabinets adequately filled, and with greater ease and convenience for the staff.

It was to be some years before a solution to the food warehousing problem presented itself, at least in the longer term. It was a fortuitous situation that the former Jersey Coal Distributors Board, of which the Society was a shareholder, was sold to British Fuels Limited, which already had a successful operation in Guernsey. Imports of coal to Jersey would now be prepacked and could be stored in the smaller of the two existing warehouses. This enabled the Society to purchase the larger building and convert a previous coal store into a modern food warehouse. This building has since been extensively refurbished and extended to become one of the largest distribution centres on the Island, equipped with the latest radio frequency technology to efficiently store and supply the food stores. Computerised ordering by the stores drives daily deliveries of products, enabling minimum stockrooms, maximum retail space and fresher stock.

A far cry from the early days.

Wishing you a Happy
Retirement ??
John Morris
CO
CO OP
DISCO
99
TEA
21
CO OP
DISCO
KIT
27
DISCO

Chapter 9

The Eighties

As the 1970s drew to a close, the Society was about to enter a new and demanding phase in its history. It was now 1980: 25 years had passed since that memorable decision to amalgamate and combine the two former Societies, and it was now time to fulfil the aspirations and hopes of those intervening years.

In retrospect we can see the fundamental difference that now became apparent in the overall direction of the Society and its several parts. For some 40 years it had been without question the prerogative of one man, with the support of the Management Committee of the day and always with the advice and guidance of Mr Booth and the CWS to lead the way, or sometimes to contain the enthusiasm of management. In later years, as General Manager and Secretary, John Morris had acquired a knowledge and experience unparalleled in the development of the Society and, even beyond that, through the darker days of the Occupation (**9.1, 9.2**). The Society owes much of its success to John and to the long-serving members of staff in shop and office who shared with him that vision of the future that was now near at hand.

Times were certainly changing ever more quickly, and pressures were now evident that could not be contained or exercised within the province of one man and the supporting staff of the office. That such dedicated service had achieved success in so many areas is beyond doubt, but the problems ahead would demand a wider approach. The Society was indeed fortunate that the staff and the means to implement this approach were already in place.

Opposite page **9.1** This home-made retirement card for John Morris in 1980 highlighted his sporting pursuits

It had became obvious that a more corporate form of management was now necessary, indeed essential, to direct the affairs of the Society. With the office of General Manager, now divested of Secretarial duties, Mr Allan Smith and his team of senior managers, Les Woodcock and Jim Hopley on Food Trades, with Fred Hamon and Brian Smith on Non-Food Trades, were about to face a new era of progress above anything that had been achieved before. But such further progress would not be maintained without a hitch or two.

Les Woodcock, like many of the Society's senior staff, began his 40 years of Co-operative service in a very modest way, as errand boy with the Barnsley British Society, collecting and delivering orders from shop to customer, sometimes by horse and dray. In the very early 1960s Les must have shown some natural aptitude, for the Manager encouraged him to attend night school. Two nights a week for four years gained him a scholarship, which led to a year at the Co-operative College at Loughborough and to an appointment as Store Manager with CRS at Huddersfield in 1968. He came to Jersey in 1976 and joined our Society where his experience brought him into contact with Allan Smith and subsequently to inclusion in the new management team as Food Trades Manager.

Les spoke with some modest pride of the initiatives that the new team introduced on training policies for the up-and-coming junior staff, on market research and in-store designs to attract the shopping public. He also remarked on the differences in management style and the social differences between the Islands, which had been observed for many years previously and were to be noted again in the years to come.

These initiatives that Les spoke of are an indication of the new direction that management was

9.2 The inside of the card shown in **9.1** gives a potted history of John Morris's achievements in over 40 years' service to the Society

now taking, with a particular emphasis on an adequate staff training policy. The planning of the new Don Street store, the biggest Co-op venture so far, had probably prompted the Board to accept that the recruitment of more staff for a rather different and specialised sort of shop also needed planning. Looking back half a century and more to the late 1940s and early 1950s, the shop manager himself took on junior staff, to be trained on the job. But the days of bacon boys and Saturday girls are now long since over. Several of those who started their Co-op careers in that simple way continued in their chosen vocation with pride and personal satisfaction to eventual retirement after long and efficient service to the Co-operative cause.

Now, in the 1980s, business was a tighter, faster affair. Staff needed adequate support in their first year or two and continuing encouragement to take advantage of opportunities available at Highlands College and Loughborough College, or through the many correspondence courses leading to certificates or diplomas in their chosen areas of work. Everyday business was far more demanding over a wider field than ever before, particularly for junior staff, who must be well informed on matters that were little heard of even a few years before. Trade union agreements, Health & Safety legislation, even credit card transactions, the ever-present risk of theft from the shelves, and other aspects of a busy shop life, all require a disciplined schedule of Training with a capital T, and not merely a drill in shelf filling, important though that is.

It was into this field of work that Richard Le Brocq was appointed in April 1982 as Training Controller, based initially at Beaumont Food offices, with access to all necessary administrative and clerical assistance. His brief was all-embracing, to cover, in addition to all food and services, the furniture, electrical and durable good and furnishing and allied business. In this, Fred Hamon was later to have a decisive and progressive influence when Don Street was completed and opened in 1981.

Richard's first introduction to the world of the Co-op was by way of a visit with Allan Smith to CWS Manchester, and to the College at Loughborough. This was followed by a further introduction to all shops and stores in Jersey and Guernsey and a full overview of merchandising.

Richard's next move was to stage a two-day presentation to all management staff at the Mermaid Hotel on the whole subject of training. Man-management and motivation from the top were two important objectives to pass on by example, particularly to the supervisors, who are responsible for the final displays and sales. This presentation was given by Ross Tew, a management consultant from the mainland.

It was inevitable that a little murmuring would arise – 'I don't need to be told how to do my job' – but grumbles were quickly lost in the overall response of satisfaction that at last the best interests of the staff and the business were being realized and that one could not exist without the willing co-operation of the other.

Having opened the subject in a positive manner, Richard's next priority was to offer a presentation on merchandising, one session of which was in a quiz form to add a little offbeat interest for the shop staff and for the night staff, who are responsible for the shelf displays and ticketing in the bigger stores. The quiz was presented by slide projection on screen, with the question – right or wrong – to be given to a pair of pictures showing slight disparities, a bottle on the wrong shelf, or perhaps on the right shelf but turned slightly to mask the label. A simple test but needing a sharp eye to detect quickly the differences and to remember them! Training can have an element of fun built in to hold the interest.

Later, a number of courses for the Greenfruit department, were successfully run for the relevant staff, in conjunction with the late Brian Ahearn, who was then Greenfruit Controller.

These exercises and presentations were giving Richard a grip on the weaknesses of the existing system and the full needs of the training programme at all levels.

As his experience of the Co-op widened other challenges surfaced. Richard saw the need for rather more personnel organisation between senior management to enable the highs and lows of activity – for example, during the period approaching the AGM and at Christmas and New Year – to be evened out as far as possible by a little forethought and anticipation. To this end Richard devised and produced a diary of priorities to enable managers and their assistants to agree between themselves the courses of action needed and adjustment of workloads, a move that would ease the pressure on the staff below at critical times. Later, a course was organised for managers covering all aspects of the Diploma of the Institute of Grocery Distribution, leading to a number of successes over the years.

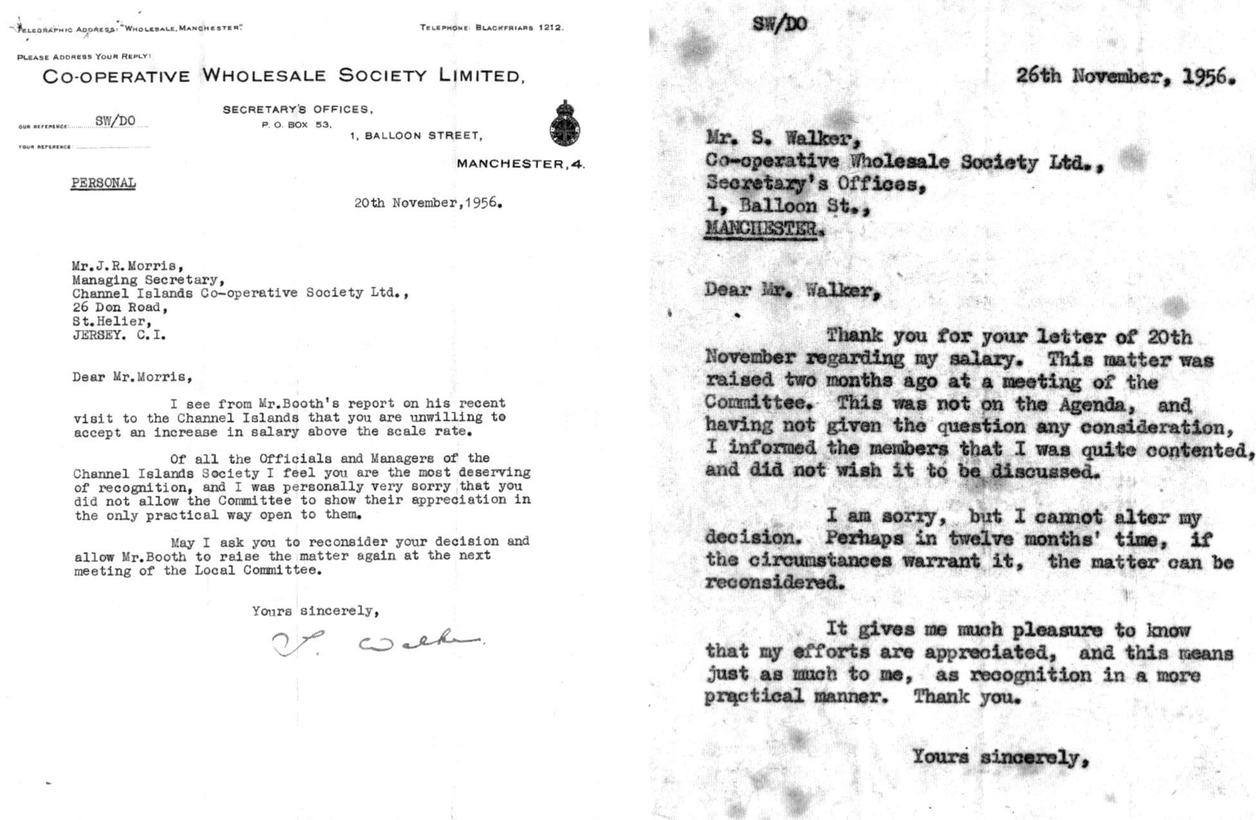

TELEGRAPHIC ADDRESS: "WHOLESALE, MANCHESTER." TELEPHONE: BLACKFRIARS 1212.

PLEASE ADDRESS YOUR REPLY:

CO-OPERATIVE WHOLESALE SOCIETY LIMITED,

SECRETARY'S OFFICES,
P. O. BOX 53.
1, BALLOON STREET,
MANCHESTER, 4.

OUR REFERENCE SW/DO

YOUR REFERENCE

PERSONAL

20th November, 1956.

Mr. J. R. Morris,
Managing Secretary,
Channel Islands Co-operative Society Ltd.,
26 Don Road,
St. Helier,
JERSEY. C. I.

Dear Mr. Morris,

I see from Mr. Booth's report on his recent visit to the Channel Islands that you are unwilling to accept an increase in salary above the scale rate.

Of all the Officials and Managers of the Channel Islands Society I feel you are the most deserving of recognition, and I was personally very sorry that you did not allow the Committee to show their appreciation in the only practical way open to them.

May I ask you to reconsider your decision and allow Mr. Booth to raise the matter again at the next meeting of the Local Committee.

Yours sincerely,

S. Walker

SW/DO

26th November, 1956.

Mr. S. Walker,
Co-operative Wholesale Society Ltd.,
Secretary's Offices,
1, Balloon St.,
MANCHESTER.

Dear Mr. Walker,

Thank you for your letter of 20th November regarding my salary. This matter was raised two months ago at a meeting of the Committee. This was not on the Agenda, and having not given the question any consideration, I informed the members that I was quite contented, and did not wish it to be discussed.

I am sorry, but I cannot alter my decision. Perhaps in twelve months' time, if the circumstances warrant it, the matter can be reconsidered.

It gives me much pleasure to know that my efforts are appreciated, and this means just as much to me, as recognition in a more practical manner. Thank you.

Yours sincerely,

9.3 This exchange of letters in 1956 between the CWS and John Morris suggests the character of the man

The accent throughout these initial stages of the training programme was to instil the spirit of leadership through example by managers and assistants down to supervisors. Ultimately, Richard ran a series of two-day Action-Centred Leadership courses for managers and supervisors. The idea here was to put over to the leaders of the Co-op 'What a leader has to do in order to lead'. These courses were well received and many of the participants have gone on to do very well, a notable example being David Palmer who, as we shall read later, eventually become involved in the Grand Marché – one of the Society's finest ventures.

In all these progressions, which of course covered both Islands, John Cuthbertson was of considerable support, being able to give the Guernsey viewpoint from personal experience. John recalls his contacts with Richard with a wry humour, telling of occasions when, while discussing a particular aspect of training, Richard would be reminded of his experiences in the RAF.

Needless to say, Richard Le Brocq would not be satisfied with his efforts until he knew that his programme was achieving results, results from which he might see a need for adjustment in detail or perhaps a slight difference in approach. He obtained a flow of feedback through a one-day course he ran at intervals to enable staff to offer comments or to enquire further on aspects of a course they had just been through.

As this programme continued and developed it became apparent that training would become a positive and regular feature of staff enhancement, giving every individual an opportunity they might otherwise have missed. With this hope and intention in mind, Richard finally resigned in August 1986 to take up the post of Assistant Secretary and ADC to the Lt Governor at Government House. He was invited to meet the Board for the last time to receive their thanks for his original work programme on training and their congratulations on his appointment to the new post.

In this openly progressive future not only was training to take a positive place but administration too. A new outlook was needed to work in parallel with the new management. In the 1956 Annual Report the name of John Morris appears as Manager and Secretary, a combined office that he continued to hold until his retirement 24 years later (**9.3**). The Annual Report for 1981 gives, for the first time, the names of Vernon Howells as Secretary and Allan Smith as Manager.

This was the moment for fundamental change. As the following pages will tell us, the Society was indeed moving forward into a new era, a time when the administrative duties would become too demanding for one man to attempt to combine successfully the increasing secretarial work with that of management as had been done so well in the past.

Vernon Howells had arrived in Jersey in 1955 from the Brecon Co-operative Society of Wales. Having served the Society for some time as Assistant Secretary he was appointed Secretary in 1980. As the Directors' Report for 1989 states on his retirement, 'he brought to the Channel Islands Society new ideas and a keen and instinctive feel for what would be best for Members and Staff in meeting the challenge of progress in a rapidly changing commercial world'. A popular man, he teamed his increasing secretarial work with new management to the lasting benefit of members and staff, the latter then numbering over 500, but the time had come for a successor to take over. Who should it be?

Looking back a little to 1960, a young Welshman, Colin Rees Davies, born in Carmarthen, was already very close to the Co-operative ideals, for his father was Manager of the main Co-operative store in the city. On completing his education Colin entered the Co-operative College to pursue secretarial studies. He then joined the staff of the Carmarthen Industrial Co-operative Society, which was eventually taken over by CRS. This brought him into contact with Mr Booth and with our Society through his contacts with the filing of Head Office Returns.

When an opportunity arose for a move to Jersey, Mr Booth, always a good friend and mentor to our Society, brought Colin over to introduce him to the Board as a Clerical Assistant to Vernon Howells. Thus accepted, Colin's first position was in the Machine Room, where he was a contemporary with Karen Young, working on the main purchase ledgers. One of his first briefs was to modernise the slow and heavy ledger procedures, spoken of so feelingly by Karen, and to introduce calculators and accounting machines. Albeit these were still mechanical they did ease much mental arithmetic and pencil and paperwork.

During this early period and anticipating a return to Wales within a few years, Colin was living in digs, but eventually he decided to remain in Jersey. He married in 1969 and settled here, though in 1971 he left the Society for a few years to go to Hill Samuel and then the Royal Trust of Canada.

9.4 Colin Rees Davies, Society Secretary from 1988 to 1999 (© Stuart McAlister Photographers)

As Vernon Howells's retirement drew nearer, John Morris, alert to the future, saw a potential in Colin and personally approached him to enquire if he would consider returning to take up the appointment of Society Accountant. Fortunately for the Society, Colin did take up this offer in 1976 to that post and, all the details being amicably agreed, on the retirement of John Morris in 1980, Colin became Assistant Secretary and Office Manager. This was followed in 1988, as Vernon Howells retired, by promotion to the office of Society Secretary.

And with that promotion the office of Secretary became firmly established 'equal but independent' to Management. In the Annual Report for 1999, the Board reported 'Colin Rees Davies, Secretary of the Society since 1988 and whose employment with the Society spans 35 years, will be retiring on 31st March 1999. The Board and Management offer their sincere thanks to Colin, a man who has given so many years of service to our Society and to the Co-operative Movement' (**9.4**).

Colin must have looked back with a smile to a particular early experience when he was called up very early one New Year's Day and told to report to the shop. It was New Year's Day 1964. Charing

Cross had suffered a serious fire during the night. One particular task was to salvage what could be recovered of files, reports and the like, but the equipment, filing cabinets and cupboards were too hot to handle. Colin and his group were detailed to bring buckets of water from hydrants near the Town Hall with which to cool down and clean up a little of the mess that was once the Society offices (see **5.1**).

The old order, which had derived much guidance and support in technical and administrative matters from Mr Booth and the professional departments of CWS, was receding. Though it would still be possible to call on them for advice, the future would involve introducing independent professionals to manage the bigger projects that were now envisaged.

Without doubt the most important and immediate of these would be the new Don Street store, the biggest and most complex venture so far undertaken by the Society. But within that complexity lay the answer to the many problems and difficulties that had defied solution for so long. The most urgent of these was the redevelopment of Charing Cross for which several ideas and plans for rearrangement had been discussed but of necessity held in abeyance for lack of space and opportunity. One of the difficulties frequently referred to was the mix of sport, clothing, furnishing, electrical goods and drapery, all remaining in close proximity to food without the clear distinction desired.

Don Street would at last enable that clear division to be achieved by taking in all the durable goods, and giving Charing Cross its long-awaited opportunity to redevelop to the full potential of the site. The terms Food and Non-Food would in future differentiate quite clearly the respective departments and their scope.

The architects were working urgently on the plans for the Don Street store to produce a design acceptable to the IDC. Although provisional planning permission had been received the IDC was more than a little particular about the elevations. This was understandable: a prime corner site within the town area demanded an elevation that was compatible with its surroundings and the adjacent buildings. To satisfy this demand new drawings were prepared, which were eventually accepted, and piling began in April 1980.

Considering the extent of the Don Street site and the bulk and design of the store itself progress was rapid despite some impatience over a delay on the piling work. But by September 1981 the Board was able to visit the site before its meeting on the 27th of the month. One can imagine the inner sense of satisfaction felt by the Board to be so soon discussing the layout of the various departments, the appointments of some of the departmental controllers and to hear of the proposed opening date of Tuesday, 24 November 1981.

Those inner feelings would have been further gratified by the presentation at that Board meeting of drawings of a new integrated shop front for the whole of the Charing Cross premises and an intimation of a new identity for the site. The redevelopment had been under discussion for some considerable time, as we have read previously, but until Don Street became a reality the details could only have been conjecture. Now they began to take positive shape and form, as the Board heard at the meeting of 9 November 1980. A comprehensive discussion took place of the problems involved in redeveloping the Charing Cross premises once existing departments were transferred to Don Street. Also considered was the necessity for the demolition and possible rebuilding of the Bakery Shop. The total reorganisation of the Non-Food operations envisaged in 1982, and the possible effects on overall profitability and the ability to maintain the rate of dividend, were discussed (**9.5, 9.6**).

The need for precise information regarding the costs of the Charing Cross reorganisation was

9.5 Charing Cross was given a full refurbishment and reallocation of departments in 1981. From left, Fred Hamon, Norman Le Brocq and Allan Smith after viewing the reopening (© Jersey Evening Post)

9.6 The Don Street, Homemaker store, opened in November 1982 (photo Ken Renault)

apparent. It was agreed that the Manager would obtain, through the Society's architect and quantity surveyor, detailed plans of the whole Charing Cross development. There would need to be sufficient separate costings to enable decisions to be made on the structural alterations required for each part of the building, and a firm timetable for completion.

So the Board faced the simultaneous challenge of integrating the move to Don Street with the many and varied stages of work necessary in redeveloping Charing Cross. This was the most important development the Society had yet planned, and a quantum leap from the move from 2 Market Street to Rectory House just 20 years before.

It might be recalled here that the early efforts of the Society to offer footwear with the clothing and drapery had never been very successful. The boots and shoes that were available at a reasonable selling price to attract the member were not always of the style and quality to suit all tastes. While there would have been a need to stock for the benefit of the working family of the 1920s and 1930s, more sophisticated tastes had become evident in these later and more prosperous years.

More limiting still to sales was the fact that the Society, still a comparatively small enterprise in its early years, could not offer the promotional clout of the big Northampton shoe manufacturers' names that were appearing in the Islands with their own shops. In the face of such competition it was inevitable that Co-op footwear tended to slip into the background.

But only for a while. Following the completion of the Don Street store and the subsequent rearrangement of several departments in the Charing Cross store and their transport to Don Street, a considerable area became available along the Charing Cross frontage, which is now occupied by Shoefayre. Members and the casual shopper passing by may have wondered at this unfamiliar aspect within the previously familiar Co-op store.

Unfamiliar it may be but Shoefayre is big on the mainland, one of the many parts that make up the whole of the Co-operatives Group's commercial activities. Because of the comparative isolation of the Islands, Shoefayre operates in Jersey and Guernsey as a concession, over which the Society exercises a nominal supervisory management. Dividend is paid on all purchases in Shoefayre shops on the Islands but they are not a part of the Channel Islands Society.

In the meantime, the pressure on both Islands for additional grocery storage space, particularly in the main stores, was becoming acute, an apparently intractable problem calling for fresh and innovative ideas. In July 1979 it was noted that the situation in Guernsey might be eased by the possible leasing of an additional Norman's warehouse adjacent to that already leased by the Society some time previously. Negotiations began.

In Jersey there seemed to be no relief in prospect, and the General Manager suggested the possibility of arranging the wines and spirits business through local traders. If this could be done at fully advantageous terms it could release a third of the present Grocery warehouse space for general use.

At about this time it was realised that the Beaumont Freezer Centre was not fulfilling its intended potential. Customer support was declining, despite presentations and demonstrations on the uses of frozen foods given by the General Manager. More to the point, perhaps, was the substantial electricity consumption necessary to maintain low, even temperatures in the cabinets. This went with the somewhat contradictory need for a reasonable working warmth for staff and customers, which would, of course, raise the cabinet temperatures and thus increase the electrical demand.

In 1981 it was reported that improved trade was necessary, and to lower the electricity demand it was proposed to reduce the number of freezer cabinets, using the space for large pack food units. It was left to the Manager to reorganise the Freezer Centre. We will return to this later, and the Beaumont site was to experience the uncertainty of several possible outcomes before final decisions were reached.

Another continuing development at this time was the ongoing efforts to find out-of-town sites for new stores in the country parishes. One such idea was for a 'centre of the island' store. John Le Sueur's site was discussed when an opportunity seemed likely in that area, but it was reported in 1980 that the owners were not interested in selling. Another possibility was the old Jersey Canning Factory in Rue de Pres, shortly to be taken up by Le Riche.

During the 1970s, particularly, encouraged by the boost in membership and an increasingly wider car ownership, as many as seven sites were studied. But excitement and anticipation over this feel for the country was calmed by Mr Mather's visit during the early part of the decade, when he certainly would have indicated how unsuitable some of these sites were. However, changing circumstances continued to keep the idea high on the priority list. A few sites were still in mind, not necessarily for new stores but for warehousing, with the constant need to maintain sufficient bulk stocks from which to service the stores. As noted previously, this seemed to be a never-ending problem, one that demanded vigilance and an eye for the future.

The General Manager was prompted to bring this to the Board in some detail during 1979, but without an immediate solution in mind. The issue had become pressing. When, during the early 1950s, the Society had only Charing Cross and Georgetown to consider, the shops could keep their continually moving supplies in-house – in other words, in the stockroom, a common term during that period. The advent of self-service and eventually the supermarket was a changing circumstance, which required a new approach to stocks, with bulk warehousing and a system for ensuring that stocks were available on demand and replenished in bulk from the mainland as required.

Five Oaks has been mentioned earlier as a potential site for a suburban retail store or perhaps an area for warehousing. Informal discussions had been held with Huelin's, owners of this extensive and valuable area, and the General Manager was able to report an initial but inconclusive response.

In August 1981 the Manager reported on discussions with Huelin's Managing Director and an offer he had made of £350,000. A price of £400,000 was then quoted by Huelin's, and this was followed by a return offer at £375,000.

The matter then rested with Huelin, and was, of course, subject to full IDC permits. Discussion of the project by the Board resulted in instructions to the Manager to obtain a legal option to purchase.

Parallel with that report, in view of the possibility of a refusal by Guernsey IDC to allow the Society to develop at Lowlands Estate, and the potential for the Five Oaks location, the Board decided to state future policy in relation to these sites in the following terms: 'In the event of IDC refusal to permit development at Lowlands Estate, any development at Huelin's Five Oaks will take place after the Anchor Market project has been completed.'

At the same time another possibility was opening up in Guernsey. The Manager reported that, in the course of discussions with the owners of Huelin's regarding the Jersey site at Five Oaks, an available large site at North Side, Vale, Guernsey, became known to him. Details of the property were presented to the Board, and the Manager was authorised to continue his investigations and to report back to the Board.

That the Guernsey site seemed the more likely to succeed was borne out a year later by a report, prepared in great detail for 'the development of a superstore in Guernsey' and for which an urgent application had been made to the IDC initially for leasing, with the option to purchase.

But such eager anticipation was short-lived; in January 1983 the Board heard the bad news that the application to develop the Huelin's site in Guernsey had been rejected by the IDC on the grounds that it was in an industrial zone and should be retained for industrial development. It was decided not to appeal against the decision but to await the outcome of negotiations for alternative premises. The Manager suggested that he could write to the press publicly expressing disappointment at the decision; the Board agreed this should be done but without implying criticism of the IDC.

So the Huelin saga was over, in Guernsey at least; there were still hopes for Jersey where negotiations at all levels were to continue for some time yet. Again, discreet enquires had been conducted between all parties concerned since the last report to the Board in June 1982. The Society appeared to be happy in 1983 to play a waiting game, realising no doubt that Huelin's at Five Oaks could be worth waiting for.

The Board heard a further report, with mixed feelings, that the owner of the Five Oaks site had submitted revised plans for a 10,000 sq. ft development with fewer car parking spaces. This was noted, and it was generally felt that little could be expected to happen until consideration of the Island Plan by the States of Jersey was much further along its path of debate and resolution.

Very soon after this report there was further news from the owners, which quickened the pace and pressed the Board to a decision to purchase regardless of the Island Plan. But this offer drew no acceptance from the owners and the matter remained dormant for some time.

Then, in April 1983, it was reported that an application would be submitted, by another developer, to the Jersey IDC during the next couple of weeks, for permission to develop part of the area for retail trading. A return of 10% had been insisted upon in the event of the developers leasing a building for our occupancy. This had not been possible to contemplate, and the Manager had requested the Board to consider the purchase of the site for the sum of £650,000. After due consideration, it was agreed that the Board would approve the purchase of the site at Huelin's, Five Oaks, subject to all necessary permits and authorisations being received from the IDC and other interested departments of the States of Jersey, to enable the Society to develop the site as a large retail outlet.

Some two years later, in February 1985, the Secretary reported at length on the capital commitments that would arise from decisions to develop several sites that were under consideration in both Islands. Huelin's, Five Oaks came up as a likely purchase, though nothing had been heard from the other side in the intervening period. A warning came through this report of the desirability of obtaining a further report in depth from Thomas McLintock & Co on the issue of capital commitment.

This was agreed. In the meantime the resulting facts and figures within the Secretary's interim report show the extent of the Society's anticipated expansion plans. While not yet firm commitments they do indicate the Society's hopes for the future, looking ahead some ten or fifteen years. Discussions with the Society's auditor centred on the following possible developments:

St Peter, Jersey	Large extension to main store and new retail shop units on the frontage
Five Oaks, Jersey	Purchase of warehouse and the redevelopment for Food and Non-Food warehousing
Castel, Guernsey	Possible development of 2,000 or 3,000 sq. ft shop to replace the existing Castel Food Shop, which was really too small to be run economically
The Bridge, St Sampson, Guernsey	Purchase or lease of a site, and to build and develop a Superstore of 25,000 sq. ft, plus roads and possibly to develop further retail outlets on the same site

It was estimated that these major projects could amount to a capital commitment of some £6 million or £7 million. The provision of capital for any one of these projects was becoming increasingly critical in view of the present heavy dependency on borrowed capital. This continued reliance on borrowings, which was not likely to diminish in the foreseeable future, was the subject of warnings every year from the auditor in his report. As stated, it was agreed that a report should be sought from Thomas McLintock & Co relative to the Society's past performance, present position and future prospects.

Within a few short years, it seemed, the quest for capital was becoming more urgent than ever, to feed the Society's enthusiasm to extend its reach to untapped semi-urban and country areas. But now, in place of the friendly exchange of views and plans accompanied by Mr Booth's kindly warnings and advice, we begin to see those warnings couched in firmer terms from accountants and auditors alike. Of course, the stakes were higher now, the possible risks greater, but the Society's aspirations remained as high as ever and, as we shall see, the risks were accepted and expansion continued.

Just a month prior to this, in January 1985, the Manager had reported to the Board on the IDC's refusal to approve a retail store on the Huelin site, a refusal that turned the Manager's thoughts towards the obvious alternative of warehousing. Allan Smith was clearly reluctant to let Huelin's slip away for lack of action while he could foresee a possible solution to the overall storage problem. To demonstrate to the Board the advantages to the Society of pursuing this particular alternative he planned a site meeting at Huelin's after the next board meeting.

That Manager's report of January 1985 on Five Oaks, previously circulated, following the refusal of Jersey IDC to give permission for a retail development of 10,000 sq. ft on this site, referred to the need to consider purchase of the site and buildings in order to provide the urgently needed new food warehousing capacity. Without this increased capacity the Food Division in Jersey would, without a doubt, grind to a halt, stated the report. The advisability of buying the site, and renovating the existing structures or demolishing them and erecting purpose-built warehouses or of endeavouring to negotiate a lease for suitable warehousing at Five Oaks or anywhere else, was discussed at length.

The Society, by way of an exchange of letters between the General Manager and the owners, had an option to buy the land and existing warehouses for £650,000. Finally, the Board agreed that the option to purchase be taken up in the sum agreed, £650,000. Any variance in the price would be the subject of further consultation with the Board. It was agreed that the Manager would arrange for the Board to visit the Five Oaks site following the next Jersey meeting.

In March 1985 Huelin's of Five Oaks was still very much alive and contacts continued. Allan Smith was a very determined Manager, who refused to give in while there was hope of a deal. Still, in that month, he reported once more on the possibilities of acquisition. He said that, during a telephone conversation with the owners of the site, he had been informed that the partners' interests had been bought out by, it was thought, Messrs Kirch and Guiton. It was clearly indicated that the price of £650,000 was now not likely to be acceptable.

Further reports indicated that by April 1985 the situation was hardening, not, on the face of it, in the Society's favour. But the Manager had not given up hope of obtaining the Huelin's site, whether by lease or purchase. A letter had been received, intimating that new offers for this site were being sought. The Manager informed the Board that the price, apparently based on a rental valuation, was expected to be in the region of no less than a million pounds. The Society would obtain its own professional valuation on a rental basis, and it was agreed that the matter be left over to the next meeting.

In the meantime, given the strategy of the new ownership, it seemed unlikely that the Society would have any influence over the final outcome of the protracted negotiations. So it transpired. The annual rent asked for the existing stores was £126,000, and it was requested that the Society declare its interest or otherwise in the property. Not surprisingly, the Board replied that it had no further interest. The Five Oaks saga had ended.

These long-continuing and protracted exchanges are an example of the difficulties and frustrations experienced by the Society in its efforts to resolve problems that paradoxically were the accompaniment to its own success. And in those exchanges it was Allan Smith and his management team who took the pressure in their attempts to reach satisfactory agreements – though there were still chances to enjoy the social side of Co-op life (**9.7**).

While much time and effort were being spent on the Five Oaks possibility, almost within grasp yet frustratingly, and eventually, out of reach, other areas were being discussed with the Board. Hopes and inclinations were towards the west, centring on the St Brelade area, truly in the west and rivalling Le Riche, which was already well established on the Red Houses crossroads and in the Quennevais precinct.

9.7 A typical Guernsey Social Club Christmas party, from 1982. Among the group (seated) are Norman Le Brocq, Allan Smith and Doreen Batiste

A possible site came up in 1980, with an adjacent house, in the Rue de Pont Marquet/Route des Quennevais area. This was to be negotiated at or within £100,000. In retrospect, and in comparison with figures quoted and accepted by the Board as reasonable for other sites, this does not suggest a site of a size suitable for a supermarket. However, a later report stated that the Society had approved the offer at £115,000 for the site, the house having been withdrawn. The Manager was also given some latitude in the event of any further negotiations.

This opportunity coincided with news of the closure of Lipton's Supermarket in La Motte Street. Readers may remember this store at the Snow Hill bus stop, now the Central Park Restaurant. While the details make interesting reading now, on reflection it seems rather strange that town sites should have been given such priority at a time when traffic congestion was increasing. Access for unloading of goods would have become very difficult if not impossible eventually. Le Riche overcame that problem with its Capital supermarket in Bath Street by allocating a portion of the Minden Place entrance for heavy trucks to park off the road and within the store. It is doubtful if the Lipton's site could have accommodated such an area for that purpose. In any event the idea was dropped in favour of the Anchor Market site in Guernsey, which the Board agreed should take precedence over any possibilities in the St Brelade area. As we shall read later, that project was not to be realised for some years yet.

In retrospect we can observe the delicate and sometimes frustrating balances that had to be maintained when forecasting and planning, along with the inevitable delays before even one development could be confirmed as clear. It was later reported that the Society's offer to take on the lease of Lipton's had been rejected. The Society took no further interest in the property.

While considerable thought and effort towards expansion was evident in Jersey, there was equal enthusiasm for various sites in Guernsey. The Society was still determined to secure a presence actually on the Bridge and several efforts in that direction are recorded. Though the old Anchor Laundry site was now the Society's property its development was in abeyance. The Leales Yard site located immediately behind the Bridge offered scope for a much larger store, of around 25,000 sq. ft, with extensive car parking. However negotiations with the owner, a Mr Zajac, were difficult and very protracted.

Negotiations continued for some time inconclusively, and the Manager reported in September 1984 that 'he hoped something may yet come of this development'. But by December 1984 there was still no clear decision, and the Board concluded, after full discussion on future plans for both Jersey and Guernsey, that development of either the Zajac site or Anchor Market be undertaken before the St Peter extension, which was also in the running.

This was at least a more positive outlook, coloured no doubt by the Manager's view that obtaining the necessary planning permits for the Bridge site could be difficult whereas the Anchor site in Nocq Road, just around the corner, was ready to go when capital forecasts permitted.

However, affairs in Guernsey were still active albeit in a quieter way. A previous chapter has covered the excitement of the Society and staff at the acquisition of Rectory House, the first extension and development of property from No 2, since amalgamation. The purpose of Rectory House initially was to relieve No 2 of the burden of the dry goods. In such a small store as No 2 it was, in retrospect, not a happy situation to have Food and Non-Food in such close proximity.

A similar situation had become evident with even greater emphasis at Charing Cross during the 1950s and 1960s, though this close proximity may not have excited too great a criticism from members who had requested the introduction of drapery, footwear and other services in the first place. However, times and customers were changing, and eventually Rectory House became the centre of much more than dry goods. The Society had kept up with the times and had introduced furniture, soft furnishings, kitchen and bedroom furniture and fittings, even a cookshop. All this was witness to the widening tastes of members – a long way from the wireless sets and brown suitcases of the 1930s.

In May 1982, Rectory House was itself undergoing transfer of some categories to the Lowlands store. A rather surprising change at Rectory House, which boasted five floors and was to undergo many more alterations during the next decade, was the introduction of a franchise to operate an Organ and Piano Section, a rather remarkable departure from established custom and trading. It is not clear now how this new department came into being, but it appears to have had the Board's blessing. However, it was opened and in operation very soon. Some disquiet was shown by the protests of staff in the Guernsey offices – in Rectory House presumably – against the nuisance of organ music, which was disturbing to office staff during the demonstrations in the adjacent area. The possibility of soundproofing was discussed.

By January 1984, the situation had become strained between the three parties concerned, and it is recorded that 'the Board reiterated its dislike of being associated with troublesome arrangements or companies'. Despite the legal agreements existing between the parties and the Society the concessionaire suddenly withdrew without notice, and the Society was faced with the problem of closing the concession and winding up outstanding accounts.

As a pleasing change to the frequent reports on development plans it was noted in November 1984 that Miss Doreen Batiste would be retiring at the end of the year after long and dedicated service with the Society, initially with the Guernsey Society. She was invited in the normal manner to meet the Board for lunch and presentations in January 1985. There is no doubt that Doreen had enjoyed a varied and satisfying career with the Co-op, commencing with her modest role as assistant at No 2 Market Street shortly after the amalgamation, later at Nocq Road, then with the mobile shops, managing several Guernsey stores and finally after retirement as a Director on the Board for a period of 12 years.

While the search for a satisfactory, and for the moment elusive, solution to the possible developments in both Islands continued, there was at the same time constant need for change to maintain standards and contain costs in existing stores. Don Street had been open and operating for three years, and it was time to assess the current situation, with reference to costs. The Don Street store had certainly been a departure from normal Co-op retailing practice in Jersey over the previous sixty years.

But, looking back for a moment to 1973, we read of the sudden death of Mr LM Jones, the Furnishing Manager, while in London on a buying trip for the Society. This was an unexpected loss for management. To fill the vacancy Mr Alfred (Fred) Hamon, previously of Langlois and Voisin, was appointed to the post of Furnishing Manager and Buyer for Jersey, separate postings being made for Guernsey. Having settled into the unexpected challenge, Fred's first innovation was the introduction of a diary system for his office and all departments, with an in and out order book so that everyone was aware of all stock movements. Gradually, he began to raise the standard and quality of the goods he ordered, an example of the dedicated care that Fred gave to his customers. In April 1979 Fred Hamon was appointed Furnishing Manager of the Society with full responsibility for the buying, and the whole operation of Furnishings, Electrical Goods, Carpets and Floor Coverings.

With the opening of Don Street Fred became the Manager of the new store. In retrospect, he recalls his misgivings over the site, based on his previous experiences of 24 years with Langlois, a similar business but just a little nearer King Street. While the passer-by may feel that the Don Street and Burrard Street junction is still part of town, in modern shopping and business terms it is removed from the mainstream of similar businesses in King Street, which had been established for a century and a half. De Gruchy and Voisin enjoyed their own individual loyalties, while Langlois, just on the fringe, maintained a similar customer loyalty, strengthened no doubt by Fred Langlois and the Auction Room. But the Society, only a few doors away, for the moment at least, needed time and experience to capture its share.

Fred Hamon could see the challenge and accepted it with a determination to arrange the departments to best advantage to attract the customer and maintain their support. A particular intention was to ensure that prospective customers were not to wait for attention; all Fred's staff were to be made aware of this and must offer their assistance quietly but immediately. But despite these best endeavours, by December 1984, there were shortcomings to be dealt with. In January 1985 the General Manager reported on a number of situations and possible improvements to be considered, to ensure the right balance between capital and revenue expenses and to encourage increased trading.

In the light of the first three years of trading and the need to reallocate some departments to different areas the changes were no more than would be expected after the trial period of a completely new store for the Society and the staff. Fred Hamon's firm ideals of pleasing the members – the customers – were strengthened by his policy of raising the general ambience of the store, as far as practicable or viably possible, to offer a welcome to all who came in.

Appointed Manager of Furnishings in both Islands, Fred made several visits to Lowlands to instigate and effect improvements there as well. On his retirement in 1987, after fourteen years in the world of Co-op furnishings to which he had given so much, the Board expressed warm appreciation of his efforts on behalf of the Society's first entry into a purpose-built store for furniture and all accompanying furnishing accessories.

Another store that needed a revamp was the Beaumont Freezer Centre. It was obvious that a change was necessary, and this possibility was eased by the IDC planning agreement in May 1986 for a change to a supermarket operation. By August a report on the conversion to a Food Centre was approved by the Board, at an estimated cost of just over £56,000. By October the work of conversion was completed, including 14 additional parking spaces on land leased from the Tenants of the Marsh. The store was open later that month.

This quick IDC approval and the subsequent conversion were in striking contrast to the situation just a few years previously when planning permission was refused in the same area on grounds of traffic congestion. The Society now had a halfway house, as it was, to St Peter where the new supermarket was trading very well but where IDC were refusing permission to extend and expand. In June 1985, for example, planning permission was refused with official reasons for refusal. As a result the Society was prompted to appeal, or, with the advice of the Architect, to submit a further application for a smaller extension. Following discussions with the Architect and the Board, an appeal against the IDC refusal was, indeed, considered an appropriate action.

The situation then became critical in that the Society believed that the IDC were acting *ultra vires* by basing refusal on principles contained in the new Island Plan, which had not yet been presented to the States. There were three such principles put forward under the Plan:

- that there should be no extension of shopping floor space outside St Helier except where there is a deficiency of shops
- that St Peter was already adequately catered for
- that additional parking space would attract more customers and thus increase traffic congestion in the area.

The issue was further complicated by action of the owners of the land intended for the car park extension by the Society should the development be approved. These owners were now insisting on the sale of the land to the Society going ahead, and were not prepared to await the result of the appeal.

The Society was thus compelled to make a firm offer to secure the land in anticipation, at a cost of £140,000.

Further discussions were held, and it was decided that the Society would call on Advocate Mourant to assist in continuing negotiations with Planning rather than to lodge an appeal. By October 1985 these negotiations were successful and approval was given for the car park extension. Following a meeting with IDC it was reported that they would treat sympathetically an application for extension to the store provided the present delivery area was removed. An exchange of land was also to be considered.

This was a fair deal. The delivery area insisted upon by the IDC for the first rebuild was right on the corner opposite the Post Office, certainly an ill-chosen situation for the frequent movement of heavy vehicles adjacent to a busy crossroads and not originally wished for by the Society. The traffic position could only have worsened with the anticipated increasing flow. These matters would be submitted informally to the IDC and to the Parish, and an official application would then be made. These possibilities were a justification of the Society's insistence on pursuing its aims.

So, as the 1980s drew to a close the prospects of expansion in the right place and at the right time were strengthening. The next decade would see positive progress towards firm establishment in the west. In the meantime one or two unusual aspects of Co-op progress were about to surface in both Islands, with impressive results.

It was to be some three years before the Board heard that these further discussions with Planning, through Advocate Mourant, had achieved some greater understanding. It is hinted at in the report to the Board in April 1989. The General Manager had met the Parish Deputy and the planning officer concerned, and alternative suggestions were proposed based on sketches for either a completely new store or an extension to the existing one.

The traffic problem had been considered in some depth. It was accepted by both sides that the volume of traffic through St Peter would continue to increase, but unlike their stance of just a few years back, over the Beaumont development, Planning now appeared more amenable to a similar development at St Peter, provided the delivery entry and exit for heavy vehicles was included in the car park area. However, in June, when the Society felt able to relax a little after this minor setback, the IDC was still expressing some concern over a development of the scale proposed by the Board, traffic problems still being the main reason for objection. In an attempt to overcome this continuing difficulty and delay, revised plans were again prepared.

But neither Board nor management were standing still while waiting for a St Peter solution. Work in Guernsey was well up to schedule on the new Nocq Road store, which was to be the Island's second major supermarket.

In the course of raising the steel framework during construction an odd but interesting complaint had surfaced from a neighbour whose television reception had suffered interference while construction was going on. The Board considered this with some understanding and responded that it was probably caused by the considerable amount of steelwork exposed during the building. A report from Guernsey Entertainment Services, whose opinion had been sought, confirmed this conclusion. An interesting situation, fortunately of short duration.

It was anticipated that construction would be sufficiently advanced to allow the ceremony of laying the foundation stone to be performed on 14 September 1989. A time capsule was prepared for the occasion, containing bank notes and coins of the period, the *TV Times*, a set of the development plans, the Society Rule Book, a current Report and Accounts, a photograph of an Aurigny plane, photographs of the foundation stone ceremony, and, lastly, a full copy of the Guernsey press containing the 70th anniversary articles. It was a most comprehensive social picture of the period and the occasion for a future generation to enjoy and appreciate.

This period around the turn of the 1990s was certainly a new one for the Society as several major projects made strong progress. By September 1989 new plans for the St Peter redevelopment were available for viewing by the Board. These plans showed an increase in selling space of 9,000 sq. ft and an accompanying increase of the car park area to 150 spaces. These adjustments had the support of the Parish and the Planning officers of IDC, and it was hoped to receive IDC Committee approval in the near future.

By February 1990 the Board was informed that a planning application had been forwarded to the IDC Committee and that overall approval had been given, subject to some improvements to elevations and a rearrangement of the new car park area. Approval in principle for the size of the store extension had been indicated.

The time taken to obtain these approvals gives an indication of the delays and frustration experienced by management when trying to move forward to 'opening day' of any new store or, as in this instance, an extension. Following on from the more promising report of February, a further meeting with Planning took place in March to discuss the elevations and the car park. In July it was reported that further delay was inevitable as final approval was awaited.

So it proved. In March 1991, over a year after the first application to IDC for approval had been forwarded, final plans for the extension were submitted. The final layout gave a total sales area of over 14,000 sq. ft. There was a parking area for at least 166 cars and two retail shops on the road frontage, one of which could be a pharmacy. After the delays of the previous eighteen months there was an air of confident finality at this stage.

It was decided that the store would remain open while the work was proceeding. Geraldine Garnier, who was on the staff at the time, confirms that the disturbance was a minor issue. Everyone wanted to see the new store open and in action. So confident was the mood now that it was decided to work on the car park area first and to engage Ronez right away to ensure a space on its road works programme.

The extended store was the flagship of the Society but the planning process had taken over seven years of frustrating delays. Sheer tenacity of purpose had brought the project to a successful conclusion.

Back in Georgetown, where the situation had been far from easy for some years past, we read in 1991 of an interesting possibility. Among the several properties adjacent to the Society's store, the rebuilding of which had taken so long to achieve, was 'Brunswick House', a lodging house likely to be available for purchase at £360,000. The General Manager had inspected the site and reported on the positive opportunities it could offer to the advantage of the store, including possible accommodation for staff and an increase in floor space for the shop. This was investigated fully by management, and purchase agreed at £330,000.

A full report on future viability was prepared indicating that despite the essential work to be done on the house, the addition of 1200 sq. ft to the existing floor space and an improved parking area by utilising the garden of the house were a justification for the costs involved. It was also evident at this stage that efforts should be made to increase the number of shoppers calling at the store and to raise their spending per head. Improved car parking would be an incentive in this direction, particularly as at that time the public car park opposite was to become a park and display area.

Plans were prepared for this proposal, and the initial response from Planning was favourable, to the extent that the IDC Committee would be shown the plans informally to gauge its opinion – a promising start. While this welcome activity was evident at Georgetown another area that had endured much delay and procrastination before its final solution in 1969 was the Beaumont Warehouse. At first so urgently needed, it had been so quickly eclipsed by the Bellozanne enterprise.

And enterprise it certainly is. Much has been written in previous pages of the ever-present and growing need for more storage space, a need brought on by two main and welcome factors – an increasing membership and ever larger supermarkets.

Allan Smith had expressed his concern on several occasions that lack of adequate storage capacity and the need for a more sophisticated delivery system could become a serious issue. It was the fortuitous circumstance of the withdrawal of the main Jersey Coal Distributors operation from a convenient site in Bellozanne Valley that enabled the Society to achieve a major objective in its search for greater efficiency in food warehousing and in stock control.

These were to become vital concerns with the rapid development of information technology, which was bringing the Society into the last decade of the century. Bellozanne and IT Central Operations were to be exciting additions to the changing face of Co-op retailing and of particular concern to the Society, which was now looking ahead impatiently, not to a variety of possible sites across the Islands, but to an emphasis on one dominant position in each Island.

10.1 The refurbished St Sampsons, Guernsey (photo Brian Green)

Chapter 10

The Nineties

As the 1990s opened the Society had many irons in the fire, to quote the old saying, but the success or failure of the many possibilities in both Islands would depend on factors such as the final availability of sites and their timing, and the need to maintain a financial balance between the issues involved. Behind everything lay planning requirements and limitations, which, as previous experience has shown, could take years to resolve.

But first a more modest idea began to emerge, a consequence of discussions during the late 1980s, which would engage the Society's attention and eventually achieve outstanding success. It was nothing to do with food or furniture – just a unique, bold and forward-looking idea.

Those readers who can remember the original Boutin's travel agent in Library Place, with its simple wooden counter, or the British Railways mailboat booking office in Bond Street, may have wondered, on return to the Island after an absence, how the seemingly limitless number of travel agents that appeared in town during the 1960s and 1970s could possibly make a living.

The answer lay, of course, in the growth of travel by air, and the social changes within society that now gave individuals, families and businesses the opportunities to widen their horizons and the possibilities for more exciting holidays. The Mediterranean resorts in particular responded with coastal developments to entice the would-be traveller to partake in this unprecedented bonanza of holiday freedom.

More available and affordable air travel and package holidays meant that travel agents could set up with certainty in an area like the Channel Islands, which had not previously commanded attention. Even Thomas Cook had not thought the Islands worthy of attention until recent years. So, in a comparatively short time the agents stepped in to an obvious niche.

The introduction of a travel agency into the traditional Co-op stores in the Islands had not seemed a possibility before. Emphasis remained for many years on the continuing programme of expansion, of modernisation of existing stores and the search for suitable sites in strategic areas for new stores. Added to which, no doubt, was the thought that travel agents were well established already, and there was considerable competition.

But the idea quickened into action in 1986, when Allan Smith approached CWS for an opinion on the opportunities for the Islands of taking up a CWS-managed services agreement. With 300 travel shops throughout the UK and forming the largest independent travel group in the country, CWS was in a strong position to advise. Discussions were held with Ray Elgie of CWS, who was eventually to find himself in command of the most successful travel business in the Islands.

All this needed serious consideration and planning. It so happened that the following year, 1987, Brian Smith, the Non-Food Manager, was taking a management course at the Warwick Business School. As part of the course Brian was required to look into the Ilkeston Consumer Co-op travel operation, and he returned to Jersey with enthusiasm and a background understanding of how Ilkeston had succeeded. Brian's experience confirmed the aspirations of Allan Smith and Ray Elgie that similar success – possibly even greater – could result from the focused efforts of the local Society.

In 1988, following discussions with CWS, a Managed Services Agreement was signed. This would enable the Society to enter the travel business in the Islands using CWS licensing and

10.2 Group Travel Manager Ray Elgie with his staff at the opening of the new Jersey Travelmaker (© Stuart McAlister Photographers)

buying facilities. Under this agreement Co-op Travel operates as a franchise under CWS but is managed entirely by the Society.

By 1989 all the necessary administration was in place, and the first Channel Islands Society travel shop was opened in Guernsey in Rectory House. The brand name Travelmaker was adopted, and it operated on conventional lines, except for one important difference. This was to attract considerable public and press attention, to the advantage of the Society.

In view of the inherent difficulties of assessing a dividend to each member when the total cost of a booking was subdivided between several agencies involved (such as the air fare, hotel accommodation, costs of a hire car or perhaps a rail connection, for all of which the member paid a lump sum), it was not possible to credit the usual dividend to the member's account. In lieu of dividend a shopping voucher was given to the member for use at a Co-op store.

These vouchers upset the travel agents in the Islands who were trying by various means to prevent the Society from entering the travel industry in what they considered to be unfair competition. What happened was that the very wide publicity given to this issue rebounded on the complainants by giving free and added publicity to Travelmaker. It was even more ironic that one of the Society's fiercest critics was the Managing Director of Preston Travel, Bob Little, who, despite his early and strongly expressed opinions, became Travelmaker's Group Travel Manager when Ray Elgie was in the UK for a couple of years. Bob's long and varied expertise in the international travel business was a great asset to the Society during the early days of Travelmaker.

The success of the Guernsey venture quickly encouraged the opening of the second Travelmaker, in Jersey, just a year later (**10.2**). And what better situation for it than the Don Street store, where it could be conveniently located on the ground floor by the windows to give light to the desks and offer a welcome to the passer-by on a dull day?

With five desks in Don Street and four in Rectory House, Travelmaker began a continuing increase in business that could scarcely have been envisaged just a year or two before when serious discussions had first begun. During 1990, the first year of Don Street, the increase of business gave CWS/Travelmaker its greatest and quickest-recorded growth.

Only a year later, in 1991, both shops gained their international (IATA) operating licence, and

10.3 Rectory House, Leisure Store, before the makeover, complete with a branch of the Co-operative Bank (photo Brian Green)

turnover hit the million pound mark. In 1994, Business Travel was opened and, despite renewed criticism in Jersey, the first Travelmaker 'all-in' tour operations began, using their own charter flights. By 1995 this had become the Channel Islands' outbound biggest holiday operation.

Travelmaker was proving to be the fastest-growing arm of all the Society's business, and a unique and forward-looking idea of just a few years previously had proved its worth. But it was time to move on, and circumstances within the Society's normal programme gave the opportunity to develop the Travelmaker image still further for the future.

Guernsey members would have noticed the rather obstructive hoarding around the frontage of Rectory House, which appeared early in 2000. Once removed, it revealed a completely remodelled Travelmaker under the name of 'hypermarket' (**10.3, 10.4**). Members find inside a quiet, welcoming

10.4 Manager Chris Roberts gives Guernsey Travelmaker hypermarket a festive launch

10.5 The Fresh Food Centrale at Charing Cross, 1995

10.6 Celebrity visit from David Bellamy to the old St Peter's Fresh Food Store, with, from left, 'Ginger' Hotton, Store Manager; Allan Smith, General Manager; Brian Ahearn, Produce Controller; and John Cuthbertson, Grocery Controller

10.7 The Homemaker retail showroom, Guernsey (photo Ken Renault)

10.8 St Peter's after its extension, 1996 (photo Ken Renault)

10.9 Pontac, 1991, with American-style wide aisles and a 'mall' feel

10.10 Bedding department, Lowlands Homemaker, 1995

10.11 The very accessible wine and spirits department in the revamped Charing Cross, 1995

10.12 An interesting use of space at the fruit and vegetable department, Charing Cross, 1995

interior with the latest facilities to encourage clients to relax and take their time while staff and the Manager, Sandy Ogier, arrange it all.

In Jersey too, in Don Street, Travelmaker has gone up, in the fullest sense of the phrase, having relocated to the second floor, where again every facility is provided for a relaxing choice of travel arrangements. This move had become necessary for the whole store was undergoing its first major refit of all floors and departments. Two previous revamps had brought advantages but during the 19 years since opening much had been learned. Only a total redesign could bring Homemaker into the forefront again and encourage members and public alike to take another look.

Travelmaker's lower-floor location in Don Street had become untenable for, apart from the booking desks being rather too close to the stairs, considerably more space was becoming essential to accommodate the increasing bulk of the latest technical equipment for making travel arrangements. Little does the traveller of the Boutin period know of the complexity involved in booking a holiday today, a complexity that would take unacceptable time and effort if written up by hand as it was just a few years ago. Add to this the new Travelmaker website, and we can begin to comprehend the progress made in the relatively few years since the idea began to take shape.

But moving ahead of competitors and creating records in travel management was not the end of the story for either Jersey or Guernsey. That complete refurbishment of Rectory House, now with its quiet air of efficiency and service, was a signal to Jersey to get Don Street Homemaker into a similar state of confidence. The comparatively minor changes made in the mid-1980s were not enough to enable Homemaker to assert itself and to bring in the additional custom needed to satisfy management and the accountants. Perhaps, after all, Fred Hamon's misgivings on the choice of site were being proved right.

Whatever the causes, it was to be some years before the necessary return was forthcoming. Not until the Board Meeting of 4 December 1994 did the relevant report on Non-Food state the situation for Don Street and Lowlands in Guernsey clearly, warts and all. The Don Street Homemaker and Lowlands required a refurbishment. In fact the decade was to see many changes, both outside and inside, to stores and shopping in general, in both Islands, a few of which are illustrated in the preceding double-page spread (**10.5** to **10.12**).

The remodelled store was to be opened in anticipation of a welcome increase in custom. Among the improvements for Lowlands was full air conditioning to improve the general ambience, relocation of several departments, introduction of new lines such as bathroom and shower fittings and extension of existing lines to offer greater choice. Discussions on the necessary market research to achieve these objectives had brought up the name of Fitch & Co., one of Europe's leading design houses, who ascertained fully the customer needs and instigated the whole project.

Another completely new department had appeared in Homemaker with the previous revamp of the whole store. The music section, comprising tapes, CDs and computer games, was installed in the area previously occupied by kitchenware. It was believed that this new departure from the previously quieter entry to the store could encourage support from the younger generation, perhaps creating the members of the future. Pulse, as the new department was called, certainly attracted a great many young followers.

The improvements made in 1994 enjoyed limited success but a more far-reaching review became evident in 1999. The catalyst to this improvement was a recently completed senior management restructuring, which saw Les Woodcock, as the new Retail Manager, take responsibility for the Homemaker shops. Recognising that the Jersey Homemaker needed a radical new approach, a strategy team, composed of himself, Jim Hopley, Jim Plumley, John Bates, Design Manager and Corsie Naysmith, leading London retail designers, commissioned market research. From that a radical new store concept was born. Two other key managers joined the team with the appointment of Ray Elgie as Non-Food Manager and Colin Gaskell as Store Manager (**10.13**).

The implementation of the totally new layout was carried out by a team led by John Bates, and this created a much more modern store with a greatly improved range of merchandise. The furniture selection was changed out of all recognition by the newly appointed Development Manager, Paul Clark, and new housewares and gift ranges were created by Colin Gaskell. Floor layouts were changed, wooded floor surfaces laid and new wall colours and signage created to offer a fresh new image.

One essential was to give each floor a less crowded appearance and a more spacious effect

10.13 Colin Gaskell, the Society's youngest manager at the time, took over the complete refurbishment of the Homemaker, Don Street (© Jersey Evening Post)

10.14 Voyager Café concessionaire Mr Mario Pirozzolo (right) offers Co-op Manager Colin Gaskell a cup of tea

while at the same time making the greatest use of floor space.

Two previous attempts to run a café restaurant through a concessionaire had not drawn the expected support of customers, who might have called in for a coffee but had not continued their visit with a wander around the store. Now was the moment and the opportunity to remedy this in a more subtle way. Previous cafés had tended to be separate areas, lacking a welcome from the main store. What better than to encourage such an active response by combining café and travel department in one open floor area, attractively coloured and furnished in restful fashion? Without conscious effort time could now be usefully spent discussing and viewing possible travel destinations and perhaps staying on for a meal – with a full menu to tempt would-be travellers as they glance through and discuss their brochures (**10.14**).

The design and completion of this major refit was the culmination of a growing awareness by the Society of customer responses to their environment within the store. As Colin Gaskell put it, 'This is very much a customer-focused refurbishment. A survey was compiled prior to deciding upon the work to be undertaken. Our aim was to update

10.15 'Help us find a garage in Jersey': Chris Le Messurier did just that and is seen here receiving a cheque for £1,000 from Allan Smith

Homemaker for the new millennium, making it more fashionable and appealing to a wider range of shoppers.'

The closing years of the 1990s would prove to be an exciting period in the Society's history. Motivated as always by Allan Smith and his team, much was to be achieved that would have been impossible just a few years previously. Though the overriding objective was still to establish a Co-op presence in key areas, there were other aims in view too. One such was to enter the petrol market for, as said before, the car was now an essential aid to shopping; and if the supermarkets provide extensive and expensive car parks for the customer why couldn't the customer buy fuel for the car as he or she bought food for the family? A simple argument, but implementing it is not so simple. Nevertheless, the determined Allan Smith set out to do just that and, despite the planning delays and objections, he achieved it eventually, only to find a happy coincidence just waiting to happen.

It was in conjunction of the St Peter's store extension and the spacious car park behind it, albeit at a cost, that the layout showed promise of space for a petrol filling station. The usual approaches to Planning raised the anticipated objections of possible traffic congestion and the loss of parking space, resulting in refusal. In January 1994 the General Manager expressed publicly the Society's disappointment at this third refusal and assured members and public alike that he would continue his pressure on Planning. Naturally there were objections from the trade too, and the possibility of a 'price war' was raised. The Parish Constable, Mac Pollard, had also objected on the grounds of traffic congestion and the fact that there were already two filling stations serving the village.

There the matter rested for nearly four years during which Allan Smith maintained his intention to open the filling station. He made a fourth application during 1997. In the meantime, the Society had achieved greater success in Guernsey with the purchase of the existing petrol station at L'Aumone, situated in a busy residential area. With a small food store already on site this was to prove the nucleus of Guernsey's first modern convenience store on a petrol filling station in line with the new generation of such stores in Britain. Though not obtained without significant cost and further investment needed to complete the 'En Route' concept the store has proved an unmitigated success, making L'Aumone one of the busiest of such petrol filling stations in the Island.

It was at this appropriate moment that Allan Smith's determined style of management received its due acknowledgement, for in November 1993 he and Mrs Lynn Smith were invited to meet the Board for the presentation of a Long Service Award in recognition of his 31 years' service within the Co-operative Movement followed by lunch with the Directors.

This success in Guernsey must have intensified Allan Smith's determination to see a similar achievement in Jersey for, having discussed the possibilities further with Planning, he was certainly delighted to obtain their consent to the fourth application in December 1997. It happened that the purchase of L'Aumone had been achieved through the initiative of a Co-op employee, Chris Le Messurier, who had heard of the possible sale of the station and passed the information back to the General Manager. In due time Chris's vital information resulted in the successful transaction, and as a token of appreciation Chris was presented with a cheque for £1,000 from the Society (**10.15**).

Prompted by this fortuitous result in Guernsey, a general appeal was circulated to staff in Jersey suggesting that a similar discovery of a filling station likely to become available and subsequently purchased by the Society could merit a similar cash award. In October 1998, only nine months after that final Planning approval for the St Peter's car park filling station, an even better opportunity became available, ready-made and conveniently situated on the main road barely half a mile from the store. Acquired from the De Gruchy family, the site already had a service shop for the station and room for replanning and expansion. This was to be Jersey's parallel to Guernsey's L'Aumone, both of them to provide the true convenience store image, the facilities to pull in for petrol and do a little shopping in a modern store at the same time. The concept of 'En Route' is now synonymous with the L'Aumone and St Peter petrol filling stations.

The outcome of this fortuitous circumstance was congratulations from Deputy Mike Vibert, Chairman of the Trade and Industry subcommittee, who welcomed the likely competition from supermarkets to challenge what he regarded as a cartel among the Island's filling stations.

So, in every sense of the phrase, the 1990s were to prove a dynamic period for the Society; continuing rapid progress it seemed was inevitable, and management was to be hard-pressed both to maintain it and to keep up with its demands. Eventually, modern technology, though still in its infancy, was to prove its worth in many ways, significantly so for the Society in those many areas of work, in shops and offices where pencil and paper, which for generations had been the accepted medium for all normal contact and recording, were now about to disappear. Telephone, the usual means of personal intercommunication, was rapidly being ousted by the fax machine and the Internet, clipboard and biros were going out of fashion!

Two departments in which this wind of change has been felt and appreciated are the General Administration Office at Charing Cross and the Member Services Office now on the second floor in Don Street. Both Karen Young, for many years Office Manager at Charing Cross, and Christine Le Blond, in charge of Member Services, have good reason to appreciate the advantages of the new IT Central Operations Centre now based at Beaumont. This is not only for the assistance they can call on if necessary through the Help Desk but for the support they gain from the computer system in covering an ever-increasing workload occasioned by the Society's commercial successes.

Karen, who began her over thirty years' service with the Co-op as a Saturday girl, recalls with nostalgic humour her early days in the Machine Room when all the members' share accounts were written up by hand in heavy leather-bound ledgers, typical of the period. She explains how all the till rolls from each branch had to be rolled up to 2"-size rolls and sent to the Co-operative Retail Society in Manchester to be entered into the computer. At the end of the year a printout of the total purchases would be sent back to Jersey. The Society Secretary/General Manager would convert into dividend value, at that time 5%, and this became the dividend, which was then transferred into the annual leather-bound customer record. In this book would be the customers' shareholding plus deposits and withdrawals, which then gave a final shareholding figure. To this was added interest, which was calculated manually, while the dividend was put into a separate column. Dividend was only paid out during the month of December by the General Manager personally at the Member Services counter. At the end of December any dividend that had not been collected was then transferred to the members' share ledger account.

And to prove how vital the new IT system is to the smooth and rapid work routine throughout the Society's stores and offices, we can see for ourselves how Karen's work is facilitated by looking at current till receipts, which show us immediately the total purchases for the year so far, the dividend earned at the time of purchase and the total dividend accumulated for the current year.

Karen also remembers Colin Davies, later to become Society Secretary, who, like herself, was a ledger clerk. One of his early responsibilities was the recording of the main purchases accounts, an area now covered by one of the Department

Supervisors. Office equipment in those early days was economical, to say the least – one hand-operated calculator and an NCR accounting machine, a cumbersome form of typewriter with a long carriage necessitating adequate desk space. Another time-consuming routine was that of writing up the weekly payments on the hire purchase agreements, 200 or more in the early days of their introduction. Now, with a more sophisticated bank account system, most of these credit sale payments are done by direct debit arrangement with the banks. Very few personal cash accounts remain in force.

Christine Le Blond, with over 30 years' service, had for many years a closer and more personal contact with members and the general public through the daily presence of her Member Services Office, now in a strategic and friendly position facing the new stairway at Homemaker and adjacent to the Café Voyager. The café, near to the office windows, is also there to tempt the member to stay a little longer.

Member Services staff deal with personal enquiries and transactions at the window, thus maintaining the close liaison the Co-op has always striven to maintain between members and the Society. While customer services have been relieved of many of the previous manual tasks, there is still considerable pressure, though this momentum is now both increased and supported by the IT system.

To give just one indication of that pressure, only a sophisticated computer system enables the Member Services staff to take in at the close of every working day the hundreds of transactions and the accompanying cash that must be totalled, checked and reconciled before banking. Without that support they could not possibly cope with the natural, and welcome, increase in membership during Christine's period of service, from 35,000 just 30 years ago to over 92,000 in 2005 and a dividend payment of over £4,000,000. This dividend payout follows the AGM and is the busiest period of the year.

Inevitably, with the opening of the new Locale at Red Houses in August 2000, the completion of Grand Marché in St Helier and the new St Martins Locale in Guernsey, the demands upon the system will increase considerably, but it will cope. How is it done? A good first step towards an understanding of the computer world in which we live and how it serves the needs of business is to think back for a moment to Travelmaker and its rapid climb to success during the early 1990s within the confines of Homemaker, as we read in the last chapter, truly an opening to a new era.

Of all the various users of IT, travel and tourism has probably embraced the technology more enthusiastically than any other industry. Travelmaker went online in 1999 with its website, at first as a method of displaying its holiday brochure and making it available to a wider audience. This was a display only, with no interactive communication available other than e-mail. Later a third-party system was introduced, making it possible for anyone accessing the site to make reservation for car hire, hotels and flights.

The Society launched its first general website in November 2001. This website contains general information about the Society, such as history, financial and stores information. In addition, there is a members' section from which members can search for purchase and dividend information. A major review has recently been completed and was launched in February 2005.

On a similar theme, there has been a significant move to transfer information electronically, mainly by e-mail, both internally and externally. Documents such as price bulletins, timesheets and cash sheets are regularly transmitted and processed electronically. Perhaps more importantly, documents are being transmitted and received electronically between external bodies such as suppliers and the Society. For example, payments and remittance advices, purchase orders and invoices are regularly processed electronically.

The use of the Internet and other electronic technology by the Society is a relatively recent trend, but has already had a dramatic impact on the way the Society carries out its business, with the IT system now linking office and store with immediate access to information. In a more general context members and the general public have become so accustomed to the modern check-out till and the speed at which a trolley-full of shopping can be passed over the scanning plate, accompanied by that musical 'beep', that they may be forgiven for their apparent lack of interest.

EPOS – electronic point of sale, to give it its full title – is the device that reads the barcode, now the universal world-wide symbol used for identifying and recording every item on the shelves. This system was introduced to the Society in 1989, the first such installation throughout its stores in the

UK Co-op movement, and the first in the Channel Islands to adopt it throughout its stores and offices and in its warehouses at Bellozanne in Jersey and at Longue Hougue in Guernsey. All these centres are now interconnected through the IT Centre at Beaumont.

It is in striking contrast to the finger-tapping cash registers still in use in the new supermarkets that were opening up in the 1970s and 1980s. It is an advance in every way; till queues are moving more quickly and business is benefiting, but this is not all that EPOS can deliver.

Moving into the Store Manager's office for a moment, we see the other end, as it were, of the EPOS system. This enables the Manager to refer at once to the sale of any item and take appropriate action. For example, as a tin of baked beans is passed over the beam the 'beep' is recording not only the price to the customer, but to the Manager it also indicates a reduction of one item in the total stock held. So at any moment during the day, the stock remaining of any item can be checked on the main computer and, if necessary, an immediate reorder can be placed with Bellozanne or Longue Hougue, or from the local supplier if that is the source of the product.

Not only do the Store Managers benefit from EPOS but also the staff involved in research into the progress and profitability of the two large stores, St Peters and Grand Marché, where daily printouts give detailed figures recording the number of customers passing through the check-outs at any period during the day and the total cash taken. These statistics are an immediate indicator of the performance of the store, and from which particular action might be desirable or necessary – perhaps varying the opening or closing times, for example, or noting the pressure on certain items requiring adjustments to the ordering schedule.

Concurrent with this more rapid, indeed immediate, facility to reorder as required is the need to ensure that the supplies arriving at the store are correct, as ordered. A glance around the enlarged warehouse at Bellozanne would give the member or a casual observer a feeling of bewilderment – how is it possible to identify individual items among the thousands that are stacked in pallets from floor to roof?

Ron Morris and Ted Tadier would give their replies with smiles and obvious relief at their memories of that Beaumont Warehouse of the 1970s, built at last after such frustrating delays. When brought into use it was no more than a vast, empty shell to be stacked only three pallets high. Once transferred from container to the building, pallets had to be positioned manually and so arranged that frequently ordered items were the most readily accessible.

Ron remembers the thirty-year old forklift that needed ballast at the rear to avoid tipping when lifting, the only mechanical help they had! When loading the delivery trucks the pallets were pushed and pulled across the truck floor, again to ensure that offloading at each store on the round was easily managed – a laborious and time-consuming procedure. Not until 1976 were the first trucks received with electrically controlled tailgates, which, with the use of Unitainers, transformed this procedure to one of comparative ease.

Now by contrast, with the IT at Bellozanne, every order from a store is accompanied by a printout of peel-off tickets, each of them a reference to a particular item or pallet. These can be quickly attached to the relevant item or pallet, enabling a quick identification for rapid withdrawals when ordered, by extending forklifts that can reach to the highest of ten or eleven pallets of each stack. The words Bellozanne and IT Central Operations were to be an exciting introduction to this changing face of retailing.

As far as the Society is concerned, the background to this remarkable technological advance within the past fifteen years or so is seen in the Annual Report of January 1990 in which appears a brief paragraph headed:

> *Technology – Computer.* During the year we have successfully launched the first food scanning operation in the Channel Islands. The pilot system has proved very successful and it will now be installed in all our Food Stores during 1990.

This was followed by a more detailed report of progress, in the Annual Report of January 1991. Among the items mentioned was:

> *Technology – Computing Facilities.* Within our Food Division we now have scanning checkouts operating in all our stores linked to our Central Food Office. Information from these scans is used to improve In-store Stock procedures, Store deliveries and Store layout.

It was rapidly becoming obvious that IT was to have a very full integration with all aspects of the

10.16 Networking in the IT Centre: from left, Chris Pugsley, Wayne Hart, Warwick Cooper (Computer Services and Retail IT Manager) and Paul Cadiou

10.17 Maureen Halliday (Computer Operations Manager) at her office in the newly refurbished building

10.18 Rena McQueeney (left) and Maria Meehan hands-on at the IT Centre

Society's work and activities, and a specialist staff would be needed to organise further developments and run the system.

It was at this stage that Mike Guest joined the staff in 1991 as IT Controller with responsibility for Strategy and Co-ordination on IT systems throughout the Society. His previous service with Littlewoods and extensive IT experience led to his specialising in computer software development.

The IT Operations now centred at Beaumont is led by Warwick Cooper, Computer Services and Retail IT Manager (**10.16**), and Maureen Halliday, Computer Operations Manager (**10.17**). From modest beginnings in 2002 they already managed over 300 PCs, 15 laptops and 115 computerised tills, on top of the central computing capacity! (**10.18**)

For the full integration and support of the whole system, there are Service and Maintenance workrooms, a Training room and, of course, the Help Desk to respond immediately to queries from any of the Society's stores or offices. As we have seen, members are also a part of this information revolution, with checkout till receipts giving them the latest figures on purchases and dividend. Take a look at your till receipt next time you visit any of the stores: you may well ask, how can they work that out so quickly?

Also, arising at this time, was the idea of a Co-op sports and leisure store to occupy the ground floor of the old bakery, an idea inspired by the success of Centre Sport at Charing Cross, which now needed to be relocated because of the extension of the food store. There was also the prompt given by the Public Health initiative of a scheme for the greater public awareness by the Over-50s of the need to take part in some form of healthy exercise for which the Active Gym had been opened at Fort Regent.

The Society could envisage some spin-off from this and also from the growing interest in and the promotion of safer cycling. An application was made in January 1994 to the IDC, which was favoured by the Planning Officers but not by the Committee. This contradictory situation prompted the Board to agree to an appeal to the IDC and intent to pursue to an acceptance by legal means if necessary. By June it seems the IDC had been convinced of the need for the Co-op idea to be supported, and consent was received. Quick to

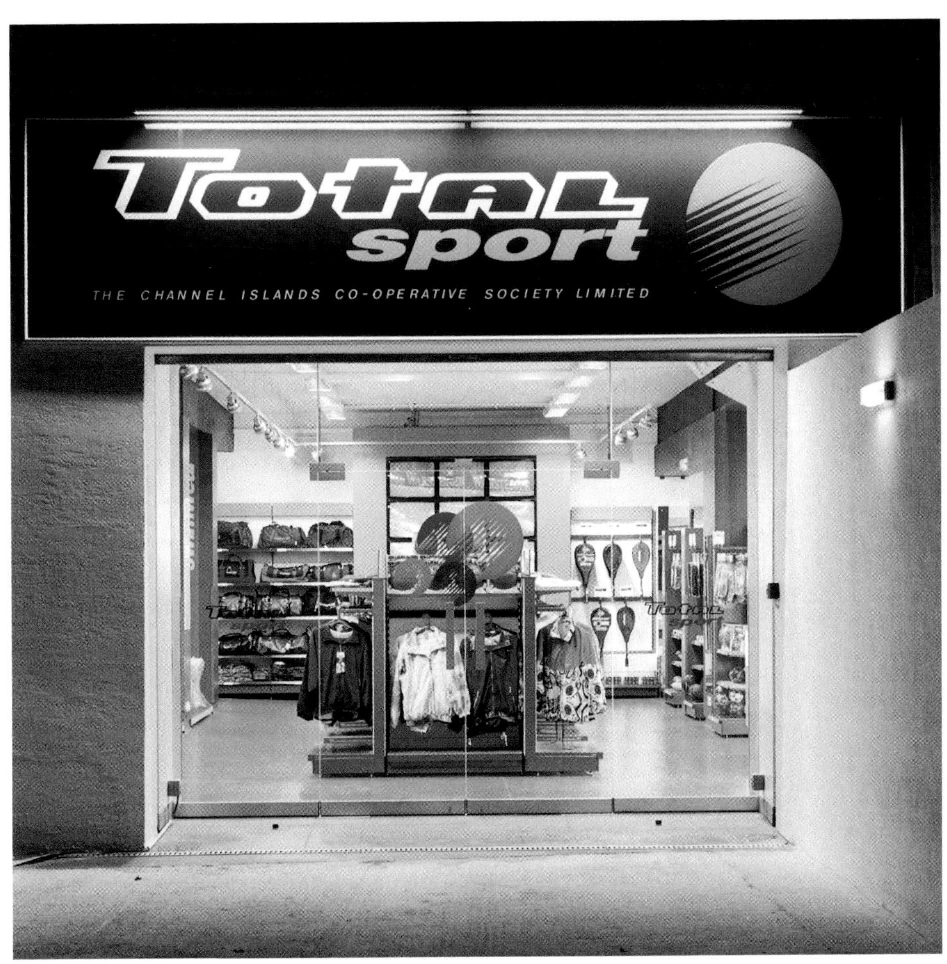

10.19 The entrance foyer of Total Sport, December 1993

10.20 The largest range of leisure clothing and equipment in the Islands: an inside view of Total Sport, 1993

10.21 The Society brought sports and sponsorship together in the 1990s: top Jersey cyclist Lynn Minchington led many cycling classes and proficiency courses for local youngsters

10.22 At the Society Presentation Dinner in October 1998, four employees celebrated their retirement: Geraldine Garnier, Derek Haines, Michael Galway and Anthony Soleil. From left: Derek Haines, Peter Grainger*, June Le Feuvre*, Jennie Vibert*, Joyce Haines, Geraldine Garnier, Anne Garnier, Kevin Mayne (* President), Betty Galway, Michael Galway, Gregory Zambon, Maureen Soleil, Allan Smith and Anthony Soleil (* Directors) (© Stuart McAlister Photographers)

follow up the opportunity, Allan Smith reported just a month later, in July, that this project would form the largest Sports and Fitness Centre in the Island, with its 4,300 sq. ft area displaying the widest range of leisure clothing and equipment (**10.19, 10.20**).

Considerable activity and preparation took place during the ensuing months. The Annual Report for 1995 announced the opening of Total Sport in December with a Customer Charter indicating a strengthened trading philosophy on price, the comprehensive range available and the presence and support of staff fully trained in the products they sell and always available to offer advice and service. Sports and Leisure was an exciting new venture. Brian Smith, Non-Food Trades Manager, was able to report in May 1995 on the widening activity of this new concept, into sponsorship with local sporting celebrity Lynn Minchington, for example, who initiated cycling classes and proficiency courses for youngsters (**10.21**). TV advertisements were shown and further-widening coverage was given through the participation of other personalities in the sporting world, suggesting a promising future for Total Sport.

While the 1990s had witnessed great activity on many fronts and very considerable progress, the closing years of the century recorded the names of several members of staff who were congratulated on completing 25 years with the Society or were retiring after long service. Notable among them were Michael Galway, with 47 years behind him, and Derek Haines with over 29 years to look back on (**10.22**).

This personal aspect of the Board/staff relationship lives on through all the pressures of present-day store life, and this is shown so fully in these reports of long service. In the same Annual Report for 1999 another event of significance was recorded – the death of Doreen Batiste on 16 April 1998 (**10.23**). She was known to many and will be remembered by many. The Board made special mention of her service in their Report:

> Her knowledge of Island life, the patois and the Guernsey character stood her in good stead in her work, and she became a firm friend of Members and Staff throughout the island. When she finally retired in 1986 she continued her involvement with the Society by standing as a Director, which office she held until her fatal

10.23 Doreen Batiste's work with the Co-op in Guernsey spanned a happy 50 years from shop assistant and mobile shop driver to Board member (photo Robin Briault)

> stroke, completing a total of 50 years' service with the Society. Doreen was the sort of person one meets only once in a lifetime; an archetypal Guernsey woman whose advice was sound and based on valuable personal experience, a legend in the Society and still greatly missed.

The decade also witnessed the changing of the guard in other ways, with the passing of John Morris on 16 May 1994 and Norman Le Brocq on 25 November 1996. John Morris has figured large in these pages, but Mr Le Brocq added some words of tribute to his colleague and friend that should be recorded here. In commenting on John Morris's wartime work, he told the *Jersey Evening Post*:

> In those days he was 'Mr Co-op'. He held the membership together and kept the organization together. He was also the architect of the merging of the Guernsey and Jersey co-operatives in 1955 ... I have to pay tribute. He really built this Society – more than any individual.

One interesting item in the Society's records relating to John Morris's period of stewardship is shown in the accompanying illustration (**10.24**), a letter of congratulation from the CWS on the first year the Society recorded sales of over a million pounds.

Norman Le Brocq was a Director of the Society for 35 years, 27 of these years as President. Under his Presidency from 1968, the Society's membership grew from 17,282 to 75,983, the number of stores expanded from four to fifteen in both Islands, and the annual turnover rose from £1.3 million to £51.5 million. As the notice placed by the Society in the *Jersey Evening Post* put it:

> Many of the Society's Directors have served for long periods on the Board, but there is little doubt that the continuity of Norman's strong leadership gave stability and a purposeful sense of direction to the expansion plans of the Society ... Jersey-born and a staunch Channel Islander, Norman Le Brocq was instrumental in the setting up of the Society's Care in the Community and environmental projects, benefiting both Jersey and Guernsey. A firm believer in the concept of the Co-operative Movement, he led the Society from the ownership of medium sized retail stores into the present span of 15 outlets, including large supermarkets at St Peter, Jersey and St Sampsons, Guernsey, Homemaker Stores in both Islands and Total Sport at Beaumont, Jersey.

The same notice records that Norman Le Brocq was twice elected Deputy of St Helier, serving the States of Jersey from 1966 to 1972 and again from 1978 to 1987, a total of 15 years, in addition to much other community and civic work (**10.25, 10.26**).

As times changed throughout this decade and the development plans for the future were becoming clearer, the Board recognised that the current management structure of a General Manager responsible for a Food and Non-Food division, managed by specialist management, along with a Secretary with executive control of Finance and Accounting, was not the ideal structure to derive the maximum benefits from a fully integrated trading and accounting management. The Society was facing its most ambitious capital development programme and needed to have an integrated management structure capable of carrying through successfully the huge developments being planned. Add to this the fact that a number of the middle management were reaching

CO-OPERATIVE WHOLESALE SOCIETY LIMITED

RETAIL TRADING GROUP

Incorporating Wheatsheaf Supermarkets

P.O. BOX 53, 1 BALLOON STREET, MANCHESTER 4

TELEGRAPHIC ADDRESS

TELEPHONE
BLACKFRIARS 1212
Ext. 314.

OUR REF WAH/DH YOUR REF

1st December, 1966.

Mr. J.R. Morris,
Managing Secretary,
Channel Islands Co-operative
Society Ltd.,
27 Charing Cross,
St. Helier,
Jersey,
Channel Islands.

Dear Mr. Morris,

At a Meeting of the Retail Trading Group held on Monday last, my Directors received details of the trading results of your Society for the year ended 1st October, 1966.

In this connection, the Directors were very pleased with the excellent results of Channel Islands Society and the fact that the annual sales had now topped the £1 million mark.

As a token of acknowledgment, they asked me to particularly write to you and offer their sincere congratulations and good wishes for the future success of your Society.

Yours sincerely,

10.24 We made a million! The CWS writes to congratulate John Morris and the Society on a record sales year, as the million pound mark is topped in 1966

10.25 A formal portrait of Norman Le Brocq (© Jersey Evening Post)

or approaching retirement – action was required, but sensitivity was also a necessary prerequisite. The managers affected had given most of their lives to the Society and deserved to be treated with respect during this difficult time of management restructuring.

Over a period of months, which included a great deal of work by the Board, a new management structure was developed and eventually approved by the Board. Following extensive consultation an early retirement package was developed which allowed managers to retire with dignity and recognised their very valuable contribution to the Society. Over a period of two years, ten of the Society's top fifteen managers took early retirement or in one case left the Society for another management position. While this caused great strain on the remaining managers it did allow for an infusion of younger managers both from within the Society and from outside to help create a dynamic management structure led by the Strategic Management Team. This comprised of Allan Smith, Chief Executive; Jim Hopley, Retail Controller; Greg Zambon, Finance Controller; David Rees, Society Secretary (**10.27**); and Brian Smith (later Colin Macleod on Brian's retirement) as Head of

10.26 At the opening of the refurbished St Sampsons, from left: Norman Le Brocq, Peter Bennett, Pam Schofield, Eric Walters, Doreen Batiste, Derek Falla and Kevin Mayne (photo Brian Green)

10.27 David Rees, appointed Secretary to the Society in March 1999 (© Stuart McAlister Photographers)

Operations. This team, guided by the Board and the rest of the central management, were directly responsible for the outstanding success of the development programmes over the millennium and beyond.

Chapter 11

The Millennium and beyond

As the previous chapter suggests, the 1990s had been the most active period of progress in the Society's history. Not only active, but rapid progress would be the norm, high expectations would arise and demands would be made upon all from Board and management to the newly appointed staff in shops and offices.

Co-op members can gain much of this sense of anticipation from their Annual Reports, while the staff are all involved in their many varied tasks and will experience it all as advances are made. But few, members or staff, can appreciate adequately the background to the pressures that beset the management teams as they pursue sometimes elusive aims and objectives, their particular hopes and aspirations that have so often faded into the past. Examples from that past would include the loss of the Five Oaks site, so accessible from town, for retailing and warehousing, and the absence of a suitable supermarket site within the St Peter Port town area, sought after for so long.

But as regrets, and disappointments perhaps, recede, so fresh opportunities occur, each seemingly more demanding than the last. In fact, two such opportunities had been hatching over a long period, one in each Island. That, in Jersey, completed and open to greet the twenty-first century, was the culmination of a long-continuing interchange between the two parties concerned, extending through many years.

Despite the pressures and the uncertainties of the period other more positive events and successes filled the later years of the 1990s. The success of Total Sport was one and the eventual redevelopment of Charing Cross another. The Fresh Food Store at Beaumont was completely refurbished and given the new Locale façade, to be reopened with a sub-post office. This new thrust along with newspapers and magazines was only possible through the acquisition of a number of smaller businesses whose key elements, postal services and news agency, were integrated into the 'Locale' format. This is now the situation in Jersey at Georgetown, Val Plaisant, Pontac, St Brelade, Beaumont and Grand Marché in St Helier and St Peter, and in Guernsey at St Martin and St Sampson. A wise move this, to invite casual callers to combine their call for stamps with a little domestic shopping and perhaps to consider membership. The opening of St Brelade's Locale in August 2000 (**11.2**) at last gave the Society a store in St Brelade, an area dominated by Le Riches. The early and continuing success of this Locale fully justified the investment by the Society, giving the members convenient shopping facilities.

In all this activity there has been a willing participation by staff at all levels, and a contribution from them towards the ends in view whether it be profit or community, often the two together, as demonstrated in *UPDATE*, the staff newsletter. Indeed, before newsletters were thought of, there existed throughout the past fifty years a happy continuation of that loyalty between Society and staff, which has shown itself in many ways. One is the long-service records of 10 to 50 years, which are

Opposite page **11.1** Mrs Rosalind Makin being welcomed by June Le Feuvre, the Society's President, and Allan Smith, Chief Executive, on a shopping visit to the Grand Marché. Mrs Makin first moved to Jersey in 1946 and has been a Co-op customer ever since. On this occasion she was presented with a Society certificate and bouquet of flowers. She hastened to point out, with a laugh, that she doesn't use a wheelchair – she might be 100 years old, but this was a shop chair brought forward for the occasion so that she could relax for the photograph! (© Jersey Evening Post)

11.2 Opening of the St Brelade's Locale, 4 August 2000. From left: Jim Hopley, Retail Controller; June Le Feuvre, Society President; Darren Le Quelenec, Store Manager; Allan Smith, Chief Executive (© Stuart McAlister Photographers)

appropriately acknowledged and rewarded; another is on those occasions when the Board has addressed a personal letter of congratulation and appreciation to staff who have made efforts beyond the normal. One example was the shared celebratory party, after the inconveniences of the Charing Cross refurbishment. Staff in their turn have shown appreciation of the support given by the Board to their charitable and community efforts, to the staff dinners and special events.

Naturally, changes have occurred over the years. One concerns Health & Safety regulations, very necessary as the Society grew in stature, which have introduced a tighter discipline in daily routines that the staff have accepted willingly as a necessary measure to their advantage and well-being. Pay and Service Agreements and the accompanying discussions have become far more comprehensive and detailed than they were fifty years ago.

In all such discussions and in matters of discipline and training the Board has endeavoured to be helpful, understanding and conciliatory. In so doing it has enjoyed a long and close association and relationship with staff at all levels. There is no doubt that the active presence and long service of Norman Le Brocq as Director and President did much to foster and maintain that understanding. And though the quickening pace of the recent and current advances and developments have put more pressure on staff at all levels, particularly at Grand Marché, it is the wish of Board and management that everyone, in office or on the shop floor, will always consider themselves an important part of the team.

Welcome among these many changes has been the growing influence of women as managers. The Society has freely acknowledged the role that women can play in office or store, and full opportunity has been given to many to show their capabilities in this sphere. Doreen Batiste, the first in Guernsey to carry the flag, demonstrated this quality of character in many ways, from patois exchanges with her parish customers to the management of several shops in turn. 'A bit of a martinet', as a nameless male put it, but always approachable, always efficient and eventually becoming a Director on the Board.

Others among the many were Jean Toop, who managed Pontac for several years, then towards retirement in 1980 had a brief spell as Manager of the new Beaumont Fresh Food Store. Also prominent in management was Roselle Rouse, who demonstrated a quiet determination to manage her shop as she thought fit; if a Senior Manager or a Director visited her and, while viewing the arrangement of shelving, perhaps moved a bottle or two, Roselle would quietly return them to their previous places – this was 'her shop'! Her staff of the period remember Roselle as strict but fair in all staff matters. And now as President of the Society, in succession to Kevin Mayne, we have Mrs June Le Feuvre, the first woman President of The Channel Islands Society and as able as any man to conduct a Directors' Meeting or an AGM.

The other, a long story in retrospect, concerns Mr Cabot of No 4 Pitt Street, whose property was of particular interest to the Society. In the Board Minutes of 28 January 1996 we read of the eventual outcome:

> **Site Purchase**
> Copies of a letter dated 23rd January 1996 from Vibert & Bridle confirmed that Mr Cabot, owner of No 4 Pitt Street, St Helier was prepared to sell the property to the Society at a sum of £125,000 subject to the existing tenancy of the shop, Gibaut's, on the ground floor and vacant possession for the rest of the building. **It was confirmed** that the shop rental was £2,500 per annum paid monthly; there was no lease involved. Contract date to be no later than 1st March 1996. **It was resolved** that the purchase of No 4 Pitt Street, St Helier be approved.

This was an important purchase for the Society in its quest to secure the properties making up the island site of Charing Cross.

The General Manager took a very close personal view of all developments within that area, reiterating the necessity to ensure that final results of all such negotiations should be to the advantage of the Society. But this was not to be achieved without continuing doubts and concerns over the remaining properties of the Foot family in Pitt Street and Dumaresq Street (**11.3, 11.4**). These were also subject to procrastination, delays and considerable expense before they were finally released for sale to the Society. By mid-1998 the purchase by the Society was completed, at last, after so many years of hopeful anticipation.

But this was not the end of story. Readers may remember a rather unusual house of French architectural design, which once stood on the corner of Charing Cross and Dumaresq Street (**11.5**). The house was demolished many years ago in anticipation of that road-widening scheme, later abandoned, leaving a very small area now derelict but for the warming feature of a wall mural painted by members of the St Helier Youth Work Project, organised by Mr Mark Renouf, and the seats, often occupied by visitors eating their lunch of fish and chips from Hector's just across the way. But again, though of very small area, this site is of particular significance to the Society, being the keystone, as it were, to the future design of the eventual full redevelopment of the Charing Cross site. This very small area has been subject of much discussion over the years between the Society and States departments. A resolution still has to be reached, which is vital if this important property is to be developed.

The island site, with the exception of the corner plot, now complete in Society ownership, still suffered embarrassing difficulties over the issue of deliveries to the store, the frontage of which faces probably the busiest vehicle and pedestrian traffic in town, particularly during the summer months when tourists are strolling through. Deliveries to the shop's in-store accommodation had for many years been made to the side door in Pitt Street by truck and then by Unitainers into the store. In recent years the paving over of Pitt Street from the Charing Cross entry still allowed access from Dumaresq Street to the store room doors. But the recent completion of the paving throughout Pitt Street resulted in the Parish compelling the delivery trucks to park illegally on the yellow line in front of the store, causing difficulties to Co-op staff, delivery vehicles and annoyance to pedestrians on that narrow pavement. However, with the election of Connétable Crowcroft a new impetus to improvements for Broad Street brought a more realistic attitude from the Parish and from late 2002 deliveries were again via the Pitt Street entrance. This allowed the improvements to the area by the Parish and States to be completed.

Sensitive and time-consuming though the Pitt Street situation had been, these were not the only

11.3 A memory of the time when Pitt Street was more than just a 'short cut', this view shows the Foot family's shops on the corner of Dumaresq Street during the 1920s, the whole very well maintained. Now owned by the Society, the area is to be restored (photo Foot Collection)

11.4 An interesting view of the interior of the Foot's shop. Some older readers may remember the evenings spent with music from a gramophone. Wireless sets were about to appear in the home, but for a while longer the gramophone reigned supreme (photo Foot Collection)

11.5 The handsome French-style house that once occupied that vacant corner with Dumaresq Street, now owned by the Society. The Cabin Restaurant was later situated on the ground floor (© Société Jersiaise)

problems facing the Chief Executive and his team. Those greater opportunities just spoken of were taking shape, and of them all the Grand Marché, which opened in November 2001, was without doubt the greatest success of the Society to date, although that success did not come easily. In fact, that culmination was reached only after several years of friendly discussion and negotiation, and occasional negation, between two parties, the Society and C Le Masurier Ltd, in which the principal protagonists were the General Manager and the late Mr Fred Clarke, one-time Constable of St Helier and Company Chairman of Le Masurier.

To introduce the first of these two men who were destined to play the major part in the long and sometimes tense build-up to Grand Marché, Allan Smith, now the Chief Executive, began his more than 40 years' service with the Movement on leaving school at the age of 15, in a Co-op shop in Bolton, Lancashire. Uninspiring though his first simple tasks may have been, he obviously showed his merit by becoming a Deputy Manager at 16 and a Shop Manager two years later. A year of professional training in management at the Co-operative College led to promotion to supermarket management, also in Bolton.

Thus launched into a career with the Co-op, Allan became Grocery Area Supervisor of Plymouth and South Devon Co-operative in 1971. In 1973 he arrived in Jersey to join the staff as the Society's Assistant Grocery Manager. In 1976, aged 29, he became Food Trades Manager and, with colleague Les Woodcock, his Deputy Food Trades Manager, had a very busy four years opening

Beaumont Freezer Centre, St Peter's and completing a major extension at Val Plaisant. In Guernsey, St Martin's was opened and refurbishment completed in a number of stores in both Islands. In May 1980, on the retirement of John Morris, Allan Smith became General Manager, with Les Woodcock becoming Food Marketing Manager and Jim Hopley his Deputy.

Allan remembers John as firm in his style and sometimes brusque in manner. When he did delegate it was in a positive, John Morris way: he would tell senior staff who might seek an opinion to 'get on with it'! As long as he knew their proposals to be in keeping with his own ideas on the particular issue in hand he was happy to give that blunt approval. At that time John Morris was holding the combined office of Secretary/Manager, a position of increasing pressure and responsibility, which no doubt was the reason for that delegation.

The Board Minutes give only a brief insight into the pressures that were growing on management during that period of development and expansion in the 1980s and later in the 1990s when circumstances and opportunities were arising in both Islands for a unique development on a larger and more comprehensive scale than any previously envisaged.

In view of his past work with the Society over the past 32 years it is appropriate here to mention a distinction received by Allan Smith in 1996 in the form of an Honorary Master of Arts Degree from Plymouth University. This resulted from his time as Chairman of the Highlands College Governing Body, which had links with Plymouth University. It was a highly fitting acknowledgement of Allan Smith's past service, and a sign of further successes just ahead. In 2004 he was to receive an MBE in the Queen's Birthday Honours List for services to Jersey and overseas charities.

During his earlier years with the Society circumstances had brought Allan Smith into contact with Le Masurier, the wine merchants, and with Fred Clarke, the Company Chairman. From the friendly acquaintance that developed came also the knowledge of Le Masurier's plans for the rebuilding of their offices and their wish to develop a large food store on adjacent land.

In June 1996, following an approach by Fred Clarke, the General Manager and Food Trades Manager were invited to walk over the site for which plans had been approved for a supermarket of 20,000 sq. ft, with car parking on three levels. These plans and the intentions were for the accompanying retail unit to be integral with the new offices, stores and warehouse of Le Masurier.

This idea of an extensive redevelopment to include the retail building within it was not acceptable to the Society, and the architects were requested to prepare an alternative sketch plan, which, if agreed, could lead to an option being secured on a separate area for the supermarket. As the site already had planning permission for a retail store there was considerable advantage to the Society in pursuing this alternative and opening negotiations with Le Masurier for a preliminary agreement to lease, possibly with an option for future purchase.

However, in September 1996, when the Society's alternative plan was discussed with Le Masurier, Mr Clarke demurred and took a different view from that discussed with Allan Smith earlier. He was also in some difficulty at that time with the States over compensation for that area of Le Masurier land that was required for completion of the new gyratory road. This was also of some concern to the Society for that new road was essential for access to the car park of the new store.

At this stage negotiations became very protracted. To assist Mr Clarke in returning to his previous understanding with Allan Smith he was invited to view the Bellozanne warehouse; he also visited the UK for two days viewing CWS warehousing. On his return it appeared that he was becoming more receptive to the Society's plans. In January 1997 Les Woodcock was able to report some progress in that Mr Clarke was about to agree a fee with CWS on the replanning of the Le Masurier warehouse, but these preliminary arrangements and agreements naturally led to the main issue of decisions on the Society store becoming ever more protracted.

The situation became even more frustrating when, in August 1997, Le Masurier indicated its intention to withdraw from further negotiations. On this more serious situation Allan Smith, now the Chief Executive, reported to the Board that Le Masurier's original plan of 20,000 sq. ft had been reduced to 16,000 sq. ft on three floors, and this was quite unacceptable to the Trading Management. In spite of this considerable difference of view between the two parties, the matter was left open and in good spirit with Fred Clarke.

Though Allan Smith maintained his contacts with Le Masurier it was January 1999 before any further progress could be reported, by which date Le Masurier had changed its intentions on the store. This was now to be a ground floor retailing area with four floors of vehicle parking. The Chief Executive had subsequently written to Le Masurier suggesting a meeting to discuss further possibilities.

However, despite the uncertainties, decision was necessary on both sides. Allan Smith was endeavouring to obtain that option on the site that had been first discussed three years previously. For the Society it was believed that plans for the retail building were now sufficiently firm for a feasibility study to be undertaken and interior designs prepared.

During this lengthy period of interchange between the Society and Le Masurier, extending over five years, the normal routine of development was continuing on other Co-op work, perhaps the most important of this period being the rebuilding of the St Martin's store in Guernsey. But this was also experiencing difficulties and delay arising from some lack of agreement with Randall's the Brewery, over the Society's existing links with the adjacent Queen's Hotel.

While this delay continued it was decided to divert energy and resources to this rather special and original project in Jersey. The need to rethink the interior design and layout led to senior managers visiting Holland to view the Albert Heijn World of Worlds superstores in and around Amsterdam. This visit drew favourable comment not only on the whole concept of the interior layout but of the range of washed salads and vegetables and the market style of the fresh foods and the overall store layout.

Les Woodcock led the survey of the several stores visited and reported very favourably and in some detail on the interior layout of World of Worlds, which departed very considerably from the usual supermarket layout. As he put it, 'no long, straight, boring lines of fixtures, instead they are like the spokes of a wheel and the lighting varies to suit the product'. This fixture layout was unique to the UK market and a bold step for the Society. However, with the success of 'Fresh Food Locales', which had also pioneered a radically different layout for neighbourhood stores, it was decided that for the store to be successful in the competitive Jersey market it needed to set new standards of large food store retailing, and the new layout was agreed.

By mid-September 1999 Le Masurier had written to the Society granting a three-month option on the site, indicating at the same time that other local and European retailers were also interested in the site. During this option period intense research into the operation of the store and its feasibility had to be completed. Among those issues was that of the policy changes emerging within CWS Retail on the mainland. Social factors were encouraging the move away from the giant superstores of the 1970s, many of which were being sold off. Custom was favouring the continuing development of the neighbourhood and convenience stores or petrol filling stations with a convenience store (of which our Society has two, one in each Island, both operating very successfully and profitably in out-of-town areas). But here was an opportunity in town to buck the trend, and to have one more large modern store firmly established for the future.

There was also the question of supplies from the Co-op Group. Would it still be able to provide the 14,000 or so lines still likely to be ordered by the Society and in the ranges needed to cover the tastes and choice of each Island? Socio-economic factors still bring out these differences between the Islands, as has been illustrated in a previous chapter, and these factors show up in the research into the ordering and warehousing patterns for each Island. One further essential requirement for the servicing of the new store was the need to expand the central warehousing at Bellozanne. This presented a major challenge to plan and construct the extended warehouse in time to accommodate the greatly enlarged produce range of Grand Marché.

These particular issues were among the several to be discussed and resolved before the option was finally taken up and decisions made on the design of the store interior and layout. The programme for the development of the whole site was received from Le Masurier in mid-2000, a programme that indicated an access date for the Society's fitting-out of 20 June 2001. Provided the programme proceeded on schedule a provisional opening date for the store was estimated at mid-November 2001, a mere five months later.

In order to ensure opening in adequate time to take advantage of the usual Christmas rush and to have the facilities and the general ambience of the store firmly established in the public eye, very considerable work would be necessary. John Bates on design and Brian Prigent on store layout and merchandising were going to be busy! Camerons, the main contractor, was facing a very tight schedule on the remaining construction work. While the basic and essential design criteria and the interior mechanics would be similar for major supermarkets, St Peter's for example, this store with its unique design would demand a great deal more than the normal.

The electrical infrastructure of the whole store and the two floors of car parking areas is indeed massive; some 10,000 metres of cabling were required for the lighting, the power supply and the fire alarms. The extensive range of refrigerated cabinets with the very latest technology to control and monitor temperatures were the result of a £2 million investment to ensure the highest standards in food hygiene. Despite previous experience gained from the redevelopment of other Society stores none has demanded the degree of excellence as Grand Marché. Outside and inside views of the store around the opening date are shown (**11.6** to **11.10**), but the Grand Marché is an evolving concept and improvements are always being made, in response to customers' needs.

One prominent feature, unique to the Islands, is the Travelator (**11.11**), a simple but essential means of bringing the customer and the shopping trolley down from the car park to the shopping floor and returning them later to their cars. A flat, rolling floor and trolleys with special wheels enable customers to browse around the store and make the most of their visit regardless of the weather. A truly innovative idea, which made the news headlines when the twelve sections, each weighing some three tonnes, required dedicated shipping arrangements and police escorts on their night journey from harbour to site. The Car Valeting service (**11.12**) is another adaptation to the needs of a hard-pressed motorist customer.

This rapid-action schedule had its repercussions up the Valley where Ron Morris, the Food Warehouse Manager, was expressing his concerns over the timetable for the extension and redevelopment of the new warehouse. This would need to be completed and ready to accept the anticipated pressures of ordering additional bulk supplies for Grand Marché as well as the normal Christmas season rush for all the other Jersey stores. The contract for this Bellozanne work had been awarded to Charles Le Quesne, and work had commenced in October 2000 but some disruption and delay had arisen.

Previous to the lease being signed future manpower needs had to be estimated, and an application was submitted to F&E in January 2000 for permission to recruit 120 people. By April Manpower Services had granted the increase requested subject to the additional staff appointed having local residential qualifications.

Now it was time to commence the appointment of these staff. In Jersey's full-employment situation this was a daunting challenge for Colin Macleod, Head of Human Resources. Already appointed was David Palmer, Store Manager, previously at St Peter's. His store management team had been recruited either from other Co-op stores or from recruitment advertisements. The recruitment of new staff entailed full-page spot colour advertisements (**11.13**), posters in all the shops and even a message on the till receipts of all Jersey food stores. Open days at a local hotel were held and a tremendous response was achieved, with over 200 applications. After careful selection an excellent team was appointed and rigorous training undertaken.

Les Woodcock, the new Retail Manager, retired in March 2000. That visit to Holland, the essential information he obtained and his subsequent report were the last major contribution Les would make to the extensive development he had witnessed and taken part in during the quarter of a century since he had joined Allan Smith in that new management team mentioned in Chapter 9. Les's place was filled by Jim Hopley, appointed as the new Retail Manager in the Strategic Team, as it is now named.

Jim Hopley has been a part of the Co-operative Movement for over 30 years, starting with the Birmingham Co-operative Society before joining the Channel Island Society in 1979. He attended Nottingham University, obtaining an Honours Degree in Economics before going on to the Co-operative College as a management trainee. Now as Retail Manager he is heading both Food and Non-Food Divisions and had overall responsibility for the product ranging of Grand Marché. A critical and demanding role this, requiring close liaison with Alan Poole, Ambient Food Manager, and Trevor Clutton, the Fresh Food Manager, and Ron Morris at Bellozanne over the choices to be made from the lines available and the ranges needed and, overall, the assurance of delivery to the warehouse in time for the opening.

The vitally important part played by Jim Hopley and his team at this time of immense pressure cannot be over-emphasised. Bellozanne Warehouse extension was only just being completed following frustrating delays by the main contractor. Grand

Marché had to have its entire product ranges of approximately 14,000 lines sourced and delivery of many new lines organised. On top of this the annual massive influx of Christmas products into Bellozanne Warehouse was in full flow. The successful launch of Grand Marché and the maintenance of supplies to all the other stores was only achieved through the dedication and professionalism of the Supplies and Distribution team.

Inevitably, for a new store of such size and importance, the building of which is very prominent in the public eye, the choice of name was also important. But this dropped into place without undue difficulty. The refurbishment of the neighbourhood stores had given a lead with Fresh Food Locale, and a new out-of-the-ordinary title was necessary to reflect the dramatic change in food retailing being created. Perhaps a touch of French to give a little more emphasis and distinction? So for the 'big shop' a bigger version of the same idea, and 'Grand Marché' was the natural outcome.

The choice of person to open Grand Marché on 29 November 2001 was also arranged with equal facility. The development of the St Peter's Petrol Filling Station and store necessitated consultation with Michael Lanyon, the Airport Director, as the site lay in the flight path. During these discussions it was mentioned that Mrs Rosalind Makin, Mike Lanyon's mother, had been shopping at the Co-operative since 1946, and that she was about to celebrate her 100th birthday. This led to a formal greeting one day at Val Plaisant while Mrs Makin was shopping, when she was met by June Le Feuvre, the Society President, and Allan Smith, and presented with a certificate from the Society for £100 worth of shopping vouchers and a basket of flowers (**11.1**).

While continuing her browse around the store Mrs Makin was followed by the press photographer looking for a picture opportunity. With her delightful sense of humour, she paused at the vegetables and looked enquiringly at him, to which he responded with 'go on, pick up a carrot and I'll take your photo!' A photograph and brief report appeared in the *Jersey Evening Post.*

A natural follow-up was to invite Mrs Makin to perform the simple ceremony of cutting the ribbon at the main door of Grand Marché. It is a chastening thought as we read through these pages to recall the progress recorded during the 82 years that had elapsed from the opening of that modest shop in New Street in 1919 to the present new Superstore, Grand Marché, a concept completely different from the normal supermarket, and then realise that when the infant Co-op opened the door of No 41, Mrs Makin was an attractive young woman of 19! A charming hand-coloured view of Market Street, Guernsey, probably from Edwardian times, gives an idea of the busy town streets during her earlier years (**11.14**). How fitting it was that she agreed to create a little more Co-op history on this special occasion.

The opening successfully and happily accomplished and publicised, the doors of Grand Marché were finally open to custom. Naturally there was still a little construction work to complete and the car park controls to fit and check, but in the store everything was moving ahead smoothly.

In practical terms, as they browse around with more than the usual ease and convenience, the reader and customer may well ask, 'but what makes it all tick so well?' It's a good question, for there are over 150 staff on the Grand Marché payroll, many of them unseen, of course. What with the employment situation limited as it is in Jersey and the controls exercised under the Regulation of Undertakings and Development legislation, there were inevitable doubts over how that number of suitable staff could be reached. For despite the Manpower Services agreement to the Society's request it could be a major problem to find them. There were the worrying aspects too concerning the time and facilities available for training of such a number, many of whom would not be accustomed to this level of shop work and unfamiliar with the Co-operative system.

To meet that challenge Colin Macleod, Head of Human Resources, had the answer. While some redeployment between stores and perhaps minor changes elsewhere could yield a little advantage to Grand Marché, the bulk of that total had to be found outside. As early as August Colin was putting out feelers, and an open invitation was spelled out in the first *Jersey Evening Post* advertisement, 'High Flyers Wanted', with a range of openings given and details of the financial and personal returns offered.

This was followed up in early October by a really bold appeal launched with an invitation to call in to the Ouless Room at the Jersey Museum, where two Open Days were to be held to encourage anyone interested to call in and talk. A very enterprising gesture this, for over 200 people turned up on the first day! Many of these were

11.6 The main entrance to the St Helier Grand Marché, December 2001 (© Stuart McAlister Photographers)

11.7 The bold frontage of the main entrance, April 2002 (photo Ken Renault)

11.8 Where did all that steelwork go? A view taken in April 2002 (photo Ken Renault)

11.9 A general view of the central area beneath the atrium feature: an invitation to browse around while shopping, November 2001 (© Stuart McAlister Photographers)

11.11 The Travelator connecting the store with the main entrance and the two floors of parking above, December 2001 (© Stuart McAlister Photographers)

11.10 The delicatessen and a corner of the wine shop, December 2001 (© Stuart McAlister Photographers)

11.12 Car valeting: an unusual but valued service at Grand Marché, December 2001 (© Stuart McAlister Photographers)

BORED

with your current job?

The same job, same people, day in day out can become tedious. At some point in life, you have to move on. Give your career a shake up and go where the action is. Right now that is with us.

If you have personality, drive and enthusiasm, then consider a career in retailing at the new state of the art Grand Marché Fresh Food Store in St Helier. This superb new shopping experience has opportunities at all levels for individuals keen to work in a fresh, challenging environment.

Why not come and see us at one of our Recruitment Open Days to discuss the many full and part time vacancies available (retired people welcome). We have a track record of promoting from within, so you'll enjoy career development prospects second to none.

recruitment open days

FRIDAY 12th and FRIDAY 19th OCTOBER 10am - 7pm
JERSEY MUSEUM (situated at the Weighbridge)

Ajuda Linguistica Facilitada

We have vacancies in the following areas:

Butchery	**Fresh Produce**	**Checkouts**
Delicatessen	**Night Crew**	**In-Store Training**
Grocery	**Warehouse**	**Car Park**

What else do we offer?

- **Industry Leading Rates of Pay**
- **Excellent Pension Scheme**
- **Staff Discount**
- **Comprehensive Training and Career Development**
- **Flexible Hours Including Term Time Working**
- **Modern Facilities including Canteen and Staff Showers**
- **Generous Holiday Entitlement**

Name: ______________________

Address: ______________________

____

____

Tel: ______________________

I am interested in Full time / Part time position.
[Please delete whichever is not applicable]

Preferred Dept ______________________

If you would like the opportunity to take your career to new heights complete the slip and return it to any of our stores marked for the attention of **Denise Coleman, Retail Office.** Alternatively, simply contact **Denise on 07797 757035**

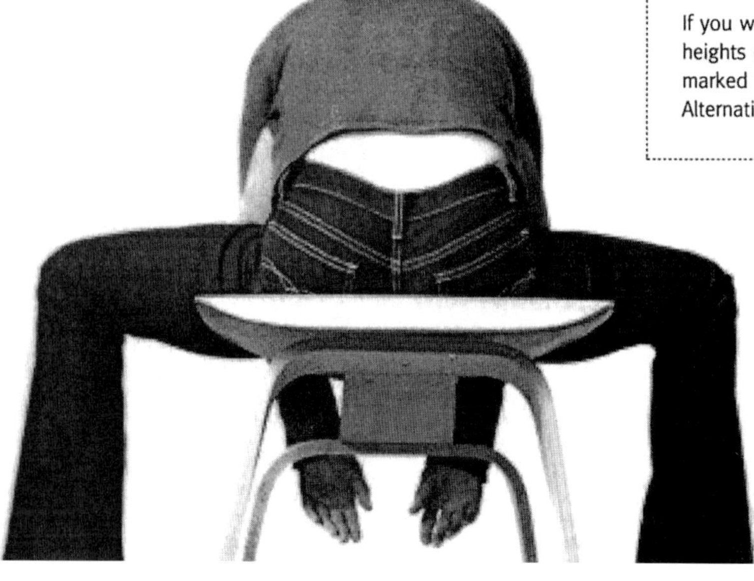

THE CHANNEL ISLANDS CO-OPERATIVE SOCIETY LIMITED
AN EQUAL OPPORTUNITIES EMPLOYER

11.13 An example of staff recruitment publicity for the Grand Marché, October 2001

11.14 A hand-tinted colour view of Market Street, probably of the early 1900s, with the future Society properties from Rectory House on the right to the Vineyard in the distance (The Lemprise Collection)

from the Co-op's competitors, the rival stores; altogether, in a wide-ranging selection of would-be employees, they were positively interested in the new opportunities conveniently available in town. Among the first of these was John Allen, who was about to create a new record entry for the Annual Report, not for his length of service, but for the length of absence!

Throughout the past six decades the Society has experienced the pleasure and satisfaction of having retained the services of many members of staff for long periods, many completing 25 to 30 years, a few even reaching 45 years of more. John joined the Co-op in 1953 as a van driver on the bread delivery rounds, working from Charing Cross and the Beaumont Bakery, where he would have been a contemporary of Mike Carter, who had just started his long service there. John remembers the fleet of seven delivery vans all finished in royal blue livery, and he recalls with nostalgic pleasure the friendly exchanges between drivers and their customers, often cheered by a cup of tea.

John left in 1956 after only three years' service but he was by no means lost to the Co-op. Noting the enthusiastic invitations in the *Jersey Evening Post* to join the staff at Grand Marché, he applied and was accepted after an absence of 45 years! He is now one of the car park attendants and 'trolley drivers'. Already well established in that role he is again enjoying the pleasures of meeting staff and customer alike in that unique environment.

Integrating into this rapidly developing situation was David Palmer, then Manager (designate) who withdrew from St Peter's Store, where he had rather apprehensively started his Co-op career in 1979, to be in at the action, ready to accept the challenge of Grand Marché. Also joining the Co-op in September 2000 was Denise Coleman from Manchester, who had gained a broad-based retailing experience during her four years' service with the Jersey Safeway, but then decided to extend that experience and interest by joining the Society.

In fact, the names of Denise and David are the first two entries on the Grand Marché payroll. Denise was then a Training Supervisor, supporting Colin Macleod in the recruitment of staff. Her early work involved the interviewing and the appointment of the most suitable candidates from the many applicants who had responded to those inviting appeals in the *Jersey Evening Post.*

The interior design of Grand Marché offers space and convenience and includes several ancillary service areas and rooms. One of these is the Training Room, which is so arranged as to accommodate groups of eight with a supervisor or manager. Here new applicants are given a general welcome and an introduction to their first manual, the Induction Workbook.

Methods and disciplines of staff training have advanced considerably since the 1970s and now embrace many personal aspects of the daily routine in a large store. This background is essential in order to gain and maintain customer confidence, for example, general hygiene and in the staff areas – the toilets here have showers. Though the workbooks are written in a light and easily readable form, there is within their pages a firm intent to ensure that every member of staff is aware of the need to attend to every need of the customer, particularly the handicapped, any one of whom may require more than the normal assistance.

All this and more is in the first workbook. Others cover merchandising and produce, the former covering inspection, arranging and pricing of all stock from the warehouse to the shelves and cabinets. And to maintain the restocking and the quality standards of all products there are the supervisors, who attend to all the divisions – Produce, Frozen Foods, Butchery, Delicatessen, Checkouts and other areas as may be needed.

Here at Grand Marché the warehouse is a model of disciplined organisation run by a staff of three, accessible off the road, with built-in freezer rooms to take the frozen foods immediately from the freezer vans arriving from Bellozanne, there to be maintained at correct temperatures until transfer to the display cabinets in the store.

Reading of these more organised procedures for the restocking of shelves and cabinets may remind customers only too well of the minor annoyance that can arise if staff are unpacking from Unitainers and stacking shelves during the day. This is unavoidable at times, but the aisles and circulating areas of Grand Marché can accommodate such an occasion without difficulty. In any event, to ensure that the normal restocking is completed before morning opening, a night crew comes in at 9.00 pm to take over the Unitainers that have been filled in readiness by the warehouse staff and the supervisors and the Night Manager whose duty hours are from 4.00 pm to 1.00 am.

Members and customers can visualise from this brief account that running a superstore of this size is virtually a 24-hour task. With such dedicated staff and all possible facilities in action, the commencement of the Grand Marché project had been very successfully completed. But opening a store is only the first step; the more difficult challenge is growing the business and the store's profitability rapidly. This was especially so in the case of Grand Marché for its growth in sales, almost doubling in the first three years of its life, would have been an enormous drain on the Society had it not achieved profitability quickly. The speed of achieving profitability, managed in the first year, was a testament to the management team led by Jim Hopley, the Retail Controller, superbly supported by his team of professional central management and a dedicated and enthusiastic store management and staff.

With the opening of the Grand Marché Superstore the Society had completed its family of food stores serving the Society's customers:

- Grand Marché, the superstore with an enormous selection of merchandise
- Locale, the neighbourhood store with a comprehensive range of stock and services including in-store – bakeries, post offices, newspapers, magazines and a full range of groceries and fresh foods
- En Route, a convenience store located on a petrol filling station.

All these stores shared common principles: the dividend, a single-price policy whether the purchase was made in Grand Marché or En Route, and a common ideal of excellent service fulfilling the Society's 'aim':

> To be a successful Co-operative business by serving our Members as the outstanding retailer in the Channel Islands.

In general terms, if the decade of the 1990s had been one of rapid growth then the early years of the new Millennium were to prove to be even more hectic. Following on from the Grand Marché in St Helier, as has been mentioned, was the completion of the Bellozanne Food Warehouse. This project was critical to the efficient servicing of the food stores, which now received stock on a daily basis. This was required because when the stores had been converted to Locales the sales area had in most cases incorporated part of the stockroom. This reduction in stockroom and enlargement in sales area was essential to the extension of services such as post offices and in-store bakeries but did demand a frequent delivery of stock 'just in time' for replenishment of the shelves.

A second and equally demanding reason for the warehouse extension was the rapid increase in range as a consequence of the Society becoming part of the national Co-operative Retail Trading Group, which co-ordinated and negotiated the purchasing of the Co-operative Movement's food purchases. This partnership of retail societies, working together for the benefit of the whole, while maintaining the societies' independence, was vital to enable the co-operative customer to enjoy prices for food products equal to those of any other store whether locally or nationally based. To enjoy this huge benefit each society has to accept a very disciplined approach to the range of food products stocked, for without this discipline, buyers based in Manchester could not negotiate with the suppliers the beneficial buying prices based upon guaranteed stocking of their product in thousands of Co-operative stores across the UK. The product range is decided upon the basis of space available for each product category in each store. This minimum range is then supplemented by particular ranges to suit each retail society's requirements, hence, for example, our range of Island products such as fresh milk, bread and locally grown produce.

This beneficial arrangement for the Society meant that in Jersey the Bellozanne Warehouse would need additional space, which along with the expansion of the business already achieved at Grand Marché and planned in the coming years, indicated a substantial building programme. This building project was completed in 2002 and is now one of the largest warehousing complexes in the Channel Islands.

Remaining in Jersey, the next project was St Peter's En Route. This ambitious development was based on the site of the petrol filling station purchased from the de Gruchy family in 1998. Following a protracted period of negotiations with the Planning department, Allan Smith secured for the Society approval for a rural petrol filling station and convenience store. The restraints imposed by the site's location were an enormous challenge to the architect used by the Society, Digby Gibbs. With the site being in a rural location Planning demanded that it should be constructed using traditional materials such as granite, wood and render, and have a large degree of enclosure so that it complemented its location in attractive design while still functional as a petrol filling station and convenience store.

This balance was achieved so successfully that the development received acclaim in the Jersey Design Awards for large-scale developments in 2004.

The completion of St Peter's En Route was celebrated by a launch in September 2003, having succeeded in the difficult balancing trick of maintaining a petrol filling service to many customers throughout an extensive building programme. The team at the store now led by Claire Sinden, a successful Manager from the management development programme, has seen the business grow enormously in the two years since the launch. Looking back at the sales levels when the Society purchased the business, it is encouraging to note that the business increase since 1998 has been over 1,000%.

The next store to be completely refurbished was the very successful St Peter's Fresh Food Store. This had been the Society's flagship store for many years but was now requiring further investment. The major project of conversion to a Grand Marché had to be completed without significantly affecting current business. This was essential in view of the importance of profitability of this store to the Society's result.

A highly detailed programme of works was drawn up, designed to minimise disruption during shop opening hours, with the major works planned for 'out of hours'.

In the event the whole project went extremely smoothly, with the store's business hardly being affected during the building programme. The project team was again led by Jim Hopley and Head of Operations, Colin Macleod, with Brian Prigent as Development Manager, Digby Gibbs as Architect and major contractor Camerons.

The Society has always sought to improve its customer service by being at the leading edge of improvements in technology, an excellent example being the self-scanning check-out tills launched at St Peter's Grand Marché in November 2004 under the 'Quick-out' programme. The ease of use for customers is illustrated by the participation level of approximately 22% of customer transactions at St Peter being through 'Quick-out'. This level of participation was testimony to the time saved by customers in self-scanning and bagging their purchases and then paying by cash, debit or credit cards, getting cash back if needed and their dividend, all in privacy and without fuss.

The store, launched in August 2004, justified the major investment by the Society. What was especially heartening to see was the loyalty of the

11.15 St Martin's Grand Marché, external view

11.16 St Martin's Grand Marché: the atrium and well-lit food area

11.17 St Martin's Grand Marché: a wide angle on a wide choice

11.18 Homemaker, Lowlands, Guernsey, external view

11.19 Homemaker, Lowlands: the ever-changing computer section

11.20 Another interior at the Lowlands Homemaker

Society's customers during the building programmes, which was rewarded by significantly improved shopping facilities.

The Society's unrelenting expansion was not limited to Jersey. In Guernsey the basis of a new generation of stores was also being planned. The major development was at St Martin's where the Society had a highly successful store but where size constraints frustrated the move to a large-store service that was increasingly required by the Guernsey consumer. The development had been in the planning process for many years but eventually an acceptable scheme was approved by the Island Development Committee.

Work on the new building began in August 2002 led by Allan Smith from the Society, Digby Gibbs as architect and the major contractor Dew Construction. The building site was based on part of the existing store's car park, a car park extension having been completed earlier, which would become part of the new store's car parking facilities. The location of this major development did have major implications on the planning of building works so that the customers shopping at the existing store could do so with minimum disruption. Again the loyalty of the customers was outstanding in accepting the difficulties that were inevitable when such a major building programme was being completed in such close proximity to the existing store.

John Lewis, the newly appointed Store Manager (transferred from St Sampson), and his excellent team of managers and staff did everything possible to help customers through this difficult time. The new store opened in September 2003, but only part of the proposed car park was available The sales area of the existing store had to be demolished and incorporated into the car park. The stockrooms of the old store are being converted into up to four shops, which will have complementary retail activities to the superstore. The goal is to make the entire site more attractive for shoppers and become the retailing centre of St Martin's (**11.15, 11.16, 11.17**).

Following the demolition and further works to the car park and roadways the 'official opening' was in February 2004. However, the development of St Martin's is still to be completed at the time of writing, with the Society hoping to provide petrol filling station facilities on site over which it is presently in planning negotiations with the States.

To conclude the development of the new store a 'time capsule', a safe built into the walls of the entrance foyer, was filled with all manner of memorabilia donated by organisations directly connected to the development. These included the architects, Randalls Brewery, the Queen's Hotel immediately next door and of course donations from the Society, store management and staff. However, the main contributions were from the community, the Church, States Deputies for the area and the local Primary School, which donated the autobiographies of the children in their final year. The whole event on 22 February 2005 was a fitting example of how the Society endeavours to be at the centre of the local community.

Following the Jersey Homemaker Store upgrading, it was now opportune to improve the Home Furnishings facilities at Lowlands Homemaker. This project again demanded the most detailed planning as the radical improvements required extensive building works but the store needed to remain operational. While keeping the store open throughout the refurbishment did mean a longer programme, it was successfully completed by August 2003. The building team was again led by Allan Smith and Digby Gibbs, with the detailed store planning being led by Ray Elgie, Paul Clark, Colin Macleod and the Store Manager, Steve du Feu. Once again the loyalty of the customers and staff working in very difficult conditions cannot be over-emphasised. The Homemaker Store is now the outstanding home furnishing store in Guernsey, giving the Society a very firm base for future expansion in this important aspect of consumer requirements (**11.18, 11.19, 11.20**).

The Society recognises that within Guernsey there are significant opportunities for further development. Two of these opportunities are presently in the planning stage. The first, which will be commenced during 2005, is at Vazon. The Society purchased Vazon Stores from Mr Langmead in April 2002. Immediate improvements were made within the existing building but the purchase of the store had been made for a more ambitious project, the building of a Locale store to serve this important area in Guernsey. The detailed plans, presently being completed as this book is being written, were to be submitted by the end of March 2005. The enlarged store will provide excellent neighbourhood food facilities for Vazon, with generous car parking facilities.

The major development for the Society in Guernsey will be Leale's Yard, located behind the parade of shops at the Bridge and purchased in

11.21 A corner of the Leale's Yard site ready for redevelopment by the Society (photo George Symons)

1998. The site is one of the largest undeveloped commercial areas in the Island, with part almost derelict, consisting of individual businesses occupying industrial accommodation and the balance an area of open land. The whole area has been scheduled for redevelopment by the States of Guernsey as a mixed-use redevelopment area (MURA), with opportunities for an extensive retail and commercial development along with housing at the rear of the site, with access from Lowlands Road (**11.21**).

The development of this important site at Leale's Yard has been a marathon task, led by Allan Smith. Negotiations with the States' planning authorities has been protracted, lasting a number of years. The conclusion of these negotiations and the planning authority's discussions with other landowners within the MURA was the Outline Planning Brief laid before the States of Guernsey on 24 November 2004. The brief was approved by the States and now forms the basis of the planning process. The Society is actively involved in this planning process as this book is being written.

The whole purpose of the Society's involvement in the site has been to provide a food superstore similar to the Grand Marché in St Helier. The building of such a store, along with the other retail facilities planned, will greatly enhance the shopping facilities for the Guernsey consumer, and additionally the whole of the Leale's Yard development will provide a stimulus for the regeneration of the Bridge as a major retailing and commercial centre in the Island.

This development provides the ideal example of how tenacity and patience are demanded of the Society's executives. The first contact Allan Smith had with the owners of Leale's Yard was as long ago as 1979. All kinds of difficulties arose, which meant that the purchase was not able to be completed until 1998, with the actual retail facilities still many years away!

The Society has plans for further stores in both Islands. Some are actively being pursued at present. However, the wish of the Society is to publish this book to help celebrate the 50th anniversary of the formation of The Channel Islands Co-operative Society through the amalgamation of Jersey and Guernsey Societies. This will take place on 15 September 2005. So, for the time being, this is the story of the progress made by the joint Society and before that the separate Co-ops on both Islands, from 1919 to 2005. No doubt there will be many more years of progress to follow, which will deserve their own book.

FRESH · FOOD · STORE

Chapter 12

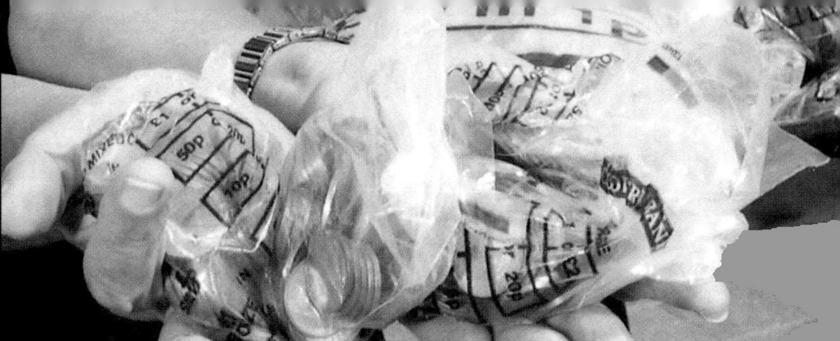

The Co-op and the Community

Life in the Islands after the First World War was a time of rehabilitation, with several thousand men returning from France and elsewhere through demobilisation camps and back to their homes. It was an historic moment of possibility and recovery, a chance and a need to make a new start, for individuals and community alike.

As we read in Chapter 1, only six months after the Armistice, in May 1919, the CWS held a memorable meeting in the Oddfellows Hall, St Helier. Here Mr Williams of London spoke for the CWS in forceful terms, urging the Jerseyman to show 'these tyrants that they can't trample on your liberties'. These were strong words and indicative of the mood of the time, for the Labour Movement was fast gaining support in English politics. At this time the CWS had been known in Jersey for many years as a local merchant, trading from No 27 Esplanade in the import and export of agricultural produce and supplies, and CWS ships were familiar sights in Island harbours. Listeners at that meeting were given an assurance of continuing support from the CWS if they formed a Society to enter the retail business for themselves. Barely a month later the Jersey Society was established, and its first trading venture, the opening of No 41 New Street, was announced in the *Evening Post.*

The Jerseyman of the day and his wife and family were a part of the Island's close-knit farming and commercial community, which viewed itself as somewhat removed from the English. David Le Feuvre expresses it well in the title of his little book, *Jersey not quite British.* It was to them that the opening of No 41 was purposefully directed. That Jerseyman and his family would have been shopping for their food and provisions at one or other of the many general shops around the country parishes or at the grocery and provision merchants in town. Where they wouldn't have shopped would have been at Le Riche or Orviss, whose three main stores in St Helier catered for the residents, providing them with chairs at the counters, tea rooms and even orchestras.

The social divide in shopping would gradually soften, but it continued into the early supermarket scene of the 1960s. In Co-op terms, the early Management Committee, comprising well-known local businessmen and women, would have tended to maintain those differences of outlook.

In wider terms of social responsibility, there would have been little opportunity or incentive for the new Jersey Society to engage in local charitable work. It was dependent on the CWS for advice, for its supply of stocks and for financial support, and it was desperately short of cash. As we saw above, within ten years of its formation the Society was facing financial crisis. A display of poppies on Armistice Day with a modest donation to the British Legion was about all members could do, while it was the Society's duty to increase membership numbers and look after individual's interests, particularly with regard to profits, the surplus and the dividend.

Given the many charities around today, it may be surprising to read that most of these everyday names did not even exist before the Occupation. Nor were the public, or the staffs, involved as they are now in organising or taking part in the many

12.1 Customer Pat English and Retail Controller Jim Hopley with a barrowful of pennies collected in the Society's penny back scheme, May 2004. More than 362,900 bags were recycled, yielding £3,629 for Jersey Hospice Care. Since the scheme was launched in 1992 over £60,000 has been raised by Co-op customers (© Jersey Evening Post)

12.2 The intrepid and ever-cheerful Allan Smith was taken away one night to spend time in the cells, but it was all in a good cause: the staff and supporters raised £1,500 to bail him out in the morning. The money went to the BBC 'Children in Need' Appeal (© Jersey Evening Post)

12.3 The Caring Award of the Co-operative Wholesale Society being presented to Allan Smith by David Skinner, CWS Chief Executive

activities we think of as commonplace for raising funds for particular or favourite charities.

As the Minutes and Annual Reports show, in the post-Occupation period to the 1950s and 1960s, the pressures of the 1955 amalgamation and the need to expand in both Islands remained overriding concerns. It would be some time before the Society could move into more socially related interests and activities. Eventually, however, changes of Board and senior management personnel also played a part in the Society's increasing focus on community causes.

There is little in the early Minutes or Annual Reports to excite attention in this respect. It was the States' decision of 1962 to abolish that clause of the Code of 1771 that restricted the interest rate to 5% that finally set the pace. Within a very short time the word had spread and Jersey was on course to reap the benefits. The money culture had begun, and the Island's present financial good fortune owes much to that decision.

This has shown positive results in arts and theatre through sponsorship, and many other benefits have flowed from it. The Society, however, has pursued a different route from the usual sponsorship, making many direct contributions in money or in kind to worthy causes, covering all ages and activities. Members have not been averse to this new projection of the Co-operative ideals, knowing that their dividend is safe; it now exceeds over £4 million a year returned to Channel Islanders who choose to shop with the Society.

It was in the early 1980s, with the new corporate form of senior management in place and Allan Smith as General Manager, that the Society took on a more informative role. The Annual Report now went into detail in introducing the community aspects and activities of both the Society and the staff. The Reports also gave more prominent and appreciative coverage of staff retirements and the inevitable obituaries of deceased members of staff and Board. Add to this a page setting out the Aims of the Society and we see how closely integrated with society and the community the Co-op had become.

As proof of this we read: 'The Society aims to play an appropriate role in the community to reflect our Society's participation in Island life and to be a responsible member of the community promoting policies which show concern for the environment and the community in which we live.' In its most positive way the Society has shown concern to promote the knowledge of and the use of a second language where needed by staff. This need surfaced particularly at the time of recruitment for the large numbers of additional staff for Grand Marché, many of whom were Madeirans who lacked confidence in their use of English. To enable them to gain that greater confidence and, in the training context, to achieve full satisfaction in their work through easier contact with customers, the Society has run, in conjunction with Highlands College, a 12-week course in the basics of grammar and spoken and written English. Future courses are planned, which will give every member of staff the opportunity to improve their career prospects, not only with the Society but in the wider world should they decide to seek opportunities elsewhere. This process has been further enhanced by the provision of Portuguese lessons for the Society's supervisors and managers – all voluntary but each series of lessons being oversubscribed!

In practical terms the Society has finally overcome any lingering doubts as to its place in today's Island society. This position has been achieved since the early 1980s when the more positive move into the ethos of caring in the community became an accepted aspect of daily life. Begun and fostered, it has been expanded into an outgoing movement.

It shows itself in the modest efforts of schoolchildren to assist a friend in hospital to the more serious enterprise of Crimestoppers whose aim it is to make Jersey more secure by tapping into the initiative and assistance of the public. As a past Chairman of Crimestoppers Allan Smith, the Society's Chief Executive, stated in an interview with the *Jersey Evening Post* his belief in the sense of community: 'To a large degree Crimestoppers reflects the community spirit in Jersey, that we want to keep this island a pleasant place in which to live.' Allan appealed to the public to call the Crimestoppers number with any information they had, emphasising that all calls were completely anonymous.

It is typical of Allan Smith to involve himself in any enterprising effort to support the community in all walks of life from children to centenarians, and always with a smile. No action is too simple to consider or too complicated to proceed. As Rotary President in 2000, Allan arranged for the Society to distribute free tubes of Smarties to primary schools, the plan being for the sweets to be eaten and the tubes refilled with pennies. Response was immediate, and St Peter's School was congratulated on its winning effort of raising £208 for UNICEF. Also done for the children was Allan's sponsored night in the Island jail, which raised £1,500 from Jersey and Guernsey staffs and suppliers in order to secure his release in the morning (**12.2**). The money was passed on to the BBC Children in Need Appeal. In recognition of his many contributions to charity Allan Smith was honoured by the CWS with the presentation of its Caring Award (**12.3**)

There is no argument now that social responsibility is important for all businesses. There are few that take this to heart more than The Channel Islands Co-operative Society. A contribution from the Society in 2004 of over £36,000, plus fundraising by staff bringing in many more thousands of pounds, is a real and meaningful contribution to the local community on top of the annual £4 million of dividend.

The Society, which has won the Co-operative Societies Caring Award five times, is one of the most active local businesses in the community. 'As a supermarket, and more importantly a Co-operative Society, our business ethos is very much community-minded,' says Allan Smith. He adds: 'Concern for Community is one of the seven core principles that every Co-op in the International Co-operative Alliance is guided by. It states that each Co-operative Society should work for the sustainable development of their community through policies approved by members.'

An early example of the Society's continuing liaison with Island schools was the Environmental Care in Schools campaign. This offered financial support to schools for environmental projects, which were usually planned, created and maintained by the students themselves, giving them a sense of ownership and encouraging their long-term ecological awareness. In 2003, to keep the liaison fresh, a new scheme began for supplying schools with sports equipment. Support was forthcoming, and 14 schools in Guernsey and 11 in Jersey joined during the school year 2004/5. The value of sports equipment supplied through Total Sport to the schools was almost £20,000 at retail prices – a meaningful contribution to the health of the Islands' children. Some of the Society's initiatives for schools are shown in the accompanying photographs **12.4** to **12.7**.

Another well-known initiative is the 'Helping Hands' fund. Each January advertisements are placed in the local media offering assistance to groups of people contributing to the Islands' well-being. Over a hundred applications are received each year, and some 25 receive assistance. While not major amounts of money, they are important to the groups concerned, who in turn have been nominated by a local supporter.

12.4 Jersey Youth Rugby Club received new kits from Total Sport in 2000. Leading the pack is Training Manager Colin Macleod (© Jersey Evening Post)

12.5 Colin Macleod, now Head of Operations, shows his versatility in presenting new recording equipment to students at Hautlieu School (© Jersey Evening Post)

12.6 Society President June Le Feuvre and Deputy Ben Fox admire the new roof garden at Rouge Bouillon School, opened with the support of the Society's Environmental Care in Schools campaign

12.7 A major Co-operative promotion, the National Music for Schools Scheme achieved great success in both Islands. In 2000 the Channel Islands were the most successful region in the British Isles, with 2,000 musical instruments delivered free to schools (© Stuart McAlister Photographers)

The Co-op dividend offers various ways of helping the community. In each Island's food stores there are containers for unwanted 'extra dividend stamps'. These stamps, worth 4p each, soon mount up to hundreds of pounds (**12.8**). Charities are asked to put themselves forward to receive funds, and four in each Island are selected to receive funds each year. During 2004 among the charities selected and the funds raised were:

- Jersey Save the Children £547
- Guernsey Salvation Army £928
- Kidney Patients Association £500
- Cheshire Home £828
- Friends of the Citizens Advice £540
- Cystic Fibrosis Trust £760

Another example of how dividend can help is by local charities having a share number and asking their supporters who are shareholders/customers of the Society to donate their dividend to their charity. This simple but meaningful help to charities given by members when shopping in stores amounts to many thousands of pounds each year. In 2003 a major fund-raising initiative by the two Rotary Clubs of Jersey, Rotaract and Inner Wheel, for the eradication of polio worldwide, Polio Plus, raised almost £4,000 by inviting members to assist by quoting dividend number 135 instead of their own. The annual Liberation Walk has long been supported by the Society in association with Rotary (**12.9** and **12.11**), while more competitive local sporting events for charity continue to arouse keen support (**12.10** and **12.12**).

On a smaller basis but of no lesser importance are the ongoing donations by members to charities of a small gift for a raffle or tombola. This practical way of stimulating charity is undertaken by many Islanders.

Supporting the environment has long been a principle of the Society. The Penny Back Scheme, whereby the Society donates a penny to Jersey and Guernsey's Hospices each time a customer reuses a plastic bag, has saved tens of thousands of gallons of oil needed to make the plastic bags as well as raising many thousands of pounds (**12.1** and **12.13**).

The Society also contributes to the Jersey Charity Auction, which raises money for the Joint Charities Christmas Appeal. Its annual offering of 'The World's Longest One Minute Trolley Dash' is always one of the most popular auction lots, having raised many thousands of pounds for the needy of the Island.

Like many local businesses, the Society's success as a fundraiser year on year can be largely credited to the enthusiasm of its staff in many fund-raising activities. The Society is one of the most active organisations for the BBC Children in Need Appeal. During the 2004 appeal, over £20,000 was raised by staff and customers, with management and staff participating in fundraisers. These included putting Allan Smith and Jim Hopley along with other senior managers in the 'Stocks' at St Peter Grand Marché, with Marie Le Hegarat selling wet sponges to be thrown by customers and staff; and arranging for Alan Poole, Head of Food Supplies and Logistics, to work in Bellozanne Warehouse during Children in Need Day. Customers also donated £5,657 in dividend to this worthy cause.

The Society's concern for the community is not just a matter of fund-raising and donations. The Society is also a leader in making its shops easily accessible for the disabled. In this connection it has formed a new working partnership with a UK charity, the Centre for Accessible Environments (CAE), to undertake greater analysis of disabled access issues when planning its new developments. The CAE campaigns to make new buildings and places more accessible to all possible users, including disabled and older people. The CAE assesses the plans of each of the Society's future developments and recommends any improvements that could assist those with disabilities or mobility problems.

When considering the plans for the Grand Marché superstore, Jersey's largest, the CAE recognised that 'access for all has been considered in many aspects of the building design', and praised the fact that 'the majority of the superstore layout has good circulation and aisle widths'. Grand Marché has a large range of disabled facilities including disabled parking, toilets, specially designed shopping trolleys for use by wheelchair users and a motorised trolley to make shopping much easier for customers with mobility problems.

At St Peter Grand Marché a further innovation was installed, that of hearing loops to aid members who are a little hard of hearing. This facility is available at the customer service desk, post office and at the checkout all the positions have a sign indicating the assistance.

Within the Society's St Peter's En Route development, the 'Service Call' system is intended to help disabled, elderly or members who find the self-

12.8 Peter Roffey, Society Vice-President, saves some unwanted dividend stamps for the Salvation Army, 2005 (© Guernsey Press Co)

service petrol filling arrangements difficult. The system works by means of a receiver mounted within the convenience store and hand-held infra-red transmitters, which are distributed to customers to keep in their cars. When used appropriately the receiver bleeps for about 5 seconds, alerting staff that a member is outside and requires personal service. A light on the receiver flashes to show the customer has requested assistance.

Taking such care is for the benefit of the Society's customers, but does benefit the Society and the wider community. This was acknowledged by the Jersey Child Care Trust awards for 2003/4 when Grand Marché St Helier was awarded overall winner in the retail category based on accessibility, cleanliness, safety, customer service and in-store facilities, including baby-changing and dedicated equipment for the disabled and for children's entertainment.

Concern for the wider community shows in many ways. One was evident in 1998 when the Society launched a petition to prevent the Constables Committee enforcing Sunday closing on all larger shops (**12.14**). Petitions against the threatened closures were placed for a week in the Society's Jersey stores, in English and Portuguese, before the States met to consider the proposition. Allan Smith led the campaign, saying that 'At present the consumer has a choice. If the amendment goes through they won't.' He explained that since Sunday opening had begun in the Society's stores in 1996 an average of 6,000 customers had chosen Sunday shopping, making it the second or third most important trading day at the stores.

The positive outcome of the campaign was acknowledged by a full-page advertisement in the *Jersey Evening Post* some three weeks later, in which

12.9 Marie Le Hegarat (third from right) ready to start an enthusiastic team of 'Co-op Rollers' on the Liberation Day Walk

12.10 The successful Society team that beat off all opposition in the It's a Knock-Out event between local Island companies, 1999

12.11 The Society joins Rotary in supporting the Liberation Day walk

12.12 Society management and staff produce an 'oarsome' performance in the Dragon Boat charity event of 1999

12.13 The 2000 Penny Back Scheme led to over half a million plastic bags being recycled, and the penny for each bag yielded £5,463 for Jersey Hospice Care. Jennie Vibert (left), a Board member since 1995, and Margaret McGovern demonstrate the rewards of looking after the pennies (© Jersey Evening Post)

the Society thanked the more than 9,000 customers who had signed up (**12.15**).

On a still broader platform the Co-operative Movements support for 'Fair Trade' by stocking a comprehensive selection of products from developing countries and guaranteeing the growers and producers a fair price. This price includes a social premium to enable real improvements to producers' standard of living within their communities. This has received enthusiastic support from the Society, making it the leading food store operator of Fair Trade Producers within the Islands.

During 2005, its 50th anniversary year, the Society has pledged to donate £50,000 to charity and is celebrating this special milestone throughout the year, involving the community in many and varied events.

The Society never forgets that it is owned and controlled by its customers. It is an article of faith that it wishes to widen the involvement of the everyday customer in contributing towards future decisions to improve Society service. This involvement is shown by an increasing range of initiatives.

They include: **focus groups**, in which members volunteer to come together with Society management and tell them about the service and product ranges across the whole spectrum of trading activities conducted by the Society. These have proved particularly valuable, and action is taken on the points raised.

Then there are **consumer evenings** at a selection of Society stores, which began in 2002. Members are invited along to the Homemaker, Travelmaker and Food Stores. Society management and staff from both Charing Cross and store management then conduct the groups around the store, advising them on how layout is planned, how product ranges are constructed and the finer points of hygiene, health and safety, training of staff and store management. These evenings are concluded with light refreshments. The idea was carried through after research revealed that members wished to know more about what made their shops 'tick'.

12.14 Allan Smith with the petition supporting Sunday shopping (© Jersey Evening Post)

Market research has been undertaken by the Society for many years. Interviews with customers as they exit the stores provide excellent and immediate information on how the service and product ranges are perceived. The results are carefully analysed and form the basis of decisions on the future requirements of the Society's customers and Islands' consumers. This is truly listening to the customer!

The heart and soul of the Society is in the community, its shops and services and Directors, Management and Staff serve that community through being The Channel Islands Co-operative Society.

Thank You!

To all 9,154 consumers who signed our petition "The Consumers Voice" wanting shops other than small corner shops to be allowed open on Sundays.

We hope your views will be appreciated in future Sunday opening proposals.

THE CHANNEL ISLANDS CO-OPERATIVE SOCIETY LIMITED
27, Charing Cross, St. Helier, Jersey JE1 1AS.

12.15 Full acknowledgement was made to over 9,000 customers who had signed the petition (© Jersey Evening Post)

13.1 Retail and financial management team at The Channel Islands Co-operative Society, 2005

Chapter 13

Allan Smith – Chief Executive
Jim Hopley – Retail Controller
Greg Zambon – Financial Controller
Colin Macleod – Operations & Human Resources
David Rees – Society Secretary

Retail is Detail: A Manager's Observations

Allan Smith
Chief Executive

A successful retail Co-operative Society did not just happen. It was the result of perceptive Directors and Managers creating customer-led successful strategies supported by a hard-working workforce.

In the Preface I stated that this book had been written through the eyes of a customer. It will be appreciated that behind the growth of the Society is the dedicated work of thousands of people for the 86 years of the Society's history so far. Retail is about people: they make the difference, they differentiate you from your competitors. This short chapter is therefore dedicated to every single one of the people who have served the Society.

Retail is detail – an often-used saying within any retail business. In the case of a food retailer, whether you are checking the hygiene routines or the presentation of delicatessen, attention to detail is critical if you are to serve and fulfil the consumer's needs. And herein lies the most important aspect of retail success: anticipating consumers' requirements into the foreseeable future. This is not a matter of luck or a natural development. It is the product of research, analysis, experience and judgement. Some of those judgements are noted in this chapter along with my tribute to a few of my colleagues. It cannot in practice be more – this is not a book, only a chapter.

I came to the Society in November 1973, a young man of 26, but already with 11 years' experience in food retailing, having started as a 15-year-old shop assistant. The position advertised was that of Assistant Grocery Manager, designate Grocery Manager on the retirement of the then Grocery Manager John Peach. Little has been said in the book about John Peach but he, along with John Morris, was an architect of the Society's growth after the formation of The Channel Islands Co-operative Society in 1955.

John Peach was an aggressive retailer and his stores' growth in business had been based on clean, well-run shops with a low price policy. During the years 1973–76 my function was to bring the stores up to date in modern supermarket techniques, which were to form the basis for our expansion in the late 1970s. Tragically, John died in 1976, prior to his retirement, from the heart problems he had lived with for many years.

The Board promoted me to Food Trades Manager and we sought a deputy, duly appointing Les Woodcock. An experienced food retailer, Les was charged with continuing the improvement in standards and also creating a Trainee Management Programme that would match any in the retail industry at that time. We knew the new stores at Beaumont and St Peter in Jersey and St Martin in Guernsey were only a few short years away, and the Society had not yet invested in meaningful management training. Both Les and I had benefited from excellent training, practical and academic, by the full year we had spent at the Co-operative College.

It was at this time that we made the first major strategic decision on fresh foods. While price remained important, we knew that if we were to appeal to an increasingly affluent Channel Island consumer we had to improve our fresh food quality and presentation. In today's market this would appear very obvious, but supermarkets in the 1970s were frankly poor at handling fresh foods. We had the major benefit of an excellent fresh meat manager in Michael Galway, who was appointed Meat Controller; we also appointed a Greenfruit specialist, Brian Ahearn, as Produce Controller and promoted a Store Manager, Robin Walker, to develop the delicatessen and dairy cabinets.

This was our investment in Fresh Foods, and it was an emphasis not taken up in the main supermarkets for another few years. Another Store Manager, John Cuthbertson, was to join the central team as Grocery Controller. This gave us the basis for the future Fresh Food Stores, our 'brand' for the food stores of the 1980s and early 1990s.

In 1979 the Board appointed the successors to John Morris: Vernon Howells would be Secretary, controlling the accounting and administration division, and I was appointed General Manager with the two main divisions, Food and Non-Food. Those appointments would commence on 12 May 1980.

My promotion to General Manager meant the appointment of a successor to myself, which naturally went to Les Woodcock. As a retail marketing specialist, Les continued to manage not only the profitability of the food stores but also the retail standards and marketing of the division.

This in itself was a change of strategy, in the move away from a 'buying'-led organisation to one led by the identification of 'consumer needs'. The challenge was then to construct a product range and services to fulfil those needs. This was a totally different approach from then accepted practice. However the job of Food Buyer for what was becoming a sizeable retail operation was vital for the Society's continuing success. The man appointed, Jim Hopley, had considerable buying experience gained with Birmingham Society and he possessed an honours degree in economics. This was a vital appointment. Jim was to have a profound effect on the success of the Society and is still with the Society as its Retail Controller and Chief Executive Designate.

Following the successful food store openings the emphasis moved to providing our customers with a wider selection of merchandise. Two of the major areas for consumer spending are clothing and home furnishings. As you have read in the book, we opened Home Furnishing Stores in both Islands. Our policy of stocking an almost complete home furnishing product range, electrical products, furniture, floor coverings and textiles remains unusual, if not unique. We could have become specialists in one or two areas but decided that our unique selling proposition (USP) was a full range of home furnishing with a 4% dividend and a price promise to match any other retailer of the same product, delivered free to the home. We would also hold the major fast-selling products in stock so that immediate delivery was possible.

Fred Hamon was appointed Non-Food Manager, and we made the strategic decision to aim our product range at growing a 'middle' market of consumers. This meant moving up the quality level from the previous ranges, as we perceived the major demand from consumers was in this category. Following Fred's retirement he was succeeded by an experienced home furnishing retailer from the UK, Brian Smith, who would further develop the Society's growing business in Homemaker, our 'brand' for Home Furnishings, Total Sport and Travelmaker.

Following the opening of the Jersey Homemaker in 1981 Charing Cross was transformed into a Style Centre, selling Ladies', Men's, Children's and Sports Clothing and equipment. The clothing market is second only to food in size and was an obvious choice to develop. We already had a Drapery department in both Islands so the progression was natural. However, following several years of only moderate success we decided to exit the Ladies', Menswear and Children's market, but retained a considerable sportswear and equipment store, Total Sport, at Beaumont. The harsh reality was that we did not have a strong enough USP. Our competitors were major multiples or well-established family businesses, and even with our 'co-operative' dividend our offer was just not good enough.

After this setback our clear strategy was only to compete in areas where we had a strong USP and could offer customers real benefits for shopping with the Society.

Allied to the Society's investment in more stores was an investment in people. One key appointment was that of Richard Le Brocq as our Training Controller in 1982. Our training programmes were geared to improve customer service, store standards and management performance. These basics have been continued through to the present day, and our investment in the Society's people has paid rich dividends both to the individual and the Society.

By the mid-1980s identifying the strengths and weaknesses in our shops was becoming ever more important as competition within the Islands intensified. We began the process of extensive market research, which we still continue to this day, to assist us in creating detailed retail strategy. It was after such research in the mid/early 1990s that we made significant decisions on the future composition of the food stores.

The early 1990s were to be difficult years for the established food retailers as new, much larger stores opened on the Island. Initially Besants opened at Grands Vaux and then Safeway bought the group of Besants' stores in Jersey and Guernsey. We opened our own superstore at St Peter's, and the mid-sized supermarkets were left fighting much larger stores with smaller product ranges, which were now less attractive to sophisticated Channel Island shoppers. Action was needed, a new strategy essential.

Following careful market research a new strategy was proposed to the Board. We would segment our stores into specialist market sectors and create unique product ranges that would fulfil customers' requirements. The four sectors in a family of Fresh Food Stores were:

- **Grand Marché**: A superstore, offering a comprehensive range of merchandise including facilities such as post offices, in-store bakeries, toilets and baby-changing facilities. There would be a selection of Housewares and Electrical products on top of a superb selection of Fresh Meat and Poultry, Produce and Serve-over delicatessen, along with an extensive selection of grocery products, newspapers and magazines.
- **Locale**: A neighbourhood store, based in local communities, which needed to be the focus of the area and wherever possible have a post office, newspapers and magazines and in-store bakery. There needed to be a product range based on fresh foods, large enough to allow a customer to obtain a full weekly shop, but the concentration would be on the top-up market, with customers' main shopping trips being done at Grand Marché.
- **Centrale**: A town centre hybrid store with a product selection geared for people who worked and lived in town. This concept was later integrated into the Locale group of stores to simplify the range to three clearly defined groups.
- **En Route**: A convenience store based on a Petrol Filling Station forecourt. Being our smallest stores, the product range here was carefully chosen to suit the particular location and size of store, although the range would still retain an emphasis on fresh foods.

There had been a growth in convenience stores within the Islands, each adopting a premium price policy. Our strategy, to give our customers a unique offer, was to have a single price policy across the whole group of stores, with 'Superstore prices' in neighbourhood and convenience stores. Add to this our co-operative difference of dividend and double dividend in Grand Marché and Locales, and dividend stamps in En Route, and you do have a clear and unique offer.

Once we had made the strategic decision we then had to go out and buy the stores that sold newspapers and magazines and had a sub-post office. Of course, you cannot 'buy' a sub-post office, and it is solely up to the Post Office to grant a sub-post office agreement. But being high-volume stores strategically placed in centres of the communities we were fortunate in getting a number of post offices transferred to our stores following the stores' purchase.

We had a new strategy and needed to create a design concept radically different from those of our existing stores. These concept designs were created by Corsie Naysmith, a leading London retail design company, in conjunction with myself, Les Woodcock, Jim Hopley and John Bates, the Society's Design Manager. However, to be successful the stores' product ranges had to be carefully tailored for each concept and also match each store's sales area. This task was lead by Jim Hopley and, once decided, the conversions to the new concept could begin. The pilot store selected was Beaumont in Jersey, which was converted to the Locale format. To create the product range required we needed to purchase the local news agency and post office, a first for the Society. This was successfully completed and the store converted. We hoped our strategy was correct, and the result proved it was, with huge increases in business. The concept of 'Locale' was born.

Following on the introduction of 'Locale' came another radical decision, at the time, for the Society. This was to apply for Sunday trading licences in all its smaller stores and to staff its stores on a Sunday with volunteers from our normal staff and specific Sunday staff. The result was a resounding success, and those two strategies of segmenting our retail offer and trading on Sundays in the smaller stores formed the basis of the Locale and En Route brands.

The conversion of the stores to the Locale format, the new Grand Marchés and En Routes is documented within the body of the book and needs no further comment here.

Another key strategic decision taken in 1996 was to join the national Co-operative Retail Trading Group, which organises the food buying for all co-operative societies. It uses its massive buying power, some £5.6 billion, to lower our cost prices, which then enables us to pass on this benefit in lower retail prices.

But there is another side to the Society story, because the Society's shops are not all food stores, and within our Non-Food division major strategic decisions were also being made.

The Society's entry into travel retailing has already been documented, but after introducing real competition into the market with a discount based on shopping vouchers, we again had to provide a unique offer. With most travel agents at the time focusing on packaged holidays starting from UK airports, the Society decided to start with 'direct' holidays from Jersey (rather than Guernsey, owing to the length of runway at the airport), to a variety of destinations. This is a challenging business, with the main 'directs' entailing the Society having to charter flights for these holidays.

The risk was initially shared with another travel agent but now, with our growth in the business, the entire seating capacity is being sold by Travelmaker. This facility has given the residents of Jersey in particular a very convenient way of taking a holiday and is the backbone of our travel business.

To compete effectively with the UK national travel operators the Co-operative Movement came together as the Co-operative Travel Trade Group to negotiate with the major providers of packaged holidays and cruises. The Society joined this Travel Trade Group soon after its formation so that we could offer both 'directs' and 'packaged holidays' at very competitive prices. 'Directs' would still attract shopping vouchers, and packaged holidays came with an offer of always matching the prices charged by other agents for the identical holiday. The travel team led by Gary Hudson still has major challenges as travel has become increasingly competitive, especially as it is easily available through the internet and numerous other sources. However the strategy outlined above, allied to experienced consultants, we believe, will provide a firm base for the future.

In Homemaker the same strategic review was carried out prior to the latest major refurbishments in Jersey and Guernsey. This review by the new Homemaker team after the Society's management restructuring in 1998 led to a major revision of our furniture product ranges, which had become too traditional, and the introduction of a comprehensive range of housewares. The new in-store design and layout was again created by Corsie Naysmith. Both Jersey and Guernsey stores were totally revamped, as explained in the book.

My opening remarks of this chapter spoke of the importance of the Society's people. Following the major restructuring of Society management a renewed emphasis and importance was given to Human Resources, and a new manager, Colin Macleod, was appointed as Head of Human Resources. With a new Retail Controller, Jim Hopley, following the early retirement of Les Woodock, major strides have been made in developing our people to enable them to fulfil their potential within the Society. A renewed commitment to training has been demonstrated by the appointment for each of the food stores of specialist in-store trainers, who report not only to the Store Manager but also to the Human Resources Team.

A major emphasis since 2002 has been succession planning as a number of managers, myself included, approach retirement age. The Society seeks to provide managers and staff with opportunities to rise to the highest management positions, always subject in more senior roles to the Board's discretion of advertising locally and nationally to ensure the Society candidate wins the position on merit. Being able to give your people opportunities to fulfil themselves gives you a strategic advantage over companies, both local and nationally based, that restrict the progression of local people.

Behind every successful organisation has to be efficient accounting and administration. The Society's team, led by the Financial Controller Greg Zambon and Accountant Brian Siney, works to the highest accounting standards, supports the retail operation and, with the IT department led by Mike Guest and Warwick Cooper, operates at the minimum cost. It also constantly seeks to use

IT to make further reductions and provide timely and accurate management and financial information.

Within the Society we now have specialists in Food, Homemaker, Travel and Total Sport retailing. We have Supply Management, IT, Marketing, Human Resources, Property, logistical and finance specialists, all focused on achieving the three-year Strategic Plan approved by the Board of Directors. It is a team totally dedicated to fulfilling customer needs.

Finally, I would like to make my own tribute on behalf of the management team to the Directors of the Society since 1955. In a co-operative society the Directors are elected by the Members of the Society at the Annual General Meetings. In Jersey and Guernsey we have been exceptionally fortunate in the people who have come forward for election as Directors. From Norman Le Brocq, who served for 35 years, 27 of those as President, to those who could only serve for a short period, we offer our grateful thanks and list on a 'Roll of Service' in Appendix 1 all those who have served the Society in this way.

This is only a chapter in a book, it is not a book. I hope you will agree that the growth and success of the Society did not 'just happen'. It was the product of an enormous number of people, from the President down, who have made The Channel Islands Co-operative Society Limited.

Appendixes

A1.1 Board of Directors, 2005. (left to right) Mrs Jean Pritchard, Mrs Jenny Tasker, Mr Peter Roffey (Vice-President), Mr Peter Grainger, Mr Nick Le Couteur (retired April 2005), Mrs June Le Feuvre (President), Mr Eric Walters, Mrs Jennie Vibert (© Stuart McAlister Photographers)

Appendix 1

'Roll of Service' by Directors of The Channel Islands Co-operative Society Limited

							Years' Service
Mr J R Jones	Chairman	1955–1957					2
Mr H K Foley		1955–1956					1
Mr J Mills	Director	1955–1957		Chairman	1957–1968		13
Mrs J Kimber		1955–1958					3
Mrs M A Rothwell		1955–1956					1
Mrs L de Ste George		1955–1984	(D)				29
Mr N Foley		1955–1965	(D)				10
Mr I G Dunstan		1955–1960					5
Mr D P Cheeseman		1955–1956					1
Mr E Brouard-Munford		1955–1960					5
Mr C A Browne		1956–1958					2
Mr W J Balshaw		1958–1961					3
Mr R W Clark		1958–1968					10
Mr H R Graham		1959–1961					2
Mr N S Le Brocq	Director	1960–1968		President	1968–1995		35
Mr C H Tucker		1961–1967					6
Mr W Horrod		1961–1967					6
Mr H H Ferguson		1961–1967					6
Mr D A Falla		1965–1990					25
Mr C A Falla		1967–1982					15
Mrs D Stevens		1967–1984					17
Mr B Geall		1968–1979					11
Mrs N Cherry		1968–1981					13
Mr W Siddle		1968–1978			1981–1984	(D)	13
Mr P Bennett		1978–1986			1987–1990	(D)	11
Mr W J Forman		1979–1987					8
Mrs P Schofield		1982–1992					10
Mrs J Le Feuvre	Director	1984–1999		President	1999–Present		21
Miss D E Batiste		1985–1997					12
Mr E V Park		1985–1987	(D)				2
Mr A D C Webber		1986–1988					2
Mr K Mayne	Director	1988–1995		President	1995–1999		11
Mr E Walters		1988–			Still serving		17
Mrs J Pritchard		1990–			Still serving		15
Mr P Grainger		1990–			Still serving		15
Mr P Roffey		1992–			Still serving		13
Mrs J Vibert		1995–			Still serving		10
Mr E C Hampton		1997–1998	(D)				1
Mrs J Tasker		1998–			Still serving		7
Mr N Le Couteur		1999–2005					6
Mr B E Shenton		2005–					

(D) Died in service

Appendix 2

Financial Results of The Channel Islands Co-operative Society Limited, 1955–2005

Year Ending			Sales	Surplus before Distributions & Members' Benefits	Reserve Fund	Members
			£	£	£	
Sept 29	1956	[53 weeks]	403,173	25,333	10,861	6,162
Sept 28	1957		434,864	26,647	12,530	6,411
Sept 27	1958		469,837	26,592	15,500	6,414
Sep 26	1959		504,740	28,062	20,000	6,750
Oct 1	1960	[53 weeks]	602,901	38,425	23,120	7,159
Oct 7	1961	[53 weeks]	676,493	37,564	37,000	7,783
Oct 6	1962		751,645	57,389	45,000	9,366
Oct 5	1963		879,057	69,213	65,000	10,885
Oct 3	1964		869,283	57,869	75,000	12,239
Oct 2	1965		962,368	63,293	111,000	13,155
Oct 1	1966		1,032,692	70,477	132,000	14,479
Oct 7	1967	[53 weeks]	1,192,981	84,266	150,000	15,597
Oct 5	1968		1,342,082	101,029	170,000	17,282
Oct 4	1969		1,637,169	134,220	190,000	18,999
Oct 3	1970		1,942,454	162,648	200,000	20,359
Oct 2	1971		2,216,570	173,124	210,000	22,625
Oct 7	1972	[53 weeks]	2,863,099	217,624	275,000	24,799
Oct 6	1973		3,336,142	291,272	425,000	26,312
Jan 11	1975	[66 weeks]	5,224,500	439,879	500,000	28,788
Jan 10	1976		5,718,317	412,410	650,000	30,849
Jan 8	1977		7,593,370	605,212	800,000	33,421
Jan 14	1978	[53 weeks]	9,480,830	849,567	1,000,000	35,899
Jan 13	1979		11,215,919	798,285	1,300,000	38,848
Jan 12	1980		14,186,908	875,516	1,500,000	41,596
Jan 10	1981		16,741,640	1,230,235	1,600,000	43,511
Jan 9	1982		19,288,153	1,273,947	1,700,000	45,537
Jan 8	1983		22,807,793	1,516,557	2,000,000	48,337
Jan 14	1984	[53 weeks]	24,874,105	1,925,728	2,418,351(i)	50,638
Jan 12	1985		26,160,399	2,118,488	2,882,613	53,393
Jan 11	1986		27,474,153	1,903,623	3,078,255	55,978

Year Ending			Sales	Surplus before Distributions & Members' Benefits	Reserve Fund	Members
			£	£	£	
Jan 10	1987		29,157,581	2,578,062	4,563,401	58,465
Jan 9	1988		30,957,945	2,703,623	5,626,150	60,882
Jan 14	1989	[53 weeks]	33,941,108	3,363,460	6,992,852	62,988
Jan 13	1990		36,616,721	3,107,855	7,789,455	64,857
Jan 12	1991		44,018,903	3,396,554	8,534,598	67,028
Jan 11	1992		45,112,643	3,201,203	9,020,830	68,854
Jan 9	1993		46,345,099	3,079,400	18,553,477(ii)	70,878
Jan 8	1994		48,489,000	3,535,000	19,669,000	73,482
Jan 14	1995	[53 weeks]	51,554,000	3,358,000	20,471,000	75,953
Jan 14	1996		52,196,000	3,855,000	23,276,000	77,756
Jan 12	1997		57,397,000	3,989,000	23,427,000	79,583
Jan 11	1998		60,880,000	4,917,000	24,880,000	81,249
Jan 10	1999		63,787,000	4,664,000	26,328,000	82,876
Jan 9	2000		65,791,774	4,138,000	30,872,000	84,157
Jan 14	2001	[53 weeks]	72,575,000	4,960,000	34,210,000	85,644
Jan 13	2002		78,147,000	5,143,000	35,801,000	87,171
Jan 12	2003		89,777,000	5,632,000	37,229,000	89,495
Jan 11	2004		96,424,596(iii)	5,757,000	39,287,000	91,628
Jan 9	2005		104,495,167	7,161,000	43,690,000	93,702

(i) 1984 Reserves increased by Revenue Reserve
(ii) 1993 Revaluation of Property Reserve commenced
(iii) Financial Reporting Standard introduced, reducing sales in Travel (where the Society acts only as agent), to recording income, not sales value. For the sake of comparison gross sales have been shown

Figures have been extracted from the Annual Accounts
The Society reports to the highest financial standards, which means direct comparisons in the years when new financial standards are introduced are not possible

Appendix 3

Shops of The Channel Islands Co-operative Society Limited in 1955 and in 2005

Shops of the Newly Amalgamated Channel Islands Society 1955

Jersey

Food Shops
Charing Cross
Georgetown
Three mobile shops
Meat stall in Market

Warehouse and Despatch Stores
Don Road

Bakery
Beaumont

Coal Store
Georgetown

Offices
Don Road

Workshop and Garage
Val Plaisant

Guernsey

Food Shops
Market Street
Bridge
Two mobile shops
Meat stall in Market

Drapery and Hardware
Market Street

Grocery Store, Garage and Mobile Store Depot
Nocq Road
Roselyn

Shops of the Society in the 50th Anniversary Year 2005

Jersey

Food Stores			
Grand Marchés	St Helier	St Peter	
Locales	Beaumont	Georgetown	St Brelade
	Charing Cross	Pontac	Val Plaisant
En Route	St Peter		
Home Furnishing Store			
Homemaker	St Helier		
Sports & Leisure Store			
Total Sport	Beaumont		
Travel & Bureau de Change			
Travelmaker	St Helier		
Warehouses			
Food	Bellozanne Valley		
Home Furnishings	St Peter		
Offices			
Finance & Administration	Charing Cross		
Retail	St Peter		
Member Service	St Helier		
Service Operations			
IT Operations	Beaumont		
Electrical Service	St Helier		
Meat Factory	St Peter		
Concessions			
Footwear	*Shoefayre*	St Helier	
Restaurants			
Grand Marché	St Helier		
Homemaker	St Helier		
Car Wash			
Grand Marché	St Helier		
Sub Post Offices	St Helier	St Peter	
	Beaumont	Georgetown	St Brelade
	Pontac	Val Plaisant	

Guernsey

Food Stores

Grand Marché	St Martin	
Locales	Longstore	St Sampson
	Market Street	Vazon
En Route	L'Aumone	

Home Furnishing Store

Homemaker	Lowlands

Travel & Bureau de Change

Travelmaker	St Peter Port

Warehouses

Food	Longue Hougue Lane
Home Furnishing	Lowlands

Offices

Member Service	St Peter Port

Service Operations

Electrical Service	Lowlands
Meat Factory	St Martin

Concessions

Footwear	*Shoefayre*	Bridge
Fitted Furniture	*Homemaker Studio*	Lowlands

Sub Post Offices	St Martin	St Sampson

A3.1 St Brelade Locale

A3.2 St Peter Grand Marché

A3.3 St Peter Delicatessen Counter

A3.4 St Peter Pharmacy Concession

A3.5 St Peter Meat Factory

A3.6 Retail Office

A3.7 Homemaker warehouse

A3.8 St Peter Fresh Food En Route

A3.9 Fresh Food Locale Beaumont

A3.10 Total Sport

A3.11 Total Sport Interior

A3.12 IT Department Beaumont

A3.13 Food Warehouse Bellozanne Valley

A3.14 Food Warehouse Bellozanne Valley

A3.15 Fresh Food Locale Val Plaisant

A3.16 Fresh Food Locale Georgetown

A3.17 Fresh Food Locale Pontac

A3.18 Grand Marché St Helier

A3.19 Grand Marché St Helier

A3.20 Grand Marché St Helier Post Office

A3.21 Fresh Food Locale Charing Cross

A3.22 Shoefayre Charing Cross Concession

A3.23 Charing Cross Office

A3.24 Homemaker Don Street

A3.25 Homemaker Don Street

A3.26 Homemaker Electrical Service Department

A3.27 Member Service Office Don Street

A3.28 Travelmaker Don Street

A3.29 Fresh Food Locale St Sampson

A3.30 Sub Post Office St Sampson

A3.31 Homemaker Lowlands

A3.32 Homemaker studio – Concession

A3.33 Market Street – Vineyard

A3.34 Homemaker – Warehouse

A3.35 Fresh Food Locale Market Street

A3.36 Grand Marché St Martin

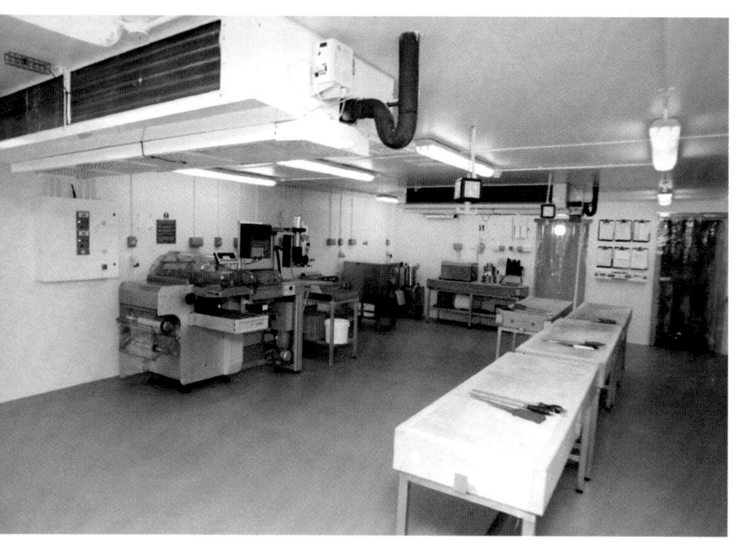

A3.37 St Martin Meat Factory

A3.38 Members Service Department – Rectory House

A3.39 Fresh Food Locale Vazon

A3.40 Fresh Food Locale Longstore

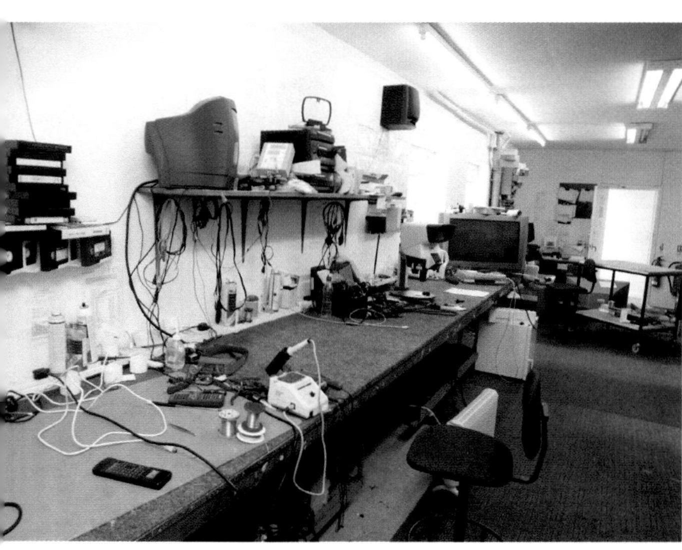

A3.41 Electrical Services Department

A3.42 En Route L'Aumone

A3.43 Shoefayre Concession

A3.44 Food Warehouse

A4.1 The first Co-operative store, in Toad Lane, Rochdale, dating from 1844

A4.2 Formal shot of thirteen of the original Rochdale Pioneers

Appendix 4

The Co-operative Movement, Then and Now

During the early part of the nineteenth century the Rochdale Pioneers and other early 'Co-operators' owed much of their inspiration to the writings of Dr William King, a physician and philanthropist, and to Dr Robert Owen, a Scottish manufacturer and social reformer.

Both King and Owen had observed the evils of the competitive capitalist system of the day, which was tending to debase the standing of skilled tradesmen by employing unskilled workers in their stead at lower wages. Parallel with this, the technical advances in the expanding industrial world enabled manufacturers to dispense with much of the labour they had previously required. This period has been described as one of chronic underemployment in which skilled trades were like islands threatened on every side by technical innovation and by the rush of unskilled or juvenile labour.

Dr King, the main advocate of 'practical co-operation', described the situation thus:

> there are persons who think that the labourer can never be anything but a marketable commodity to be bought and sold by capitalists like a log of wood, a hat or a pig …

Robert Owen, uniquely, was a wealthy man who had made his fortune in the cotton trade but practised co-operative ideals. His factory, at New Lanark in Scotland, had become one of the most enlightened of his day. Here Owen founded an industrial community within its own purpose-built village and housing and, although he adopted a form of ticket system in part payment of wages, the tickets were exchanged at his own village store for food and clothing but at fair prices, and profits were used to provide schooling for the workers' children.

Other forms of Co-operation were promoted and tried with limited success but none stood the test of time. It was to be 1844 and the Rochdale Pioneers who became the founders of the Co-operative Movement that still exists today.

These 28 Rochdale men, imbued with their ideals and determined to succeed, scraped together a meagre capital sum of £28 and opened a shop in Toad Lane in Rochdale where they sold wholesome food at reasonable prices (**A4.1, A4.2**). A share of the profit, or surplus as they preferred to call it, was returned to members in proportion to their purchases – the famous Co-operative dividend or 'divi'. From the decisions and practices of the Pioneers, the Rochdale Principles of Co-operation were formulated. These included: voluntary and open membership; democratic control, with one man, one vote; payment of limited interest on capital; surplus allocated in proportion to a member's purchases – the dividend; and educational facilities for members and workers.

It is not claimed that the Rochdale Pioneers Society was the very first Co-operative in Britain, nor that its shop was the very first Co-operative store. There were earlier societies, some of brief duration, but even those that survived came to adopt the Rochdale pattern of Co-operation as the best means of operating a Co-operative Society and fulfilling its aims. Rochdale became a model for the formation of similar Co-operative societies throughout the United Kingdom. By the end of the nineteenth century there were some 1,400 Co-operative Societies.

In the Channel Islands we look back now from 2005 to the beginnings of our Society in 1919, eighty-six years ago, still within the span of living memory. From 1919 back to 1844, the year the

Pioneers set up their little business, seventy-five years, would have been still within the memories of some of those who tossed in their shillings at the Oddfellows Hall. In this context we can understand the rather bombastic manner adopted by Mr Williams at that meeting and can grasp mentally the strides the Movement has taken, and continues to take, now dictated by the rapidly changing financial constraints and influences of the present day.

And behind it all is the Co-operative Wholesale Society, now renamed the Co-operative Group, of which we have read so much through earlier chapters of this book. The CWS was established in 1863 as a wholesaler for the support of the growing Co-operative movement and for the manufacture and supply of the goods that the emerging and fast-growing Societies were demanding. For example, in just one area of growth of the retail societies – dairy and kindred products – it has become Britain's biggest farmer (**A4.3, A4.4**).

But looking back to the 1850s and 1860s, when the Movement was really becoming a force for change, a very real problem for those fledgling Societies was the difficulty of obtaining regular supplies of even the basic foods they needed for their members. These early Societies were entering an era of retailing on a larger scale than ever previously experienced, and the loose and inefficient form of retailing of the time could not be relied upon to satisfy this growing demand for a reliable source of supply of their basic needs.

Another factor that was having serious effect was the tremendous growth in population, particularly among working-class families. For though trade and industrialisation eventually led to a flood of cheaper goods becoming available, this was not to the benefit of the working class whose shopping habits remained much as they had been for their parents and grandparents.

In terms of shops themselves, where would the new working class have shopped? The 'proper shops', such as grocers, chandlers, drapers and haberdashers, with trained staff and the support of apprentices, were expensive, and, being mainly in the bigger towns and cities, were difficult to reach (**A4.5, A4.6**). At the other extreme, basic needs of produce, food and clothing could be found in the street markets that abounded in many towns and bigger villages of the time, but choice and quality were not to be relied upon. Then there were the 'general shops', which stocked a variety of groceries, chandlery, hardware, drapery and often a range of quack medicines and home remedies. These shops were usually run by a family, with perhaps the help of untrained staff. The goods, particularly the groceries, had to be packaged and weighed in the shop so, again, quality and weight could not always be relied on. Often sales were made on credit, leaving customers in debt who could ill afford it.

This haphazard and uncertain form of retailing, with no overall and reliable main supply of goods through a bulk wholesaler, is summed up in Johnston Birchall's book *Co-op, The People's Business* (1994) as follows:

> One reason why retailing was so inefficient was because the wholesaling of goods was not very well organised. Imagine the thousands of small producers, factory or workshop owners, self-employed tradesmen and farmers who needed to make contact with many more thousands of small retail shops, in an age when travel was slow and difficult. Under such circumstances, direct selling from one to the other was not always possible, and in the growing industrial towns and cities was certainly very inefficient, and so wholesalers began to fill the gap.
>
> These 'middlemen' have often had a bad reputation, seeming to do nothing but increase prices to the consumer, but they actually filled some vital roles: organising the buying from several producers, keeping stocks of goods, organising transport, undertaking some of the intermediate production work such as processing or packing of the goods, and then selling them on to the shops ... this wholesaling function became very sophisticated, but in the mid-nineteenth century it was as haphazard as the retailing, with producers not being able to sell their goods very easily, and the more enterprising shopkeepers filling the gap by doing some wholesaling for other retailers ...

The take-off of a retailing revolution was still not guaranteed; it needed a revolution in transport. In the mid-nineteenth century, transport remained slow, with wagons on the turnpike roads being used to bring food to the towns, and with cattle being driven into the markets on foot (the canals were really only useful for carrying grain and fuel). While small market towns were still able to draw their food from the surrounding countryside, this became more and more difficult for the growing industrial cities.

The Pioneers were lucky in their timing, because the railways, which began to be built in the 1840s, provided a network of lines and stations (far more than we have now in 2005), which created a national market in food. They allowed for regular delivery to even the remotest areas, and for the first time working-class people were able to obtain a reliable supply of fresh fruit and vegetables, to drink enough fresh milk and eat fresh fish. John Burnett points out:

> The greater reliability of such transport allowed shopkeepers to stock a wider range of goods, to have a much faster turnover of stock, and to lower their costs.

Even so, it is very probable that those early Societies would have experienced a hint of suspicion and reluctance on the part of some manufacturers and suppliers to provide them with their basic groceries and provisions given the unplanned form of retailing that prevailed despite much-improved means of communication. These delays and frustrations were a nuisance to the young, growing Societies, which could do little on their own to alleviate the situation.

Our Pioneers could foresee this as a problem for the future of the Movement and one to be resolved quickly. Overcoming criticism and trading difficulties in the early stages, in 1850 the Pioneers began hesitatingly to engage in wholesale trading to supply other Societies, of which there were now several in the Manchester area. That they began at all is a tribute to their continuing enterprise for, prior to 1852 they were not legally able to trade with other Societies. However, an Act of that year cleared the way, and by 1855 wholesaling had become a department in its own right with its own committee to oversee it. Regrettably, financial misjudgements arose during those early years, and a general meeting was called with a Resolution to cease wholesaling altogether. Fortunately for the Movement's future, the Resolution failed to obtain the necessary majority and wholesaling continued.

From 1863 onward the newly formed Co-operative Wholesale Society was in a strong position, rapidly becoming established as the main supplier of goods to the ever-growing number of independent Societies. The Societies and the CWS were virtually synonymous, growing in status and number together. By 1914 the CWS had become a massive and formidable business, with its own bank, a turnover of £35 million and a workforce of 22,000 people. On the retail side Society membership had risen to over 3 million in 1,385 Societies, with an annual turnover of £88 million, an awesome amount of money in those days.

All this was achieved without the need to attract any major capitalists as shareholders, or reliance on ruthless entrepreneurs to provide the driving force. In fact, though there was an abundance of capital it was the combined strength of 3 million tiny share accounts that financed it and the combined wisdom of thousands of unpaid directors that drove it, a true 'rags to riches' story.

From those early hesitant days of the mid-nineteenth century the CWS made tremendous strides forward and upward. Branches sprang up in Newcastle, Liverpool, Birmingham, Leeds, Cardiff; factories were purchased, new ones were built. Within 50 years there were branches in New York, Rouen, Copenhagen and Hamburg. A fleet of CWS ships began trading links with the Continent, importing direct to the central depots in London, Manchester and Newcastle. These central depots served the Societies established and flourishing in the surrounding areas.

As we have read in Chapter 1, CWS ships were well known in Channel Island waters as frequent visitors to the Albert Pier in the 1920s and 1930s when CWS had its merchants' stores on the Esplanade and in Kensington Place for the export of the Jersey potato crop and the import of agricultural supplies.

By the 1890s the CWS had firmly established international trading with Montreal, Gothenburg, Spain and Denmark. In 1906 the Rochdale and Oldham flour mills were taken over and, combined with the purchase of the Sun Mill, CWS became one of the biggest flour millers in the world. Further afield, tea estates in Ceylon were purchased in 1913.

This progress and achievement were accomplished within 60 years of the Rochdale Pioneers and their first modest store in Toad Lane, at a time when the social conditions and circumstances of the common man and his family were at a low ebb. Regrettably, Cooper, Ashworth, Howarth and Smithies, four of the Pioneers who had played a leading role in the establishment of that first shop,

A4.3 CWS milk on the roundabout (photo CWS)

A4.4 Harvesting on a CWS Broadbank contract on the Castle Howard estate near York, the home of the Howard family (photo CWS)

A4.5 An early small-town Co-operative store. The errand boy with his hand truck would deliver customers' orders; the sides of bacon and the joints hang in the open (photo Johnston Birchall)

A4.6 The Ipswich Co-operative store in the typically elaborate architectural style of the 1880s or 1890s (photo Johnston Birchall)

A4.7 Leaving nothing to chance: a large notice in this early Co-op self-service store explains to the customer exactly how to carry out the new-fangled form of shopping

A4.8 Plaque commemorating the Portsea Island Co-op's claim to fame, 1948

all died at an early age and were unable to see the ripening of their 1844 crop.

While progress continued into the twentieth century, the two World Wars and a world depression between them naturally had far-reaching effects, and the Movement had to adjust to them. In addition to normal trading developments, time and circumstance during the 1950s and 1960s were introducing fundamental social changes to the shopping scene in both retail and wholesale (**A4.7**, **A4.8**).

During this time of formative change the Movement was entering a period of intense pressure, which was to prove decisive for its future. But it can be said with confidence that in times of crisis the Co-operative Movement maintained its principles in an exemplary manner not only to its members but also to the community. This was first shown in 1913 when the people of Ireland, particularly in the Dublin area, were suffering the effects of a long-drawn-out transport strike that threatened near starvation for many, particularly for the children of Dublin.

The CWS stepped in to a situation that seemed likely to continue indefinitely. With the help of a £5,000 credit from the Trades Union Congress, the CWS made up 30,000 food parcels, chartered a ship, the SS *Hare*, and delivered the goods. The

Dublin and Belfast Co-operative Societies added their contribution of 12,000 loaves of bread for distribution. Despite the scorn of local suppliers, employers and shopkeepers who said it could not be done, that shipment and the several that followed during the next three months proved that the British Co-operative Movement had not only the initiative but greater resources at its disposal for meeting and overcoming a crisis than any other organisation of the period.

It was not surprising then that during the first few weeks of the war in 1914 the CWS was turning out 10,000 uniforms a day for the Army, had stockpiled 70,000 blankets and was continuing to supply government needs at prices as close as possible to cost. As the war wore on the CWS continued its contribution to the country's needs; Co-op drivers went to France to drive for the Army, Co-op Halls were requisitioned for troop accommodation, and, on a personal level, the CWS made a particular gesture in proof of care for their members – they agreed to pay the difference between all their employees' Army pay and their Co-op wages and to give three months' wages to the families of any member killed in action. Nearly 6,000 Co-op employees were called up of whom 810 never returned.

Despite opposition to the Co-op system by the normal retail suppliers and tradesmen and tacitly by government, which declined to defend it against unfair competition, the Movement emerged from those four years of extreme pressure stronger then ever, with 4 million members.

Following that war experience, through those twenty years of comparative peace, though marred by the Depression of the 1930s, the CWS entered the Second World War at the peak of its development, with 1,100 Societies, 24,000 shops and a membership of 8.5 million. But 1939 was not to be a rerun of 1914; this time there was no way by which the government could ignore the Movement, with sitting Co-operative Members of Parliament to fight the Co-op's corner. It is fitting to recall that while many in the Islands were enduring the Occupation our fellow members of the Co-op in Britain, now stronger than ever, were contributing to the war effort in a tremendous surge of activity to cope with the highly technical military demands of the 1940s. With the frightening power of the Nazi bombing the Movement suffered widespread damage and destruction to its shops, warehouses and factories, as did so many of its competitors. During this war 15,000 CWS employees served in the forces, of whom 545 lost their lives and 400 were taken prisoner. All this is still too vivid in the memories of many of our members and readers for us to dwell on it.

Looking ahead into the immediate future, it became obvious that by the mid-1950s, when rationing and other restrictions were ending, time and circumstance were introducing fundamental changes to the shopping scene that both retail and wholesale were compelled to accept and adjust to. During that period of the new Channel Islands Society's expansion, particularly in the 1960s, plans were constantly in a state of flux, as advances towards a more open shopping experience demanded rapid transition from the conventional counter shop, with its leisurely counter assistant service and the wicker baskets carried by the ladies to the self-service open plan. Self-service required removal of the main counters and the provision of display shelving and cabinets, with bold notices to guide the customer, unaccustomed to such freedom.

This idea was quickly adopted in Britain. In fact, as early as 1948 the Portsea Island Society converted one of its shops to a full self-service store; a plaque on the wall commemorates it as the first in Britain. This was followed in Jersey and Guernsey later, in the 1960s, but with so few shops and those being of restricted size and shape it could not reach its full potential. Only Charing Cross and the 'Food Hall' of Market Street were converted to a limited degree.

But self-service was only to have a short life. This was because the adjustment just mentioned was not only a matter of rebuilding shops damaged during the bombing, or bringing other older shops up to date. Society itself was changing and the Movement had to change with it. Growing affluence at all levels was integrating class distinctions to a degree never before experienced in the UK. The car was a lively agent in this change and now more affordable to more people it enabled customers to travel distances to shops of their choice. These were now becoming mini-supermarkets with car parks to accommodate them.

Many of the big Societies in the London area and other big cities with no parking facilities of their own now found themselves unable to adjust fully. Some of these main stores occupying perhaps a whole block and built, as one illustrator described it, like cathedrals, now hemmed in by streets closed

A4.9 A typical Co-op superstore of the 1960s, many of which have since been sold off to be replaced by the modern convenience store (photo Johnston Birchall)

to car parking and more difficult of access to delivery vehicles, presented a problem that demanded a completely new approach if the Co-op was to stay in business (**A4.9**).

During the early years of change this demand could be partially met by rebuilding or moving out to the suburbs where space could perhaps be included for car parking, which was becoming a problem of its own. With ever-increasing charges for nearby commercial car parks this charge tended to demean the 'divi'.

These are the very problems that our own Island Society was becoming aware of in the 1960s when Board and management made many forays into the parishes to view likely sites for supermarkets, always with the need for adjacent parking space.

Other pressures too, eventually combined to compel the Movement to take the same bold step its competitors were taking, moving right away from the town or city area and building superstores that provided everything the members could wish for, including cafés, banks, limitless car parking and the ultimate attraction then still to come, petrol filling stations on site offering reduced fuel prices and the 'divi'. It could not have been foreseen that the impact of those early supermarkets followed by continuing growth of car ownership and the extension of the road network around the towns would lead to the development of huge new superstores and retail warehouses on the outskirts of urban areas, which would threaten to undermine the Movement's reliance on small shops.

A paradox indeed, but that is the way it was going. That major Co-op refurbishment of 1968, Operation Facelift, in which 1,300 shops were modernised and the familiar national Co-op symbol designed and adopted, was not enough. A major rethink was necessary, not on supermarkets but on the smaller stores. In 1958 there were about 30,000 shops open nationally; by the early 1980s there were only 9,000 left. It was significant that 60 per cent of sales was still attributable to the small neighbourhood shops and the smaller supermarkets. This led to a further and deeper assessment resulting from what could be seen among the competition. In the late 1980s it was noted that some traders had recognised that the small shop in the right place could complement the superstore or supermarket by opening long hours in convenient locations.

So this brief résumé of Co-operation over a period of 160 years leaves it in a very substantial modern form – the Co-operative Group, now much changed over the years, is still a formidable force in the Movement, smaller perhaps, but tighter, and still ready for the future.

Parallel to the CWS has been the Co-operative Retail Society, the CRS, with over 900 shops and funeral homes in much of England and throughout Wales. It is claimed that there are few items that

A4.10 Stanford Hall, home of the Co-operative College for 57 years (photo `Co-operative News`)

A4.11 Rae Hall/Haskins Dining Room at Stanford Hall, upgraded with a donation from the Channel Islands Co-operative Society (photo Charnwood Photographers)

A4.12 Wall plaque at entrance to Rae Hall/Haskins Dining Room commemorating the lives and work of John Morris and Norman Le Brocq (photo Charnwood Photographers)

the Co-op does not sell, and as an indication of its purpose for the future, the biggest merger of all was announced in April 2000 when the CWS and CRS finally merged. This created a £5 billion business operating about 1,100 food stores and the biggest funeral service in the UK.

Co-op banking, insurance and travel have extended their areas of business within the Movement with impressive results. But perhaps the most commonly talked of item or aspect of the Movement is the dividend or 'divi', that share of the profit, or surplus as the Pioneers preferred to call it, returned to members in proportion to their purchases and viewed by members as virtually sacrosanct.

The Co-operative Movement has grown up through the generations to achieve a very professional stature and now boasts the widest range of initiative, effort and meaningful activity from the purely local, social and Society levels right through to representation at national government level. During this sometimes stormy course, progress has continued and the Movement has endeavoured to maintain the paramount purpose of serving its members and the general public to a degree of disciplined service and courtesy that results from training, from the practical shop work through to professional management.

Supporting this local need for a minimum and disciplined level of service to the community through training was the Co-operative College set up at Holyoake House in 1919. This carried on the earlier efforts of the Co-operative Education Department, which as far back as 1906 was organising classes in economics. These early efforts were expanded and strengthened so that even during the Second World War the college continued correspondence courses, which through the medium of the Red Cross were made available to prisoners of war.

As the war drew to a close a fund was set up, which quickly resulted in the purchase of Stanford Hall in Loughborough situated in 300 acres of grounds. In 1945 this was opened as the home of the Co-operative College (**A4.10**). The Channel Islands Society, in response to the report of a general refurbishment of the college carried out in 1996, donated £10,000 for the upgrading of the Rae Hall/Haskins Dining Room, in particular acknowledgement of the lives and work of John Morris and Norman Le Brocq. A plaque commemorating this event was placed on the wall at the entrance to the room (**A4.11, A4.12**).

The property at Stanford Hall has now been sold. The delivery systems for training have changed beyond recognition and the expensive facility was no longer required. The Co-operative College, now located in Manchester within an existing building occupied by the central federal society, Co-operatives UK, continues to provide excellent distance learning courses and will operate training seminars in Society premises around the UK. The Movement has changed and in response so has the College.

Yes, the Movement continues to thrive, though, as the *Co-operative News* portrays, it engages now in a wider, deeper interest in world issues as well as in the routine but exciting affairs of its local Societies.

As examples of its continuity in a changing world we may look back to Robert Owen's New Lanark co-operative mills and model village of nearly two hundred years ago and ponder the invitation to take a luxury weekend in the New Lanark Mill Hotel; or we could celebrate with a weekend at the Gilsland Spa Hotel in Cumbria, which has celebrated its hundredth year in Co-operative ownership.

Truly, it can be said that the Movement continues to change in company with our changing world, yet it remains steadfast to the principles set for it by Robert Owen and the Rochdale Pioneers.

Index

References to illustrations are in **bold** type. (G) = Guernsey, (J) = Jersey

CAR VALETING
POST OFFICE